Managing Int
Media Projects

MW01098029

Tim Frick

CENGAGE
Learning·

Australia • Brazil • Japan • Korea • Mexico • Singapore • Spain • United Kingdom • United States

CENGAGE
Learning·

Managing Interactive Media Projects

Managing Interactive Media Projects, Source Edition
Tim Frick
© 2008 Cengage Learning. All rights reserved.

Senior Project Development Manager:
 Linda deStefano

Market Development Manager:
 Heather Kramer

Senior Production/Manufacturing Manager:
 Donna M. Brown

Production Editorial Manager:
 Kim Fry

Sr. Rights Acquisition Account Manager:
 Todd Osborne

For product information and technology assistance, contact us at
Cengage Learning Customer & Sales Support, 1-800-354-9706

For permission to use material from this text or product,
submit all requests online at **cengage.com/permissions**
Further permissions questions can be emailed to
permissionrequest@cengage.com

This book contains select works from existing Cengage Learning resources and was produced by Cengage Learning Custom Solutions for collegiate use. As such, those adopting and/or contributing to this work are responsible for editorial content accuracy, continuity and completeness.

Compilation © 2013 Cengage Learning
ISBN-13: 978-1-285-91457-2

ISBN-10: 1-285-91457-0

Cengage Learning
5191 Natorp Boulevard
Mason, Ohio 45040
USA

Cengage Learning is a leading provider of customized learning solutions with office locations around the globe, including Singapore, the United Kingdom, Australia, Mexico, Brazil, and Japan. Locate your local office at:
international.cengage.com/region.
Cengage Learning products are represented in Canada by Nelson Education, Ltd.
For your lifelong learning solutions, visit **www.cengage.com/custom.**
Visit our corporate website at **www.cengage.com.**

Printed in Mexico

Table of Contents

Preface

INTENDED AUDIENCE

Managing Interactive Media Projects is a resource guide for students, designers, developers, marketers and project managers to help manage expectations when creating interactive media on a large or small scale. The book focuses primarily on communication and organization in client-vendor relationships with the understanding that designers and developers sometimes work alone on interactive media projects and sometimes they work as a team. The book outlines processes that make up both simple and complex projects. While its content is primarily geared toward college level students studying interactive media, it will also be a helpful tool for entry-level project managers or marketers who want to get up to speed on the interactive media creation process but don't need to know how to code Web pages or use Flash. Its focus is on organization, communication and managing expectations when building interactive projects of any size.

Although this book touches on tips and tricks for streamlining production tasks, you do not need to be a Flash whiz or a crack JavaScript programmer to get something from its content. The tips outlined herein are typically contextual to the greater task of meeting a deadline or maintaining project expectations. A fundamental understanding of various applications associated with interactive media creation—Photoshop, Illustrator, Final Cut Pro, After Effects, Flash, Dreamweaver, and so on—will be helpful but not necessary.

In a college environment, this book would feasibly work well for students who have already spent a year or two studying design concepts, typography, copywriting, programming and other elements that form the structure around which most interactive projects are built. In a professional scenario it would work well for marketers or professional project managers who do not need to know the aforementioned applications or programming languages but need to know how to speak the language of those who do.

EMERGING TRENDS

There are *always* emerging trends in interactive media. New technologies, design trends and cultural shifts such as users becoming active project collaborators (think YouTube or MySpace) ensure that change is a true constant in this field. This necessitates professionals keep their skills updated on a near daily basis and forge into new, sometimes unknown territories in order to stay competitive. If you don't enjoy the steady challenge of a continuous learning curve, this is definitely not the field for you.

BACKGROUND OF THIS TEXT

As an instructor in the interactive media department at Columbia College Chicago, I often ran across students with incredible design, animation or programming skills, or, in rare cases, all three. Almost every class had that one person who just 'got it.' Their natural talent allowed them to whip up flawless interface designs or produce full projects in the time it took the other students to pick a font and a color palette.

Unfortunately, it was far too frequent a case where those students with the most natural talent were also the ones who had the greatest difficulty getting their projects in on time or meeting expectations outlined by a class syllabus. It was disheartening when a year or two later, I would hear that this person who showed so much promise in my class was unable to get their career off the ground or make a go of it in the freelance world because they could not find the proper balance between right and left-brain skills to make their business work. I often found that while many of my students could produce impressive designs and complex rich media applications with ease they typically had not the slightest notion how to apply their ideas to real world scenarios and keep a client happy, maintain deadline schedules, and so on.

This book hopes to bridge that gap. As a professional who hails from the creative side of interactive development, I cannot help but impart my experience from that perspective. This book is ultimately borne from my own personal experiences as first a freelance designer and animator, then as the owner of a company that creates a wide variety of interactive and rich media solutions for clients of all types. Devising unique visual and experiential solutions is the heart of what we do at Mightybytes but without a succinct understanding of how to manage our client's expectations, meet deadlines, and keep projects on track we would have been out of business long ago.

Where applicable, I tapped into the deep wellspring of our clients' knowledge base as well, interviewing them on various aspects of their process and best practices. Thus, the text features a wide variety of useful 'real world' perspectives from industry professionals that, in my experience, is often overlooked in college curriculum.

From a professional standpoint, the company that needs to outsource interactive projects will often look for resources with a proven track record of projects similar to their own that utilize current technology trends and up-to-date standards alongside a solid visual aesthetic. But just as important is the fact that they will regularly turn to a vendor they can trust. Since successful project management is ultimately about building relationships based on effective communication, those relationship built on trust and mutual respect are far more likely to stand the test of hard times and longevity than those that are not. If the client respects the vendor for her visual and technical expertise as well as her ability to communicate, and the vendor respects her clients' need to stay on track, on schedule and on budget, these relationships will be strengthened even further. The vendor who can strike a perfect balance between earning trust and understanding the bleeding edge of interactive technology and application standards will be the one with staying power. Earning that trust starts with implementing an effective process.

Overall, this book attempts to transform a somewhat dry topic that many creative individuals may not want to think about into something that is friendly, accessible, and easy to follow. Hopefully, it will make a difference once readers begin to apply the concepts they learned herein to a professional scenario.

TEXTBOOK ORGANIZATION

Managing Interactive Media Projects attempts to follow the life cycle of a typical interactive project in as close to a step-by-step manner as possible: it begins with concepts surrounding a project's initial planning and conceptualization and ends with a project's launch or release and long-term maintenance and promotion strategies. Because the process for creating interactive media is so iterative in nature with many production tasks occurring simultaneously, it is difficult to write any kind of process guide in a true step-by-step fashion, however. The overall 4D process of Define > Design > Develop > Debug does apply to most if not all interactive projects, but the typical interactive project will rarely be that simple. *Managing Interactive Media Projects* attempts to outline as many of the steps in a typical project's life cycle as possible and encourages the reader to adapt the steps outlined herein as necessary to devise a process that works for each individual project. Some steps will be relevant to smaller projects but not to larger ones, some may be relevant to team projects but not to those developed by an individual, and so on.

To illustrate process-in-action, the book follows an interactive project—the design and functionality overhaul of a Chicago theater company's web site—from concept to completion. Developer, client and user—key players on any interactive media project—work together chapter by chapter to get their needs met from the site as it is being developed. When appropriate, each chapter ends with information relevant to the production cycle of that specific project as it relates to the chapter's content, the hope being to provide information that readers can apply to their own real-world projects.

Each chapter is also supplemented with relevant project profiles, case studies, exercises and sidebars that complement various topics discussed throughout the text.

The book content is organized as follows:

CHAPTER 1

Introduction

Chapter one serves as a basic introduction to the book's concepts and stress the fundamental importance of effective communication and organization during all phases of design and production on an interactive project.

This Chapter Discusses:

- ◎ Who should read this book
- ◎ What kind of projects this book will cover
- ◎ How to use this book

CHAPTER 2

Conceptualization and Initial Planning

This chapter focuses on idea development and how to begin the planning stages of your project. Whether or not a designer/developer's intent is to create something based on a prospective client's request, revamp or overhaul a project that currently exists, or start something from scratch, many of the same concepts apply when it comes to bringing that idea to life. The first task after fleshing out a concept is to define the project in as detailed a manner as possible. Then, individual phases of work and the process by which they will be accomplished are defined.

This Chapter Discusses:

- ◎ How to define your idea
- ◎ Things to look for in an initial interview
- ◎ Defining initial creative ideas with wireframes, sketches, and so on.

◎ How to refine and qualify your idea as a viable Web project
◎ How to outline a plan to create your project
◎ How to create a rough outline of time, materials and resources

CHAPTER 3
The Initial Proposal

Chapter three discusses the kind of information one needs in order to put together a solid proposal, how to get that information or as much of it as possible, and how to present information in your proposal to cover as many details about the project as possible.

This Chapter Discusses:

◎ What makes a good proposal
◎ What elements to include in your proposal to win business
◎ How to 'cover yourself' with the terms outlined in your contract

CHAPTER 4
Defining Project Specs

In chapter four, the deliverable's primary target audience is defined and a consensus is developed as to what kind of technology will be used to access the content. Once established, these specifications will serve as the benchmark against which all functionality and design usability are compared for the final product. It is essential to determine project specs up front in order to define the environment one is designing for.

This Chapter Discusses:

◎ What project specs are and why they are so important
◎ How to define target users
◎ How to create a technology profile
◎ How project specs affect the production process
◎ The importance of getting a sign-off
◎ What can go wrong with improperly defined projects

CHAPTER 5
Content Assessment and Treatment

Chapter five focuses on conceptualizing what will engage the end user and initial content development. Assess whether or not the defined project specifications affect your initial ideas. Create a content development schedule that plugs into the flexible timeline from chapter two. If you are a development team of one, working alone or with a client, it is still important to set up realistic expectations and a timeline that you can meet. If schedules and goals are defined appropriately, possible conflicts with content development should arise at this point and can be dealt with accordingly, thus alleviating problems down the line.

This Chapter Discusses:

- ◎ How to define content for your project
- ◎ How to create a content development schedule
- ◎ How to define team members (if applicable)
- ◎ How to develop the project's voice and personality
- ◎ How to create a treatment/content outline for your content
- ◎ Outline options for peer review

CHAPTER 6

Information Architecture

Chapter six discusses how to outline the flow of information for an entire project. The success of many projects is often determined by the intelligence and extensibility of the overall architecture. Information to be published on the project must be outlined in intuitive content categories. Naming conventions for files are defined. The key is to create a project where users can access all of the information with as few clicks of the mouse as possible while segmenting the content in such a way that users are not overwhelmed with huge amounts of information. It is important to include potential content structures in the navigational flowchart even if they are not implemented in the initial release. Planning for the future will ensure that the project is flexible and expandable over time, not obsolete within a few months or weeks.

This Chapter Discusses:

- ◎ How to outline information flow for your project based on content assessment
- ◎ How to define project naming conventions for files and directory structures
- ◎ How to create navigable content segments
- ◎ How to define relationships between content segments
- ◎ How to loosely define media elements as established by content segments
- ◎ How to create a visual chart outlining your project's content

CHAPTER 7

Creating a Script and Asset List

In chapter seven we determine exactly how a project's story will be told and what script formats are appropriate for different kinds of projects. We begin at the main screen/home page and detail the kinds of information that will be found throughout the project, how the interactivity works, how the text will read, and so on. The book works through subsequent screens based on information provided by the navigational flowchart. The script should not only tell the story and break the content down into manageable segments, but attention to details such as user activity and experience, media inventory for each screen, etc. should reflect previous steps of the process. The result is a comprehensive overview of the entire project, providing everyone with a common point of reference to begin the design and production phases.

This Chapter Discusses:

◎ When it is appropriate to use a more traditional script format

◎ How to transform your navigational flowchart and treatment into a working script

◎ How to format your script so it outlines all media assets and interactivity

◎ How and where to use naming conventions in your script

◎ How to cross-reference your content for consistency

◎ How to create a supplemental asset list

CHAPTER 8

Art Direction and Interface Design

In chapter eight we select several hierarchical screens in the flowchart to begin exploring interface design solutions. These static screens, selected from various content segments, serve to test consistency of message, intuitiveness of navigation, and how the overall user experience will be. We explore effective typography, color, use of screen real estate and the overall voice and personality of the project. Refinements are made to improve the screens' effectiveness in communicating the intended message based on client input. It is important to refer to the project scope document as to the proper protocol for dealing with extensive revisions. Once these screens are approved, a prototype can be created and screen layouts for the entire project can be designed and approved by the content management team (if this is applicable).

This Chapter Discusses:

◎ Exercises and resources for kick starting the design process

◎ How to conceptualize your design comps

◎ How to work with existing design standards

◎ What to include in design comps

◎ How design templates can be useful

◎ What to include in a design rationale document

◎ Options for presenting design comps to a client

CHAPTER 9

Revisions, Approvals, Scope and Feature Creep

Chapter nine concerns itself with the process of making revisions, managing approvals, sticking to a project's scope, and outlining strategies for addressing 'out-of-scope' requests. It emphasizes the importance of effective communication up front and discusses in-depth how defining detailed project specs early in a project's life cycle can save significant time during production.

This Chapter Discusses:

◎ How to approach revisions

◎ How to define the approval process

◎ When to get it in writing

- ◎ How to define when a request is 'out-of-scope'
- ◎ How to address feature creep and out-of-scope revisions

CHAPTER 10
Prototyping and Scope Creep Redux

Chapter ten focuses on the important communication role prototypes play in interactive production. It discusses in detail how designers and developers can integrate prototyping into their workflow and provide navigable interactive media models that demonstrate key features such as screen interactivity, layouts, and other functionality throughout a project's life cycle. The chapter also discusses various tactics for approaching additional revision requests upon prototype reviews.

This Chapter Discusses:

- ◎ What prototypes are
- ◎ Why you should build them into your production process
- ◎ When to build prototypes
- ◎ Rapid prototyping and its advantages
- ◎ Real world scenarios for prototype deployment

CHAPTER 11
Design Production

Chapter eleven covers the process of creating screen designs for an entire project and offers time-saving tips for reusing elements and integrating design templates into your workflow. The chapter also includes important information on staying organized by implementing established naming conventions and directory structures as well as how to track approvals on your designs once they have been presented.

This Chapter Discusses:

- ◎ How to approach design production
- ◎ How to get the most out of a template design
- ◎ Applying naming conventions to your design files and folders
- ◎ The logistics of presenting designs for review and approval

CHAPTER 12
Production and Programming

Chapter twelve touches on many production tasks and ways to approach programming an interactive project from a project management perspective. Communication strategies are proposed for maintaining expectations, tracking approvals and and keeping project timelines. Informative passages on topics like building an asset library, understanding media formats, working with content management systems, and the importance of using a detailed script or asset list complement the communication strategies outlined in this chapter.

This Chapter Discusses:

◎ The importance of standardizing production elements
◎ Important differences between Web, Flash, and disc-based projects
◎ How to create and organize an asset library or server
◎ How to use a script, asset list, or flowchart to drive your project
◎ Important team environment considerations
◎ Time tracking and progress report tips

CHAPTER 13
Testing, Revision Tracking and Quality Assurance

In chapter thirteen, project progress is monitored throughout programming to track status and identify errors or missing content. Strategies for checking interactivity and functionality on multiple machines that reflect the target users' technology profile are outlined. The concept of using testing matrixes to answer key questions essential to the project's success is introduced. Tactics for tracking revisions and managing multiple rounds of iterative testing are outlined as well.

This Chapter Discusses:

◎ Why you should thoroughly test your projects
◎ Standard testing procedures
◎ How to develop and use a testing matrix
◎ How to track revisions
◎ The pros/cons of internal vs. external testing

CHAPTER 14
Final Revisions, Launch, Promotion and Maintenance

Chapter fourteen focuses on the final steps required for completing an interactive project. Included are tactics to make the project's launch successful, promotional ideas for getting the word out about the project, and strategies for maintaining the project over an extended period of time.

This Chapter Discusses:

◎ How to devise and stick to a revision cutoff point
◎ What to include in a release/launch candidate
◎ What constitutes a final deliverable
◎ When to deliver a completed application/site vs. source code

◎ Launching your site, distributing your product

◎ Strategies to extend your services beyond an initial contract

BOOK'S BEST FEATURES

Visual Preface:

◎ Follows a typical Web design and development project from start to finish.

◎ Every chapter includes 'real world' case studies from industry professionals offering insights into process and best practices.

◎ Provides templates for important project documents such as RFPs, proposals, contracts, testing matrixes, and so on.

◎ Outlines step-by-step processes in an organized and easy to follow manner for the non-technical.

E. RESOURCE

The CD guide developed to accompany this book will assist instructors in planning and implementing their instructional programs. It includes a sample syllabus for using this book for a 16-week semester interactive production class. It also provides chapter review questions and answers, exercises, project documents, and additional instructor resources.

ABOUT THE AUTHOR

Tim Frick has provided creative media services to an extensive client list since the early 1990s. His work has received design, video and interactive awards and has appeared in many publications, Web sites, and television broadcasts as well as at Chicago's Museum of Contemporary Art. Tim's company Mightybytes has been creating design-driven media solutions for a wide variety of corporate, educational, arts, and not-for-profit clients since 1998.

Tim received his Bachelor of Arts in English with a certificate of Film Studies from Michigan State University and completed his graduate coursework in Film and Video at Columbia College Chicago. He was an instructor for several years in Columbia College Chicago's interactive media department and has been teaching classes for Ascend Training on various design, animation and interactive topics since 1998. He has held positions on the board of the Association for Multimedia Communications (AMC), as well as on advisory committees for the Illinois Institute of Art's Animation and Interactive Media Departments and the Interactive Media Departments of Columbia College and Westwood College. He has been a featured speaker at numerous engagements and conferences, including the American Marketing Association's seminar series on Technomarketing: Using the Tools of Tomorrow to Reach Your Customers Today, the AMC's FlashFest, Adobe Users Group seminars, and the Chicago Motion Graphics Festival.

ACKNOWLEDGMENTS

I have been humbled by the amount of work putting together this manuscript has necessitated. I always wondered why the acknowledgement sections in books I read were so long-winded in their proclamations of gratitude. Now I know.

That said, there are, of course, a bundle of folks without whose patience and willingness to help I could not have completed the tasks assigned to me in completing this book. I will try to keep my long-windedness in expressing gratitude to a minimum.

First of all, my hat is off to some of the folks at Mightybytes—Adam Clark, Eric Beestrum, Travis Chandler—who kept things at the office stitched together while I was away, often for days at a time, wrapping myself up in pixels and participles in the name of higher learning. In addition to keeping the fort held down and the deadlines made, they were instrumental in finding old projects, taking screen grabs, creating graphics, and engaging in hours upon hours of tedious Photoshop production work for the many images that pepper this manuscript. This book would never have happened were it not for them.

And speaking of patience, my partner Jeff Yurkanin has a seemingly endless supply of it, from which he doled out copious amounts without question throughout the year plus it took me to put this book together. He eloquently suffered a lot of complaining, frustration and my often curmudgeonly and overtaxed demeanor while simultaneously offering sage advice and never once slapping me upside the head when I know for a fact that he wanted to. How can I not be grateful for that?

Darren McGarvey at Word's Worth Writing Center in Dayton, Ohio provided abundant help with research, sidebars, and general writing/editorial support. Getting to the bitter end was made much less bitter because of his help.

Many thanks to Bret Grafton for coordinating and shooting much of the book's photography and patiently dealing with fickle publishing requirements and sliding deadlines.

I must extend gratitude as well to the venerable Patrick Boomer, one of my oldest friends, for pushing me through those last organizational crunches to meet deadlines . . . and then taking me out for decompression time afterward. Cheers.

Thomson-Delmar Learning's Ed Nolan made the introductions that facilitated the book contract in the first place. Thanks to Ed for his networking prowess.

I also have to send big props to the clients, friends, contacts, and professional associates who allowed me a glimpse into their work process and gave me the freedom to publish their candid interviews, suggestions, and process in this book. The book is a far better tool and resource guide with the inclusion of their information.

This goes double for The Neo-Futurists. Sharon Greene and Lindsay Muscato were instrumental in assuring this book has a real world edge and will appeal to those with a creative bent. Many thanks for allowing us free access to your resources and all the files used to develop http://www.neofuturists.org for the greater pedagogical good.

Writing has oftentimes taken the back burner to other endeavors in my life and I have to thank Catherine Kaikowska, Dale Heiniger, and StoryStudio Chicago's Jill Pollack for helping me get it on the front burner where it arguably belongs. Jill Pollack single-handedly rekindled my love for the written word at a time when I'd pretty much given up on writing for any other purpose than to draft emails and devise copy for the company Web site. Also, she was kind enough to open up the StoryStudio space for our photographic endeavors and for that I am grateful as well.

And perhaps most importantly, thanks to Mac and Jan Frick. Supportive parents cannot be underestimated when you set out to accomplish your goals in life and mine should be the spokespersons for that particular cause.

Below are some resources that made the process of creating this book easier.

Word's Worth Writing Studio
http://www.wordsworthdayton.com

StoryStudio Chicago
http://www.storystudiochicago.com

Bret Grafton Creative
http://www.graftoncreative.com/

The Neo-Futurists
http://www.neofuturists.org

QUESTIONS AND FEEDBACK

Thomson Delmar Learning and the authors welcome your questions and feedback. If you have suggestions that you think others would benefit from, please let us know and we will try to include them in the next edition.

To send us your questions and/or feedback, you can contact the publisher at:

Thomson Delmar Learning
Executive Woods
5 Maxwell Drive
Clifton Park, NY 12065
Attn: Media Arts & Design Team
800-998-7498

Or the author at:

Mightybytes, Inc.
5235 North Clark Street
Chicago, IL 60640
773-561-7529
info@mightybytes.com

CHAPTER 1

Managing Interactive Media Projects

Objectives

IN THIS CHAPTER YOU WILL LEARN:

1. WHO SHOULD READ THIS BOOK.
2. WHAT KIND OF PROJECTS THIS BOOK WILL COVER.
3. HOW TO USE THIS BOOK.

FIGURE 1-1
STAYING ON TOP OF CHANGES IN WEB AND INTERACTIVE MEDIA
DEVELOPMENT IS A FULL-TIME JOB IN AND OF ITSELF.

INTRODUCTION

In the ever-changing, always expanding world of the Web things change at hyper speed and staying on top of the new developments is a full-time job in and of itself.

As time has progressed and technology has become more sophisticated, the Web has transformed from a collection of static pictures and text to a robust arena in which communities are built, transactions are processed, hotel rooms are booked, photos are shared, etc.

Web content creators are constantly pushing the envelope of what is possible within the confines of a browser window. Upside: Users benefit enormously from this change and innovation. Downside: The "how-to" development changes faster than skill sets. Trying to keep up with every approach to creating Web content has become a virtual impossibility.

And more importantly, in this ever-changing environment how can Web developers create projects that are not outdated before they are even launched? How can they manage expectations without getting in over their heads or letting down those to whom they must answer?

This book will guide you through the tangled path of creating and managing basic Web projects from a content and usability standpoint. It focuses primarily on front-end content, media and seamless, intuitive user experiences, in addition to occasional forays into application development and server-side technology.

WHO SHOULD READ THIS BOOK

As you might expect from the title, this is not a book about the nitty-gritty production details of how to tween key frames in Flash or code button rollover states on a home page. Instead it looks at the bigger picture: How to manage expectations and execute projects by breaking them into individual production tasks and proceeding accordingly based on parameters you define at the project's outset.

To figure out how this book could work best for you, consider how your current skills suit the many facets that comprise a typical Web or interactive media project. Are you a writer, designer, programmer, an interactive media student, a project manager just getting started? Whatever your role, knowing what the other roles entail can be an asset to your achievements.

Whatever your skill set, this book will provide you with guidelines and a general formula you can use to manage interactive media projects. The steps and concepts can be applied to projects as simple as banner ads or as complex as data-driven rich media applications.

FIGURE 1-2
PROJECT MANAGERS, DESIGNERS, WRITERS, PROGRAMMERS AND
MARKETERS CAN ALL BENEFIT FROM THE CONTENTS OF THIS BOOK.

Party Line

Scenarios in this book will be applicable to three typical parties involved in most Web projects: the client, the user, and the developer.

FIGURE 1-3
THE THREE MOST RELEVANT PARTIES ON ANY INTERACTIVE
PROJECT: CLIENT, DEVELOPER, AND USER.

The Client

The client is the driving force behind your interactive endeavors. Typically, it is the client who approached you about creating a site or project. You must answer to the client and be accountable to him or her during every step of the development process. The client has an obligation to you as well as to the claims and commitments made at the project's outset. Your ultimate goal with the client is to build a relationship of trust and mutual respect in an environment fraught with challenges.

The User

Although you may be answering to the client, it is ultimately the user whose needs must be kept at the forefront of all production decisions. Users should be defined, researched, and catered to every step of the way. If they are the least bothered or perplexed by the content it can spell disaster for your project.

FIGURE 1-5
THE USER'S NEEDS SHOULD BE AT
THE FOREFRONT OF ALL YOUR
PRODUCTION DECISIONS.

The Developer

The term *developer* is being used rather loosely here, but ultimately, this is you. Your forté may be copywriting, design, programming, etc., but for the purpose of this book let us assume you are in charge of all production tasks on some level and have at least a fundamental working knowledge of each. The basic premise for this book is that a client has asked you to develop a Web site or an interactive media project and it is your job to efficiently make that happen. Thus, you will be responsible for developing all Web content from the first through the last step. If you do not know how best to address a particular task required of you, typically it is your job to find someone who does. In many cases Web and interactive content is developed by a team of individuals, each with a particular specialty. To best define your role, we are going to assume the developer is in charge of all of them.

FIGURE 1-4
THE DRIVING FORCE BEHIND YOUR INTERACTIVE ENDEAVORS:
THE CLIENT.

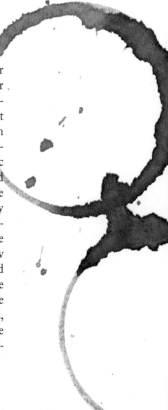

FIGURE 1-6
FOR THE PURPOSE OF THIS BOOK
WE WILL ASSUME THAT THE PERSON
IN CHARGE OF ALL PRODUCTION
TASKS IS THE DEVELOPER.

The Book Project

Throughout this book we will follow a client, a developer, and a user chapter-by-chapter through the process of a typical site overhaul. Perspectives from each entity will be highlighted and we will showcase the triumphs and challenges of each project process from initial conceptual notions to a launched Web site, promotional options, etc.

Not every scenario referenced will apply to this particular project. Much of the content on scripts and treatments, for instance, will be more relevant to story/script-oriented training modules or Flash projects and appropriate materials will be referenced within those chapters. The project we have chosen, however, does utilize many of the tasks outlined in this book and is exemplary of a typical medium-sized Web project. That said, let us meet the, uh, *players*.

MEET THE NEO-FUTURISTS

Why This Book?

This book was born from the need to educate individuals involved with any step of the media creation process on the fundamentals of meeting or exceeding expectations on interactive media projects. It offers a project process breakdown geared toward designers and developers familiar with the production process as well as writers and producers or project managers just getting started in this field.

The book assumes you have a fundamental understanding of the tools used to create Web sites. It does not cover tips or techniques for those tools, but rather how to control their output to meet the needs of a project's larger scope. In other words, you will not learn how to code Web pages or create Flash movies. You will, however, gain valuable knowledge for communicating project expectations that will keep your boss or client happy and your timelines and budgets on track.

It is doubtful that many people enter college with dreams of being a project manager. It just is not one of those lofty goals that tantalize high school students with dreams of grandeur. Let us face it, there is not a lot of glamour in project management and if you are of a remotely creative bent—a writer, designer, photographer—project management is more than likely considered a "necessary evil" rather than an important skill set essential to your professional growth.

Yet the ability to effectively maintain control of a project—any project, not just interactive media—is a skill set necessary for most careers. Good project management skills will transcend industry and application and ultimately make you successful at your chosen career path.

Projects this Book Covers

The types of projects where this book could be helpful fall into two categories: Web sites and Flash projects. Of course, Web sites can contain Flash files and Flash projects can import HTML files, so it is understood there is definitely a gray area between the two. And although a Web site is defined as something a user accesses via his or her browser, the actual content that defines a particular Web site can be developed in any number of ways using a vast array of tools, services, and technologies.

It is important to distinguish between Web sites and Flash projects in terms of production, because although many tasks overlap

FIGURE 1-7
IT IS IMPORTANT TO DISTINGUISH THE DIFFERENCES IN PRODUCTION TASKS BETWEEN WEB AND FLASH PROJECTS.

CHAPTER-BY-CHAPTER, WE WILL FOLLOW THE PROCESS OF OVERHAULING THE NEO-FUTURISTS' WEB SITE.

CASE STUDY:
Theater Company Web Site Overhaul

Meet the Neo-Futurists

Chicago's **Neo-Futurists** has been a key voice in the city's While The Neo-Futurists are in both Chicago and New York, the site we reference in the book is specifically for the Chicago Neo-Futurists independent theater scene for nearly twenty years. Creators of the seminal late night show *Too Much Light Makes the Baby Go Blind*, the company is well known for its offbeat and quirky productions and is so highly regarded that it has inspired a spin-off ensemble in New York City. *Too Much Light* offers thirty plays in sixty minutes with admission fees based on the roll of a die ($1 to $6 added to a base price of $7). New content is also based on the roll of a die, with two to twelve new plays written every week. The show has been a weekend staple in Chicago's independent theater scene since its initial premiere in December 1988, at the Stage Left Theater.

"People consider *Too Much Light Makes the Baby Go Blind* to be more of an interactive, live event rather than a theater performance," said Sharon Greene, artistic director. "There's a lot of audience participation, and the mood is generally a bit more raucous and irreverent than your typical performance. Most other theaters are closed by the time we open our doors at 11 p.m., so our competitors are usually live concerts or nightclubs rather than the latest rendition of *Macbeth* or *The Zoo Story*. Plus, all the *Too Much Light* material is both original and constantly changing, so it makes for a unique experience every week."

"PEOPLE CONSIDER TOO MUCH LIGHT MAKES THE BABY GO BLIND TO BE MORE OF AN INTERACTIVE LIVE EVENT RATHER THAN A THEATER PERFORMANCE," SAYS ARTISTIC DIRECTOR SHARON GREENE.

With sold out shows nearly every weekend and a desire to expand, the Neo-Futurists wanted to grow its Web presence and educate its audience about various performance offerings.

"We realized with our typical target audience being between the ages of eighteen and thirty, the best way to reach them was digitally," Greene said. "Postcards and fliers will always be part of our promotional repertoire, but we realized if we truly wanted to reach people outside Chicago or our general neighborhood, we needed to do it via the Web."

So the Neo-Futurists theater company set itself to the task of creating a new online presence that would address its revised needs.

"We already had a Web site," Greene said. "But it wasn't doing what we needed it to. While on the one hand we liked its mashed-up D.I.Y aesthetic, we also found that its non-intuitive interface was putting some people off. The buttons and jargon used were too cryptic, updating content was difficult, and it didn't provide an easy way for users to purchase tickets or allow us to keep in touch with them. So we realized something needed to be done."

The Content Developer

The Neo-Futurists approached Mightybytes, a media design firm in Chicago with a ten-year track record of creating dynamic online media, about overhauling its site from the ground up: new design, new content, new functionality, and a new server. The Neo-Futurists theater company did its homework and held several meetings to discuss site parameters prior to considering a vendor. By the time it met Mightybytes for an initial interview the project had a defined framework that included a first draft navigational flowchart, initial technical specifications and user profiles, and rough design guidelines.

Kristala, a content developer at Mightybytes, led the charge to find out the Neo-Futurists' needs and how Mightybytes might be able to fit the bill.

"WE ALREADY HAD A WEB SITE," SHARON SAYS. "BUT IT WASN'T DOING WHAT WE NEEDED IT TO."

THE NEO-FUTURISTS CHOSE MIGHTYBYTES TO OVERHAUL THEIR WEB PRESENCE.

KRISTALA FROM MIGHTYBYTES
AND SHARON MEET FOR THE
FIRST TIME.

A Typical User

Mightybytes' office was just around the corner from the Neo-Futurists',
so it was easy to facilitate several initial interviews to define project
logistics. During one meeting it was agreed that the average site user
would likely be representative of the people who made up *Too Much
Light's* audience, which was typically college-aged individuals between
eighteen and twenty-five.

Enter Max Crowe, a twenty-four-year-old volunteer for the Neo-
Futurists. He sometimes works the door during *Too Much Light* shows
in exchange for free tickets and membership in the theater's community.

Max's interest in the show, coupled with the
fact that he fits the profile of an average
attendee, makes him the perfect candidate for
a typical site user. His feedback on interface
options, navigation, usability, and other site
elements will make him invaluable to the
project's success.

With the addition of Max, the communication triangle was complete. Throughout this
book we will follow the Neo-Futurists' Web
overhaul step-by-step, getting feedback from
all three parties. We will document their opinions on key project considerations as they
relate to topics covered in each chapter and,
where possible, present options on how to
address each issue. Project sidebars will typically be found at the end of each chapter.

MAX TYPIFIES THE AVERAGE
NEO-FUTURIST AUDIENCE
MEMBER.

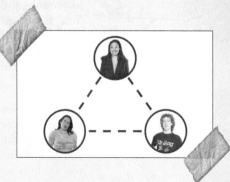

OPEN LINES OF COMMUNICATION BETWEEN ALL PARTIES ARE
CRUCIAL TO A PROJECT'S SUCCESS.

between Web development and Flash production, many are inherent to one but not the other. Depending on its intent and purpose, elements of a Flash project may need to adhere to production steps more akin to film, video or animation production than to those necessary for Web development. If you design or develop both types of content it is important to be fluent in each approach and know where one is appropriate over the other. For example, storyboards, treatments, and scripts may not be useful when putting together a company's corporate Web site, but they can be essential tools when creating training modules or story-driven educational sites using Flash. And while a navigational flowchart is indispensable to developing most Web sites, it may not be as critical when your Flash project is more linear in nature, where the only navigation might be "Next," "Back," or "Exit" buttons.

It is also important to note that, depending on the nature of your project, several overlapping terms exist that contextually mean very different things. A script to a Web developer, for instance, typically refers to code written for the purpose of accomplishing a specific task on a Web page, whereas a script for an online training module created in Flash usually refers to a document that defines action, media elements, voiceover, written content, etc. The nature of your project will determine what approach is best and where to use each term.

Step-by-Step

This book will guide you through a variety of interconnected steps used by professionals to produce and manage Web-based projects. You will explore these steps chapter-by-chapter in a linear format. However, when you apply the steps to your projects you will find that some occur concurrently while others are iterative.

You will explore project timelines early on in this book, something you will revisit and hone throughout the book and your projects. As you follow the steps of a typical project you will see how some steps are dependent on the completion of others while other steps can occur concurrently during a typical project.

FIGURE 1-8
THIS BOOK WILL GUIDE YOU THROUGH THE STEPS OF CREATING A WEB OR INTERACTIVE MEDIA PROJECT.

Although the prototyping and design chapters are in the middle of the book, for example, these iterative tasks typically occur throughout a project's lifespan. Communicating early and often about a site's visual aspects and constantly testing how proposed functionality works in tandem with the design direction is crucial to project success.

In addition to concurrent project tasks, if you adopt a rapid prototyping production philosophy throughout the lifespan of your project, its visual identity, story, media, and interactivity will be developed alongside one another and regularly loop back to address critical design, content, or functionality issues as they arise. The intent of adopting this philosophy is to incite a more collaborative communication environment during production.

Specific topics covered in this book are:

◎ Idea development
◎ User profiles and technology
   specifications

- ◎ Developing a treatment and assessing content
- ◎ Writing an effective proposal
- ◎ Information architecture and developing a solid navigational chart
- ◎ Interactive script development
- ◎ Feature/scope creep
- ◎ Art direction and interface design
- ◎ Prototyping
- ◎ Design production
- ◎ Revisions and how to handle them
- ◎ Interactive production and programming
- ◎ User testing and quality assurance
- ◎ Launching
- ◎ Promoting and maintaining a finished project

FIGURE 1-10
SUCCESSFUL INTERACTIVE MEDIA WORKS BEST WITH SUCCESSFUL COLLABORATION.

Effective Communication

Communicating concepts and ideas clearly is what design and interactive media are all about. If something is going well on a project, let the appropriate person know and your efforts will be returned. If things are going poorly, you owe it to yourself and the people with whom you are working to inform them. An occasional e-mail may do the trick, but you would be surprised at how much more effective a phone call or impromptu meeting can be. The most important thing to remember is to stay in touch. Essentially, much of this book is dedicated to that simple, but often, overlooked fact.

Collaboratively Yours

In some respects this book is a survival guide to help you communicate and work with other people. Many times creating a robust interactive media project can be a long, drawn-out, and arduous process. Many steps are involved even for a simple project and the process—more often than not—requires collaboration with numerous parties, including designers, programmers, photographers, producers, project managers, and key decision makers who hold the purse strings. Attention to details is mandatory. Although applying the concepts herein will help you stay organized and on track when working on projects by yourself, the book's usefulness will become most evident when you are required to collaborate with others.

Seeing a project to its end requires a certain amount of fortitude and the ability to check your ego at the door. Few have the wherewithal to fully flesh out their ideas to ready a project for production. Fewer still have the tenacity to see them through to fruition. In a classroom scenario, you are usually afforded the luxury of creative autonomy. This is not so true in the professional world, where you must receive approval for your work every step of the way.

Project Scenarios

Many project scenarios in this book are somewhat biased toward a corporate client/vendor

FIGURE 1-9
COMMUNICATING IDEAS IS WHAT INTERACTIVE MEDIA IS ALL ABOUT. YOUR WORKFLOW SHOULD REFLECT THAT.

scenario. Although a project funded by venture capital scenario might be different than corporate communications, venture capital endeavors mostly fall into the client/vendor relationship structure as well since the expectations of the entity paying cash are often what drive timelines and deadlines. And although it is understood that you may try to create a project purely born from an artistic or pedagogical rather than monetary need, this book is primarily about making deadlines and meeting expectations, be they your own or imposed on you by some other source.

Stay Flexible

Most importantly, when implementing tasks outlined in this book, stay flexible. Walk that fine line between keeping others happy and maintaining your own integrity. You need to figure out what works for you. For as detailed as the steps and processes outlined are, once you get a handle on them and find out what works for you, many of them will become second nature and, depending on the size and scope of each project, you will be able to hammer out much of the documentation in an afternoon or two for most projects. Although figuring out technology specifications and user profiles has its own chapter, for instance, you can probably figure out answers to many of the questions in just a few minutes by sitting down with the right person once you know what you are doing.

Remember, every project is different and carries with it a unique set of challenges. The information outlined in this book is meant to be used as a guideline for creating a variety of different interactive media projects from simple to complex. It is on large complex projects where all the chapters on documentation will come in handy. It is on short, quick projects where your ability to think on your feet and devise solutions in minutes rather than days will benefit you. This book aims to provide you with tools to address both scenarios with equal proficiency.

Additionally, the wide range of software tools used to create these projects changes every few months. Designers and developers have many tools available for creating interactive content and should use those with which they

FIGURE 1-11
STAY FLEXIBLE: WALK THAT FINE LINE BETWEEN KEEPING OTHERS HAPPY AND MAINTAINING YOUR OWN INTEGRITY.

are most comfortable. This book is not meant to address specific software concerns. As a creator of interactive media, it is your responsibility to stay on top of these tools and learn how they can best be integrated with your workflow.

Although sidebars and certain passages in the book reference specific applications for individual tasks, they are supplied as additional resources only and should not be construed as an endorsement of the application as a preferred route of production.

Get Crackin'

Now that you have perused topics covered in this book, let us take the first steps toward managing your own interactive media projects.

EXERCISES:

If you are teaching a group production class, consider assigning a full project to your class throughout the semester. You, as the teacher, will play "client" while the class breaks up into groups based on individual talents, preferences, etc. Each group should assign a project manager who must give regular reports to the client (i.e., in front of class) as the project progresses.

FIGURE 1-12
NOW THAT YOU KNOW THE BASICS, LET'S GET TO WORK.

CHAPTER 2
Conceptualization and Initial Planning

Objectives

IN THIS CHAPTER YOU WILL LEARN:

1. HOW TO DEFINE YOUR IDEA.

2. HOW TO REFINE AND QUALIFY YOUR IDEA AS A VIABLE WEB PROJECT.

3. HOW TO OUTLINE A PLAN TO CREATE YOUR PROJECT.

4. HOW TO CREATE A ROUGH OUTLINE OF TIME, MATERIALS, AND RESOURCES.

INTRODUCTION

At this juncture knowing what kind of interactive media content you are going to create is the first step toward a completed project. Will it be an arcade game that teaches kids how to floss properly?; a portfolio Web site showcasing your decoupage talents?; a "How-To" module that outlines Uncle Bob's drywall techniques and how they will revolutionize the construction industry? Idea development is a huge part of selling yourself as a creative person. Solid concepts that consider the "big picture" and still succeed strategically without being cliché or trite are rare. If you can consistently muster those from the depths of your brain you are an exceptional commodity. But if you are not one to breathe brilliant notions, what is the best way to develop a solid concept for your project?

Although creating Web content is an exploratory process, you still need a solid foundation upon which to build your ideas. Some projects start with that *"Eureka!"* moment wherein a great (or maybe not so great) idea suddenly pops up—out of nowhere—in the author's mind. Others are the result of countless brainstorming sessions between numerous individuals over an extended period of time. Then there are the projects where a prospective client drives the idea development process. Regardless, every project begins with an idea.

Get the Hook

So, what will your idea entail? It does not have to be thoroughly fleshed out yet, merely a scant notion of the direction in which you want to head. We will address how best to flesh out conceptual details throughout the upcoming chapters. For now the goal is to solidify at least one idea you can build into a completed project.

If, as in most corporate communications and client/vendor situations, an external party has approached you with its own idea, you are not excused from brainstorming. Find ways to improve the initial idea (i.e., devise a new approach to the content). Also, consider the end result of the project. How can you increase the project audience? What will make it easier—or more engaging—to use. You do not need to have the answers to these questions yet. However, if you keep them in mind during brainstorming, the easier they will be to address once you are in full-fledged production.

Remember, the definition of what your project entails will likely change before the project is completed. Creating engaging interactive media can be a lengthy and time-intensive process, even for simple projects, so though you may not know *exactly* what the end result will entail, you should consider staying within a range of topics that offer some interest to you if that is a luxury you can afford. You run

FIGURE 2-1
DEVISING A SOLID FOUNDATION UPON WHICH TO BUILD YOUR
PROJECT STARTS WITH A SOLID IDEA.

FIGURE 2-2
JOT DOWN AS MANY IDEAS AS YOU CAN FOR STARTERS.

much less risk of losing interest in a project centered on topics you are passionate and/or knowledgeable about. Unfortunately, that does not apply if an external party, such as a client or boss, has provided you with the original nugget upon which you will build your project. Still, the ability to build conceptually on someone else's idea and find ways to improve it will be a very valuable asset to you.

Honing an Existing Idea

Idea generation is one thing, but it is a much more common situation to be approached by a prospective client who already has an idea regarding what he or she wants. When someone supplies you with a concept, what do you do to make it better?

Developing someone else's idea is often more challenging than developing a concept yourself, because you are typically given specific guidelines under which to create. However, the same approach still applies. You should proceed as follows: Hone your idea development skills to focus on the single notion presented; do a competitive analysis of similar existing titles; and conceptually think through all angles of the provided topic. Through this process, you will hopefully find new, invigorating ways to convey the same information. Typically, most of this information can be gleaned from an initial interview.

FIGURE 2-3
IF YOU HAVE ALREADY BEEN PROVIDED WITH AN IDEA FOR YOUR PROJECT, CAN YOU FIND WAYS TO MAKE IT BETTER?

DESIGN EMPIRE: THREADLESS.COM'S JEFFREY KALMIKOFF, (LEFT) JAKE NICKELL (MIDDLE) AND JACOB DE HART (RIGHT).

PROfile:

Threadless.com
A Good Idea for the Right Audience

The possibility of winning a prize, coupled with the satisfaction of peer recognition, prompted Jacob DeHart and Jake Nickell to enter a T-shirt design contest sponsored by a forum in which they had both participated. Nickell won the contest and the prize: three T-shirts, which he never received. But he did earn something worth a lot more than three T-shirts: an idea, a very profitable and worthwhile idea.

Nickell and DeHart, who were both Web developers with an eye for the visual, got an idea for an ongoing, online T-shirt contest in which artists would submit designs and vote for their favorite. Then the two budding artists would print the winning design on a T-shirt, which they would make available for sale on their Web site. From that idea Threadless.com—*http://www.threadless.com*—was born.

"We started Threadless.com as a side project of our parent company skinnyCorp, the umbrella under which we did all our corporate Web design and development," DeHart said. "Every three months or so we would totally redo the site, add features, or take away features based on what our users would tell us. We'd only do orders once a week and print new shirts once a month. As we

(Continued)

(PROfile: Continued)

IN ADDITION TO ONGOING T-SHIRT DESIGN CONTESTS, THREADLESS.COM FEATURES MANY SPECIALTY CONTESTS AND PROMOTIONS AS WELL.

grew, the more time and energy we put in the site, we noticed the faster it grew and the more buzz there was about it. It went from three new shirts every month to now where we're doing six to ten designs every week."

SkinnyCorp's corporate projects provided Nickell and DeHart with bread and butter for several years while Threadless.com got off the ground. When Threadless.com took off, it was time to reassess priorities and decide if the Web design jobs were worth it.

"When you have clients calling every day it reminds you that you have money coming in," said Jeffrey Kalmikoff, who joined Nickell and DeHart to help with design and marketing. "But it came to a point when Threadless was regularly making the same amount of money as skinnyCorp and then jumped ahead by leaps and bounds. Suddenly it was a no-brainer."

Eventually the three were able to reassign their clients to friends in the business and take on Threadless.com full time, which is now the venture capital for all other projects they pursue.

The momentum behind Threadless.com has snowballed. In 2005 it brought in $6.2 million through sales—the fourth consecutive year of roughly quadrupling sales. Threadles.com has been wooed by retail corporations and in mid-2006 sold its millionth T-shirt. Its third location—

in as many years—tops out at 25,000 square feet, and the staff has increased to twenty, showing no signs of slowing down.

Threadless.com's first site took Nickell, who had worked on e-commerce sites, about a month to build. It was a bare-bones online presence: artists submitted designs, users rated them, and a basic shop allowed visitors to buy winning designs. The site currently has hundreds of features, including a full catalog, blogs, shirts for kids, type T's and specialty shirts, news, photos, songs, podcasts, and interviews with designers. It also invites you to join a twelve-month club, through which customers receive a unique T-shirt every month for a year. New content and feature enhancements are added on a daily basis.

When you look at the numbers it pulls in, it is easy to conclude Threadless.com is a success. The site grows four to five times a year along with its user base, which in the fall of 2006 was 350,000 and steadily increasing. It sells an average of 80,000 shirts a month with large spikes in sales near the holidays.

All this success is generated by word of mouth. Threadless.com has a strict zero advertising policy.

"We won't spend a dime on advertising," Kalmikoff said. "What we do is ridiculous stuff to get people to talk about what we're doing. We give incentives to get people

(PROfile: Continued)

THREADLESS SELLS AN AVERAGE OF 80,000 T-SHIRTS PER MONTH WITH LARGE SPIKES IN SALES DURING THE HOLIDAYS.

THREADLESS REGULARLY ADDS NEW FEATURES AND CLOTHING LINES TO THE SITE, INCLUDING A T-SHIRT OF THE MONTH CLUB, SELECT T-SHIRTS, AND A LINE OF TYPE ONLY T-SHIRTS (SHOWN ABOVE).

coming back or to tell their friends about us. We try to make sure it's fun and interesting for everyone."

Nickell and Kalmikoff attribute much of their success to knowing what their customers want because, in effect, they are their own target demographic. In fact, they know their customers so well that they turned down offers to design shirts for Target and Urban Outfitters. They knew being associated with the retail monoliths would ultimately hurt their business.

"We are very aware of the way people view us," Nickell said. "Working with giant companies like Target or Urban Outfitters or getting our stuff in their stores is going to be viewed as a sellout. The cool thing about Threadless is that with the exception now of major cities, in most smaller cities there are only a few people who wear our shirts. There is a certain exclusivity to our products."

On the Threadless.com blog people brag of how they do not let others in on where they found their shirts to maintain the shirts' uniqueness and individuality.

Other successful guidelines Threadless.com sticks by are: no branding on shirts, sticking close to the target demographic, maintaining an artistic slant to the site, and making smart promotional decisions to increase site traffic.

"It helps to show our community that we are people," Nickell said. "As we grow as a company I don't want to be that nameless, faceless corporation that's running something that's supposed to be fun. I want them to know we're real people."

FIGURE 2-4
AN INITIAL FACE-TO-FACE MEETING CAN GO A LONG WAY IN
CONCEPTUALIZING YOUR PROJECT.

The Initial Interview

When working with someone else's ideas, an initial face-to-face meeting can go a long way in helping you not only to define what the client has in mind for the content's creative treatment, but also to gather the key technical and navigational information about the project. We will cover questions for a project's creative treatment in this section, while technical and navigational considerations are addressed in chapters four and six.

Remember, you should be able to walk away from most first interviews with the information necessary to create an initial estimate for the project, if you ask the right questions: the client's creative aspirations and goals for the Web site, the project's technical specifications, who the typical user is, general navigation structure, brand and identity guidelines, etc. That is, of course, providing the client or project's initiator has answered your questions and given you the materials needed to accurately bid the project. If he or she does not, try to get a timeline from him or her on when you can expect answers.

Sometimes it can be helpful to enter an initial meeting with a list of pertinent questions. Or better yet, e-mail them to your prospect prior to the meeting, so he or she can get the opportunity to look them over. It will be beneficial on your end as well to research the company or individual requesting your services thoroughly prior to the meeting. If the prospect has an existing site, review it. Do an online search. Find out the company history, size, revenues, past projects, relevant decision makers within the organization, etc. Do a thorough review of its competitors as well. If you know enough people in the industry, ask other designers or developers to see if they have worked with the prospect and what the experience was like. The more information you have going into an initial meeting the more impressed your prospect will be.

You will be able to gauge your prospect's knowledge and experience level pretty quickly upon entering an initial meeting. Seasoned clients will often have an idea of what your questions will be ahead of time, whereas those with little or no experience will need to be helped throughout the process. Remember: A project proposed by the latter will take more time, money, and effort on your part.

Some questions to ask during the first meeting might include the following. (We will cover technical and architectural considerations of such meeting in subsequent chapters, but as the focus of this chapter is on creative conceptualization we have focused primarily on conceptualization questions.)

- ◎ What is the project's primary purpose?
- ◎ Who is the target audience?
- ◎ Do competitive sites exist? (If so, review them.)
- ◎ What are your ideas for visual concepts on the project?
- ◎ Are there existing brand and identity guidelines that must be adhered to?
- ◎ What kind of materials (logos, photos, etc.) can the client provide you with and how quickly can you get them?
- ◎ Will the site necessitate dynamic data requirements? (Depending on tools used, this may affect how you design the site's structure.)
- ◎ Is there a specific budget range in which the project needs to stay? (Budget will dictate how much time and energy you can commit to creative concepts.)

The initial meeting is where you will get most of the information necessary to compile an

estimate, so ask a copious amount of questions, take meticulous notes, walk away with as many materials as possible. This is also your chance to make a lasting and great first impression. Just as walking into the meeting with an educated knowledge of your prospect will impress him or her, your ability to dig deep during the meeting will reinforce that he or she made the right decision to call you in the first place.

If you have an idea of what you want to create and are not restricted by the requirements of others, jot down the idea and immediately come up with five or six more. For as good as you may think your initial idea is, a better one could be just around the corner. If you stick with your first notion and do not explore other possibilities, you might miss out on a great idea. Also, this early in production it is difficult to know if an unforeseen development hiccup will prevent you from exploring your original concept. A contingency plan is *always* a good idea.

It's All About the Details

If your mind is a blank slate, begin brainstorming by generating topics that interest you. For starters, write down anything that comes to mind, the sole point being to get as many ideas out as possible without letting your natural internal editor take over, which it is wont to do. Freeing your mind from the constraints of "weeding out the bad ideas" will allow you to look at things in a new way and draw similarities between ideas that perhaps were not obvious. Focus on generating as many ideas as possible. The only commitment you have to make at this point is the one that will drive you to finish your project.

Once you have a nice array of topics, delve into each, searching for a small nugget or kernel of information that could serve as inspiration for your project, a unique angle that can make the idea originally yours. Broad topics do not tend to make for engaging stories, so find an angle you can elaborate on to keep your story focused and of constant interest to the user.

Mind Maps

The hardest part of starting a project is often finding the perfect idea to get your creative juices flowing. Most times it takes a weighty list of "How about this?" and "What about that?" to engage your brain and creative abilities. So how do you generate that list?

There are many online resources available to assist in the creative process. Innovationtools.com— *http://innovationtools.com*—features a large number of articles, blogs, discussion threads, and software to help spark the imagination. MindManager 2002, a link from the Innovation Tools site, is a mind-mapping program that helps you visualize the many paths of a project from start to finish.

If you have the time, sitting down with a good book can sometimes inspire you. *The Artist's Way*, by Julia Cameron, is a helpful resource. It offers direction

FIGURE 2-5
MIND MAPPING, THE PROCESS OF CHARTING THOUGHT PROCESSES WITH FREEFORM DIAGRAMS AND IMAGES IS USED TO GENERATE AND CLASSIFY IDEAS IN AN INTUITIVE MANNER.

through thought-provoking exercises, as well as advice about defeating many of the roadblocks to creativity. Natalie Goldberg's *Writing Down the Bones*, *Wild Mind*, and *Thunder and Lightning* contain idea generation exercises and tricks to jump-start your creative process. Although not geared specifically toward interactive media, many of the exercises included can be customized for specific unique ideas, be they Web-based or not.

You can also try journaling, attending art exhibits, visiting the library, or talking to someone who inspires you. Often, the right idea will come if you give yourself the space and time to find it. The key is finding the right space and allotting enough time to fully explore as many notions as possible.

FIGURE 2-7
DRAWING A BLANK? ASK A LOT OF QUESTIONS IN AN INITIAL MEETING TO GET YOURSELF ON THE RIGHT PATH.

FIGURE 2-6
JOURNALING IS ONE OF MANY THINGS YOU CAN TRY TO FIND THE RIGHT IDEA FOR YOUR PROJECT.

For example, if you have decided you want to do something on the environment, is there a particular facet of that topic you think could be well served by an interactive media piece? On its own, the environment may be too ambitious a topic to tackle. An individual component of environmental issues, however, could be more manageable and more engaging. Perhaps you could focus on mercury poisoning in local rivers and how it affects the food supply. It is all about the details. They make a story rich and immersive and—if you keep them specific and pointed—the topic will take on a universal resonance all its own.

We have heard several stories about corrupt lawyers or politicians, struggling pioneers trying to eke a living off the "fat-o-the-land," healthcare providers facing moral challenges inherent to their jobs, alcoholics wrestling with addictions, etc. Treated in a broad manner, these topics or characters can easily become mere two-dimensional stereotypes. We roll our eyes at stories we have heard over and over. Unlike more passive mediums like film or TV, this is particularly problematic with interactive content since the user is armed with mouse and finger and typically is not afraid to use them on buttons like "Next" or "Close Window." Sure, one could always change the TV channel or walk out of a movie theater. However, the very nature of computer-based media means your audience is even less patient than it would ostensibly be were it watching TV or at the movies, because the power to move on is so immediate. Focusing on individual traits and the mechanics of what makes a specific situation unique, however, allows us to suspend our disbelief over stereotypes and transcend them, instead focusing on the individual moment and making us less likely to quit our browsers or press "Eject" on the disc drive.

The Other Side

Once you have decided on the specifics of your idea, outline both sides of the story. Conflict of some sort is at the heart of every great story. Try to think objectively when developing the pros and cons of your story. Although you ultimately may want to present a single side of your argument, it is essential you weigh both sides. This will arm you with the information necessary to present a thorough and well-researched case.

If we use the example of local mercury poisoning, research the reasons why corporations along riverbanks may want to dump their mercury-riddled waste into the water. What is a specific company's stance on this issue? Why is it taking this stance? How does it benefit the company? You may or may not like the answers, but they will allow you to make informed decisions regarding the nature of your content and often will provide you with some good dramatic tension around which to build your story.

Develop a Thesis Statement

After your brainstorming is completed, you need to develop a statement of your thesis, a sentence or two that sums up the goal of your project in as succinct a manner as possible. If you were writing a movie script, this would be the "pitch" to get the studio's approval. Feel free to use comparative analogies—"It's like *Cats* but with mermaids and Bernie Mac"—if you feel this will help you get the point across. Paring down your idea like this will help solidify the concept to its single defining point, the foundation upon which the project will be built. It will be the first statement you use in a proposal, the

Back to the Drawing Board

Here is an unfortunate truth: No matter how well you define your project at this juncture, you will likely change nearly every single aspect of its creation as you move forward. Although picking a single idea to develop will help hone your process, planning for flexibility is one of the most important elements to remember as you develop your content. Your project will change repeatedly, so build that into your process from the outset. If you are working in a client/vendor scenario, now is the time to gently remind your client that until the necessary project elements are properly defined you cannot provide him or her with a realistic breakdown of financial resources or a project timeline.

FIGURE 2-8
DEFINE, REFINE: MANY OF YOUR INITIAL IDEAS MAY NEED TO BE RECONSIDERED DUE TO BUDGET OR TIMELINE CONCERNS, SO STAYING FLEXIBLE WILL HELP YOU BE PREPARED SHOULD THAT HAPPEN.

FIGURE 2-9
PENCIL IN A VERY ROUGH TIMELINE AND RESOURCE LIST FOR CRE-
ATING YOUR PROJECT, BUT DO NOT GET THE PEN OUT JUST YET.

springboard from which you will build your concept and develop your project.

THE INITIAL PLAN

Now that your project's intent has been loosely defined, figure out how you will accomplish your goals. It is still too early to define many aspects of the process, but you should be able to identify general goals and development phases, as well as pencil in a rough timeline and a broad list of resources for completing various tasks. This will move you closer to gathering the information necessary to draft a proposal of realistic fees for producing the project.

Define Your Audience

The specifics if defining target users and their needs are covered in chapter four, but from the outset it is essential to decide who will access your content and consider how his or her needs will affect your project. In the client/vendor scenario, initial conceptual development often is the client's responsibility as he or she must define a project sufficiently in order to communicate his or her needs to prospective vendors. Defining the audience for a Web site or media project usually falls under this umbrella. If you are a client putting together a proposal request, a good developer will ask this question in the initial interview, so it is best to arm yourself with this information. Often it can be helpful

to simply make the distinction between whether your site is geared toward consumers or business-to-business, that distinction alone can tell you volumes.

Define Your Goals

Now that you have an initial idea or have plundered the depths of your prospective client's ideas, how will you proceed? How will you mold the broad scope of what you want to create into something that is viable within the constraints of your timeline or (if you know this information) budget? Somewhere in the idea development process you need to begin defining the project goals. Defining your goals will help you compile a treatment or creative brief you can include with an initial proposal.

To start, ask yourself the following questions:

- ◎ **How much information must your concept disseminate?** Can you get your point across in a few well-written paragraphs or will it require a tome of content? Will the content be nonlinear or will it be better served by more linear story-telling?

- ◎ **What media format(s) will best serve your content?** Should you tell your story with text, narration, a video demonstration, animation, or all of the above? Will some of the content be best served by using Flash and if so, which version will you target? Remember to keep your audience in mind when defining this.

- ◎ **How will you make your content interactive and engaging?** Telling a story is one thing but how will you keep your users engaged with multiple avenues for navigating through your content? Can you keep your content detailed while still clearly and concisely disseminating the information? Remember, less is more when it comes to reading content on a screen versus on the printed page.

- ◎ **How will the above considerations affect your timeline and budget?** Video and audio production can be more involved and time-consuming tasks requiring more resources and equipment than written words and images, but their impact can be significantly greater. If you add a dozen video clips to your Web site, how will that affect its timeline and cost?

◎ **Can you create the entire site with your own internal resources or will you need to outsource portions of the project?** If you need to outsource portions of the project or bring on additional resources to complete it, where will you find these resources? How much will they cost?

Broad answers to these questions will provide you with a base framework for defining your project goals. Now you can address individual phases of work and the process by which they will be accomplished. You can also begin to define a realistic—but flexible—schedule for completing necessary tasks. Again, *flexible* is the operative word here. Although reigning in the conceptual elements of your project is helpful and essential, many details are unclear, and many questions unanswered. As solutions reveal themselves, you will often be required to alter your production approach in order to move forward.

Define your Tools

It is a good idea at the outset to attempt defining what tools you plan to use for developing the site. Consider what you know about the project and how that knowledge may affect the tools you need to use for development. Keep in mind that you will likely revise the specifics of which programming languages will best serve the project, whether the site will require custom media elements—such as photography, video clips, or Flash files—and, if applicable, how the server configuration will affect content development and pages being served. A list of proposed tools, applications, and programming languages will help you define resources for creating your project—such as hosting providers, programmers, etc.—and will allow you to build a rudimentary framework for how your project will be constructed. Remember, the framework can easily be changed at this juncture based on the

resources you line up. It is less of a problem if you decide to switch from a Microsoft to an Apache server at this point, for instance, than it is once you are far into the development process. If you will outsource portions of your project, collect input on the definition of tools that will be used for the project as well.

Set a Launch Date

Once you have defined general project goals, set a very tentative launch or release date for your project. If the project concept was provided to you, most likely it was accompanied by a requested completion date. If the requested date seems unrealistic, offer suggestions for a more manageable timeline. Shoot for something you feel confident you can implement. Remember, depending on the information that has been provided, you may not have a firm grasp on project details, so be realistic. If your suggestions for an alternate timeline are met with resistance you may want to rethink whether you are the appropriate party to complete the job. There is no sense in setting a precedent this early in the project wherein your resources get tapped out right from the start just to make an impractical deadline. Little happiness lies at the end of that road. If a client has waited until the eleventh hour to begin work on a sizable site that needs to be done in a week, it is a pretty safe bet that procrastination is exemplary of his or her overall work habits and an unrealistic timeline is just the beginning of your problems.

When you are considering schedules, remember to be realistic above all other things. The job *will* take longer than you think it should. Give yourself ample time to complete all the documentation, writing, design, production, programming, and testing/debugging you think the project will require. Then double—or triple—that amount in order to allot time for revisions, scope changes, delayed approvals, etc.

Find Resources

The scope of your project will likely drive the resources that can be realistically procured in order to complete it. A larger project will require more time and a wider range of specific expertise than a smaller one will. If you are one of the few people who can write,

FIGURE 2-10
UNREALISTIC DEADLINES ARE NOT ONLY EXHAUSTING, THEY CAN
SET YOU UP FOR FAILURE AS WELL.

design, program, test, debug, and manage with equal proficiency, then perhaps finding external project resources will not be required. Those people are few and far between, however, and often are prone to taking too much. Knowing your own strengths and weaknesses is an important part of implementing a successful project on time and under budget.

Most likely you will want to define a team of people who possess specific expertise in areas where you lack competence. Assess your own strengths and weaknesses to know what areas these may be, then contact potential team members and alert them to the project prospect. Depending on the nature of your project, these will be co-workers, freelancers, independent contractors, or other companies on which you know you can rely. Make no commitments at this time, but rather line up possible resources willing to clear schedules to suit your needs and those of the project. The purpose here is to put out feelers and discover what your options are, it is not to sign contracts and make legal commitments you will no doubt need to change later.

The Money Question

Ultimately your project will need to adhere to a specified budget. In the real world, whether you are a client or a vender, employee or free agent, *someone* has got to pay for your time. Paying in cash is often far less painful than paying in drama, or worse yet, lawsuits. A good idea will not get you very far if you have to

fight every step of the way to accomplish it due to budget constraints. Facilitating a proper dialogue up front regarding project finances will go a long way toward a smooth and relatively painless production process. It is important to broach this topic with the appropriate individuals as early on as possible, so neither party is wasting the other's time.

That said, when is it possible to define a project's budget? Can you do it without knowing the project's content or structure? Typically not, especially if you have not lined up production resources. Herein lies what is often the biggest challenge of creating Web content: committing to a budget before defining project details. The more information you can get out of your initial meeting the better chance you will have of providing an accurate estimate of fees for your services and a realistic timeline for executing required tasks.

Sometimes it can be very helpful to know a project's budget range up front. There is no use tailoring a $100,000 project to a $10,000 budget. Knowing how much money you have to work with, can go a long way in helping you define the constraints of your project and customizing production to a specific figure range. This is true from idea development forward. If you are a vendor, however, the people holding a project's purse strings (your clients) are not typically very forthcoming about the figures they have allotted for a particular project. Sometimes they will request an initial bid then confess to having half the amount outlined in your proposal. At that point, it is up to you whether you want to do the project for half the budget you originally proposed or attempt to refine the content to work within their budget.

To avoid this time-wasting hassle, use your initial meeting to ask whether the project must stay within a specific budget range. It can be very helpful to both your bidding and conceptualization process if you know what number not to exceed. It will help when defining resources as well. A $300/hour illustrator will not get much done, for instance, on a $4,000 project, so it might be best to exclude that idea at the conceptualization stage.

Ultimately, a project's finances will drive everything you do. Like it or not, you will

FIGURE 2-11
TRY TO FACILITATE FRANK DISCUSSIONS ABOUT A PROJECT'S BUDGET FROM THE GET-GO.

need to have a firm grasp on them from the beginning of a project to its end.

Summary

Once you have completed brainstorming ideas and compiled an initial plan on how best to realize your goals, you should have a solid idea of the direction in which you want to head as well as a rough idea of how to get there and even perhaps how long it will take. You will first need to hone down the results of your initial brainstorming sessions to a solid researched concept and assess how that will make the site viable to target users. Depending on the nature of your project, you can do this alone or in a group. Notes and sketches from an initial meeting will help you outline creative goals and put together an estimate. A preliminary discussion of technical and budget concerns can go a long way in getting you the information needed to effectively create an initial proposal, as can a few phone calls to key resources that can help bring the project to life.

As long as you ask the right questions, specific details of which will be covered in more detail throughout later chapters, the results of an initial interview should typically yield enough information to provide a first draft proposal.

CASE STUDY:
Conceptualization and Initial Planning

Brainstorming with the Neo-Futurists

When faced with the task of defining how its site overhaul would be executed, the Neo-Futurists went through a number of committee meetings and ensemble-wide brainstorming sessions to define the company's needs and goals prior to approaching any external resources.

"Having a few technology-savvy ensemble members really helped us compile the materials we needed to talk to Mightybytes," Sharon Greene said. "It also helped reign us in a bit. We are people used to imagining something first and figuring out how to do it later. It was very helpful in the initial stages to get insights regarding the workload our brilliant ideas might actually be generating and how much money executing those ideas may actually cost."

The committee held several meetings to outline overall goals before approaching the entire ensemble.

"We knew that since we generated our own content, the site would always be unique and funny, so we decided we should focus on making the design as user-friendly as possible," Greene said.

Once the committee felt it had several solid ideas with which to work, it presented them to the entire ensemble. The committee took copious notes while the ensemble reviewed ideas

THE NEO-FUTURISTS GOT FEEDBACK FROM THE ENTIRE ENSEMBLE BEFORE DEFINING THEIR GOALS.

THE NEO-FUTURISTS WERE WELL-PREPARED BY THE TIME THEY APPROACHED VENDORS ABOUT OVERHAULING THEIR SITE.

THE NEO-FUTURISTS WERE IN AGREEMENT THAT WHILE THEY LOVED THE ORIGINAL SITE'S IMPERIAL RED AND THE TOO MUCH LIGHT BABY HEAD WAS A DEFINING IMAGE FOR THEM, THE SITE'S REMAINING ELEMENTS WERE SOMEWHAT CRYPTIC TO THE AVERAGE USER.

and generated more. Once a general consensus was reached among cast and committee members, the Neo-Futurists readied its materials and gave Mightybytes a call.

"We considered other developers," Greene said. "And many of them had impressive design and systems credentials. Our primary reason for choosing Mightybytes was their communication style. They responded promptly to our e-mails and came to our office to meet our entire staff after an initial phone conversation. They listened intently to our needs and asked smart questions regarding our visual aesthetic, the tone we

wanted for the site, etc. What set them apart was their quick, friendly, and accessible staff. They made us feel like our project was their highest priority."

"The Neo-Futurists were a lot more prepared than many clients who have approached us," said Kristala from Mightybytes. "In our initial interview they provided us with a completed flowchart, specifically outlined their business and creative goals for the site, took us on a tour of their entire facility, and revealed a complete company history. This gave us a contextual overview on which we could begin building our own creative notions as well as an idea of the project's scope."

Kristala also noted that the Neo-Futurists was forthcoming about budget concerns right from the outset.

"They were very upfront about the fact that grant applications had been filed to fund this endeavor and that project implementation as a whole may need to be piecemeal based on which grants they received," Kristala said. "With this in mind, they specifically asked Mightybytes to provide an initial bid as though they were any other corporate client, so they could use that information on grant applications. We not only appreciated their candor but by revealing this information up front it showed us that the Neo-Futurists were looking to forge a long-term working relationship, which we always find more fruitful for both parties in the long run."

"WE APPRECIATED THAT THE NEO-FUTURISTS WERE LOOKING TO FORGE A LONG-TERM WORKING RELATIONSHIP," KRISTALA FROM MIGHTYBYTES NOTED.

Idea Generation

The idea of randomness plays a key role in the Neo-Futurists' approach to theater. Each audience member's admission to *Too Much Light Makes the Baby Go Blind* is between $8 and $13, determined by the roll of a dice at the front door. The thirty plays performed in sixty minutes are chosen randomly by what the audience says, what the ensemble hears, and how well they pull the thirty random numbers (one for each play) off a clothesline strung across the theater's ceiling during each performance. Each audience member is given a nametag with a randomly selected name on it when he or she pays the admission. Also, a dice roll delineates how many new plays will be written and performed the upcoming week. Knowing this, Mightybytes aimed to extend that concept of randomness to the Web presence as well.

"In the brainstorming sessions it became apparent to us that utilizing as many randomly loading site elements as possible would not only be consistent with the Neo-Futurists' approach to making theater, but would also give their site a fresh and unique look every time a page was visited

RANDOMNESS PLAYS A KEY ROLE IN THE NEO-FUTURISTS' PHILOSOPHY.

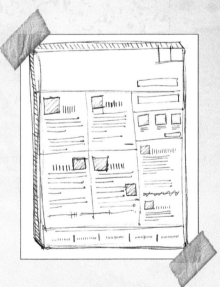

THE FIRST MEETING BETWEEN MIGHTYBYTES AND THE NEO-FUTURISTS RESULTED IN A COPIOUS AMOUNT OF NOTES AND SKETCHES THAT WERE ESSENTIAL TO COMMUNICATING KEY GOALS AND CREATIVE TREATMENTS.

as well," Kristala said. "So we made sure to keep that idea in mind as we conceptualized our creative treatment and prepared to put a proposal together."

Over the course of the initial meetings between Mightybytes and the Neo-Futurists, numerous reference sites were reviewed and many creative ideas were thrown on the table, revised, embraced, or cast aside. The end result was a stack of notes and sketches on both sides as well as a clear definition of what was expected from each party moving forward.

One of said sketches provided the information necessary for Mightybytes to develop and revise a hand-drawn wire-frame inventory of assets and elements the home page might include. Although not meant to imply design decisions or art direction intent, this document successfully conveyed how information and interactivity on the home page might be structured and helped in creating the site's navigational flowcharts.

"Our first meetings were very productive for both sides, I think," Kristala said. "If only every client who approached us was that prepared and forthcoming. It would make our jobs so much easier. I think this will be a fun project and I am really looking forward to working on it."

"OUR PRIMARY REASON FOR CHOOSING MIGHTYBYTES WAS THEIR COMMUNICATION STYLE," SHARON FROM THE NEO-FUTURISTS NOTED. "THEIR QUICK, FRIENDLY, ACCESSIBLE STAFF MADE US FEEL LIKE OUR PROJECT WAS THEIR HIGHEST PRIORITY."

EXERCISES:

- ◎ Brainstorm initial ideas for your project.
- ◎ Make a list of twenty-five project ideas based on your brainstorming.
- ◎ Write up thesis statements for five of your twenty-five projects.
- ◎ Decide on a final topic for your project.
- ◎ Define rough project specs: users, technologies, tools.
- ◎ Make a list of resources to bring your project to life.
- ◎ If you are teaching a group production class, consider the following:
- ◎ Break the class into groups based on clients and content developers.
- ◎ Have each group assess another's ideas and vice versa. Offer feedback based on what will make an idea viable for the target demographic or the Web in general.

TOOLS

Sample documents are included on the CD-ROM included in this book:

- ◎ Mind Map Activity

Files can be found in the folder labeled with the corresponding chapter number and title.

CHAPTER 3
The Initial Proposal

Objectives

IN THIS CHAPTER YOU WILL LEARN:

1. WHAT MAKES A GOOD PROPOSAL.

2. WHAT ELEMENTS TO INCLUDE IN YOUR PROPOSAL.

3. HOW TO "COVER YOURSELF" WITH THE TERMS OUTLINED IN YOUR PROPOSAL.

Now that you have brainstormed ideas and done some cursory initial planning for your project, the next inevitable step is to build a proposal. But what kind of information should you include to ensure your bid ends up on the top of the heap every time? How do you keep your costs competitive while still maintaining some margin of profitability? How do you prove that you know the client's problem better than anyone else and can offer the best solution? How do you offer just enough information to whet their whistle without giving away too much information and finding out later that the client hired someone else to implement *your* solution? Sadly, there are no foolproof answers guaranteed to win the business every time. But let's take a look at several tried and true options for creating a solid proposal that shows you have done your homework and are the right choice for the job.

HOW MUCH DOES A WEB SITE COST?

A friend of a friend has just launched a new line of hair products. Your cousin wants to put his portfolio of driftwood art online. Your doctor is looking to increase his client base. Whatever the situation, it is inevitable a client or prospective client will pose you this question: "How much does a Web site cost?"

Often this is the first question asked by uneducated clients. They do not want to know what a good site can get them, how it can help their business strategy, or what and how much content they should include on it. They just want to know how much it is going to cost. Beware this scenario.

If you have even the foggiest notion of the development process for Web or interactive

FIGURE 3-2
IF YOU ARE BEING ASKED TO PUT A PROPOSAL TOGETHER, MOST LIKELY YOU ARE IN SOME KIND OF CLIENT-VENDOR SCENARIO.

media you know what a ridiculously unanswerable question that is at the outset of any project. And if you answer it without considering the ramifications, you are setting yourself up for failure.

It may not be possible to gather all the information needed on a job before you have to put together a full-blown proposal. However, it is in your best interest to gather as much information as possible about the project content and deliverables before you broach the topics of costs and timelines. Ultimately, you will have to gauge your price based on how many "unknowns" there are and how forthcoming your prospect has been regarding budget and the details of project scope.

FIGURE 3-1
HOW MUCH DOES A WEB SITE COST? DON'T ANSWER THIS QUESTION UNTIL YOU HAVE ASKED A LOT OF YOUR OWN FIRST.

Let us take a step back for a second. If you are being asked to put together a project proposal, you are typically in a client-vendor scenario, so that is the primary focus of this chapter. This is not to say if you are an in-house agent you will never be asked to create a proposal. However, the chance is much greater that you will be asked to do so if you are a freelancer, vendor or independent agent.

If you commit to figures prior to finalizing content, your client has the freedom to add functionality, information screens, revisions, etc., with no consideration for how much time it will take to implement them. Ultimately, if you signed a contract for a "per project" fee, prior to defining said project you could end up working around the clock for a pittance. A few projects like that and your interactive media career will be over before it gets off the ground. If you are in the rare situation where development money is no object or you are being paid by the hour, then this is obviously less a concern. Unfortunately, most projects do not play out like that, which is why you have to be *extremely clear* about how much work you are willing to do for the money and timeline agreed upon. And to know how much work will be expected of you, you need a clear idea what you are going to create.

The reality is that most clients do not understand the amount of labor it takes to create interactive media. They do not comprehend the ramifications of requests such as, "Just add another button here" or "Make it work on the Mac." Nor should they. As their vendor, it is your job to understand their requests and provide them with a realistic estimate of what it will take to get the job done based on a clear understanding of their intent. And rest assured, if you miscalculate the amount of work it takes and have signed on the dotted line, they are not going to be sympathetic when you ask them for more money. Most times they will just shrug their shoulders in a "not my problem" stance.

There are many factors that will come into play when deciphering the scope and budget of your project: existing relationships with the client, perceived worth of the project, corporate budget restrictions, technological requirements, definition of content, etc. The list goes on and every project is different. It is your responsibility to know as many of these factors as possible before committing a figure or timeline to any one of them.

It is essential to note that the production process for Flash projects, like computer-based training modules or linear "click-through" presentations, often require a different set of production tasks than most Web sites. Will you need someone to write a narrator's script? How much animation, video or audio will be necessary to get the point across? What will each animation screen entail? Will you need to shoot your video on a blue or green screen and composite while editing? Will the project require original or stock music? You will be required to ask different questions to define the specs for rich media projects like these versus standard image and text-driven Web sites.

Subsequent chapters will address many of the questions you should ask prior to bidding. This chapter is included early on in the book because 95 percent of all Web or interactive media projects will require *some* sort of financial commitment prior to commencing full production. Remember, if you do not have enough information about a project's scope to make an accurate financial commitment then *do not* make a commitment. Do your research and remember to pad your proposal accordingly to compensate for the time it takes to properly define and bid a project.

Proposal Precursors: Defining Projects

Before we address what goes into a good proposal, let us talk about a few scenarios that may affect how you might put together a proposal.

The RFP

A well-produced Request For Proposal (RFP) can help take the guesswork out of defining your project. An RFP is typically compiled on the client side (although it can be equally helpful within a single organization) and outlines as much information about a potential project as possible, including creative concept, technical specifications, timeline, navigational flowchart,

FIGURE 3-3
A DETAILED RFP CAN SAVE LOTS OF TIME AND EFFORT WHEN PUT-
TING A PROPOSAL TOGETHER.

and sometimes even projected budget range. A well-written and thorough RFP will go a long way in defining your project and should generate solid ideas on how best to produce it. If the document is thorough and well written, it will save you a lot of time and the information included therein will become the building blocks you use to create your proposal. If a prospective client has approached you about a large Web project and has not provided an RFP you may want to request one. Typically, if clients are requesting quotes from multiple vendors they will have done at least *some* legwork toward defining their project's details.

First Contact

A detailed RFP can get you off to a great start, but what if a prospect asks for numbers yet cannot define the project any further than, "My company needs a Web site"? What do you do then?

There are a couple options for addressing this scenario: You can blindly suggest a random number and hope it is enough to cover the project, or you can dig deep to define the project and apply figures based on what you discover. Of the two, the latter is the more sensible approach but is also fraught with its own set of challenges. Do you handhold prospective clients through the process of defining their project? And if so, how do you get paid for doing so? Research takes time and unfortunately most prospects are not willing to devote the financial resources typically necessary to obtain the right information prior to awarding an entire project to a specific vendor.

If your project is one that requires a narrative-style script be developed, such as in the case of Flash-based training or educational modules, the matter is complicated even further. You cannot assess the content until a script is written, but you cannot write a script until someone agrees to pay for the time for you to do so. So what do you do?

Digging For Gold

The best-case scenario is arguably one in which you provide the client with a preliminary figure to develop his or her content then build in an option to present a fully fleshed-out project bid once all content has been defined. The client pays you an initial deposit to define his or her project with the understanding you will provide him or her with a detailed proposal and documentation once the process is complete. This may include defining users and technology profiles, developing navigational flowcharts, finding resources, drafting up a script, and developing rapid prototypes to serve as a rough sketch of how a project's interactivity will work. It all depends on the terms of your negotiations.

An initial deposit based on defining a project will give you an opportunity to wade through the process of knowledge transfer with your prospect before committing to a final development figure. This offers two advantages: 1) The client gets a much more realistic idea of budget and timeframe based on the fact that his or her project is now well defined; 2) Your thorough understanding will allow you to allocate resources toward getting it done on budget and within the proposed timeline.

Smaller projects may not require this level of commitment and, as was noted in the previous chapter, you may be able to acquire all the information necessary to bid a project during the course of an initial interview. The larger your prospective project is, however, the more opportunities it will have to sprawl beyond your grasp without proper definition. If a prospective client is forging new career territory and has never done this before, the chances for a project to careen out of control increase exponentially. If the project requires a detailed script and extensive video or audio production, the chances are greater still. An initial project deposit based on proper scope

FIGURE 3-4
FULL-FIGURED: AN INITIAL DEPOSIT CAN GO A LONG WAY IN HELP-
ING YOU DEFINE A PROJECT'S CONTENT. UNFORTUNATELY, MANY
CLIENTS MAY REQUIRE A BUDGET COMMITMENT FOR THE ENTIRE
PROJECT PRIOR TO HIRING YOU.

definition can go a long way in alleviating many production problems down the line.

But let us be realistic. Although it may seem like a logical step for a company to hire and pay an external resource to assist in defining an ambiguous project scope, the reality is that this typically only happens on large-scale projects and sometimes not even then. Many job prospects will expect you to give them an estimated development figure and hold you to it, regardless of whether the project scope changes. With that in mind, your proposal needs to be *very* specific about which tasks are and which are not included.

FIGURE 3-5
BIDDING BLIND: COMMITTING TO A PROJECT BUDGET WITHOUT
FIRST KNOWING ITS SPECS CAN BE FRAUGHT WITH POTENTIAL
HAZARDS.

If you are bidding on the project against other prospective vendors, asking for a project definition fee up front will likely not be an option. Then you will have little choice but to build the time necessary for project definition into your proposal. If you do not get the job it will unfortunately be lost time you will not be remunerated for. Hopefully the client will have done his or her homework and can provide the details you need upon request for easy and efficient project definition and thus a quick proposal turnaround.

Bidding Blind

But what if the client does not want that? What if he or she wants the figures now? Often times, annual budgets will not wait on process or proper project definition before allocating money. Your client is being pressured by his or her boss to get an estimate, so it can be put in the budget.

In this situation it is smart to bid high and plan for the worst. If you know the project scope is going to change as it becomes further defined, you want to be certain you have allotted enough time and money to cover that. Since you are not sure what you are bidding on, you have to presume the project definition process is going to yield unforeseen factors. Always leave some "wiggle room" in the budget and timeline to account for extra revisions, enhanced functionality, etc. If upon presenting the proposal you note your prospect exhibits the telltale signs of "sticker shock" suggest alternative options to moving toward a figure all can agree on without selling yourself short.

Rare is the client who does not have some sort of idea how much money he or she is willing to spend. Prospects who are not forthcoming about their budgets are typically shopping for vendors based solely on price and, unless you desperately need the work, best avoided. Remember, although the end result of what you will produce could, in some circles, be construed as a product, you are ultimately providing a service and must charge accordingly. Prospects who will not give you an idea of their general budget range most likely consider your work a product rather than a service and want a single price they can fixate on, regardless of how the project is defined. Thus, if the project scope changes all they see is the end result, and they will not understand why the budget must change along with the scope. Those who are happy to offer up a general financial range in which to custom tailor a solution are typically more willing to negotiate on specs and timelines, and they tend to be more flexible when surprises arise.

Knowing the client when bidding blind can help a great deal. If you have worked with him or her before and remember he or she is prone to requesting revisions or requiring a multi-tiered approval process wherein half the company needs to sign off on your work before you can proceed, you can plan accordingly.

But even when you build flexibility into the budget you must be as explicit as possible regarding what you will or will not do for the proposed price. Be certain to define how many rounds of revisions your price includes. Tell your client you will present him or her with a contract addendum once your project has been defined. Explain that the addendum will state how many information screens will be included with the price, how many images will be licensed from stock companies, etc.

The Dangling Carrot

Unless they offer something up in writing—and usually even then—do not be fooled by clients dangling the prospect of future business under the premise that you will create their current project for free or for a lesser budget. It rarely works out that way. Few long-standing, mutually beneficial relationships flower from the seeds of a project done for free or little money.

This scenario usually plays out on a more intimate level: an entrepreneur, friend or family member approaches a young designer/developer looking for experience and samples for his or her portfolio. The situation varies, of course, but the dynamics are usually the same: one party needs the work, the other needs the work done but cannot afford or is unwilling to pay to make it happen.

This relationship is typically doomed from the beginning. The root of the problem—although often financial in nature—is typically flawed

FIGURE 3-6
DON'T BE FOOLED BY THE PROSPECT OF POTENTIAL FUTURE BUSINESS IN EXCHANGE FOR LOWERING YOUR RATES. FEW LONG-TERM RELATIONSHIPS FLOWER FROM THE SEEDS OF A PROJECT DONE FOR FREE OR LITTLE MONEY.

on a deeper level because the relationship starts off without the mutual respect needed to make long-term client/vendor relationships work. Thus it begins a downhill slide almost as quickly as first contact is made. The client wants to cut corners any way he or she can, including paying less (or nothing) for digital media services. The developer, in turn, is not inspired to do a good job because he or she is not compensated appropriately. What is even worse, the developer might be forced to find a second project to make ends meet, which is time spent away from the first client's project. Deadlines are missed. Features are dropped. Tempers flare. And then it starts to get ugly. Ultimately, no one is happy and more often than not the two parties part ways, usually with the client still owing the developer money and the developer threatening a lawsuit.

If the relationship does make it beyond the first project, a precedent has been set between the two parties. When project number two shows up, the developer is rarely offered the opportunity to make up cash lost on the previous project or even get paid a realistic amount for the work involved on the new project. Sticker shock sets in on the client side while resentment begins to overshadow the relationship from the developer's perspective. Because the developer was willing to do the first project for a truncated fee, the client will not hesitate to attempt cutting another deal with the developer by offering less money for the second project. Eventually, this disparity will rear its ugly head, undermining any hope the two parties may have had for a synergistic relationship.

Although it is unfortunate that many startups and entrepreneurs lack the financial resources to fund effective digital communications, you too need to make a living and those you work for need to understand that. Your time is worth money. However, do not price yourself out of the ballpark, but do not work for peanuts either. Clients need to respect your abilities as well as the necessity to be paid for them. If there is no mutual respect in your client relationships, there can be no relationships. It will only be a matter of time before the bottom drops out. Why set yourself up for failure? You should save your "bridge burning" cards for when severing ties works to your advantage, which is rarely if at all.

This kind of relationship might work if the designer or developer has little to no real-world experience and needs to build up a portfolio he or she can use to acquire more work. Even in this case, however, it might be better to find a not-for-profit organization you are passionate about and offer your services to it rather than trying to help out a friend or family member. If you believe in the work you are doing, it will show, and in this case you can supplement the lack of financial gain with your passion for the organization's cause.

Spec Work and Creative Solutions

Occasionally when a client requests that you bid on a project, he or she will also request that you submit designs as part of the proposal. This request shows a lack of respect for your expertise as well as a lack of understanding that you need to be paid for your work. If a client is asking you for designs up front, then he or she does not possess a fundamental understanding of process and will likely fight you tooth and nail on monetary issues. You also likely do not have enough information or materials to accurately represent what the client is requesting in an interface design comp. As we have discovered, there are many questions that need to be answered before you can begin the interface design process with any remote expectation of accuracy.

Also, do not to be too detailed in your proposals regarding the specifics of your creative solutions. It is perfectly acceptable to outline your process, but remember the client is under no contractual obligation to choose you as the developer when you submit a proposal unless you have him or her sign a non-disclosure agreement (NDA)—which he or she probably will not do (although he or she may ask you to sign one). There is nothing to prevent the client from taking ideas presented in your proposal and offering them to a vendor who will do the same job for less money.

Your primary goal when submitting a proposal is to show the client that you thoroughly understand the project and give him or her a peek into your production process without giving away too many details.

FIGURE 3-7
BEING ASKED TO DO SPEC WORK SHOWS A LACK OF RESPECT FOR YOUR EXPERTISE. DON'T LET PROSPECTIVE CLIENTS GET AWAY WITH IT UNLESS YOU *REALLY NEED* THE WORK.

Elements of a Good Proposal

Once you have gathered enough information to create a good proposal and procured the tools with which to create it, what information should you include to help you get the

Proposal Tools

How you choose to create and present your proposal is up to you. Much of how your proposal information is conveyed will depend on your relationship with the prospect. Some clients may be perfectly fine with brief, bulleted copy pasted into an e-mail from Microsoft Word. Others may insist that you include details on every production element for the entire life of the project along with a company history, work samples, and references. A long-term client, as opposed to a new client, will be more flexible in how you present information to him or her.

The complexity of your project will often dictate the details of your proposal and the tools you use to put it together. Larger projects may require that you present proposal information using text, imagery, charts, graphs, Web links, etc., in which case you may want to use a page layout program that gives you more control over your proposal's look and feel and can output to Adobe PDF or another widely accepted document format.

From a project management standpoint, a discussion of proposal tools cannot be considered thorough without at least a brief mention of Intuit's QuickBooks software. An industry standard accounting and business management tool, QuickBooks may seem a bit daunting to the uninitiated but once a company file is set up and configured, it really is easy to use. After pertinent contact information for a prospect is input, QuickBooks' estimating tools allow you to break down projects in terms of services, associated descriptions, notes, terms, etc., auto-tallying the total for each new proposal element you add. You can associate a different hourly rate or flat fee with each estimated service as well. More recent versions include an estimate/invoice layout designer and the ability to track hours clocked per job via an online tool, the latter feature being extremely helpful on jobs that require multiple parties.

One of QuickBooks' primary advantages is that its built-in estimate building tools are fully integrated with the rest of its functions, allowing you to utilize the information from your estimate throughout a project's life cycle, cross-referencing it with tracked time, overall business profitability, previous jobs for the same client, etc. Once a job has been completed all the information associated with that job can be used as the basis for final invoicing with a single mouse click.

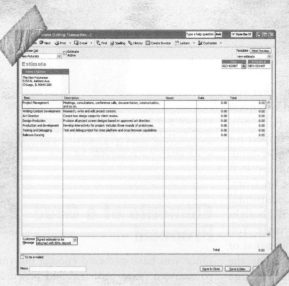

FIGURE 3-8
INTUIT'S QUICKBOOKS MAKES EASY WORK OUT OF CREATING ESTIMATES.

FIGURE 3-9
CREATING A SOLID PROPOSAL THAT WILL WIN BUSINESS AND POSITION YOU AS A KNOWLEDGEABLE PROFESSIONAL REQUIRES A NUMBER OF KEY ELEMENTS.

FIGURE 3-10
STATE THE PROJECT'S GOALS IN A CONCISE MANNER AT THE BEGINNING OF YOUR PROPOSAL.

Project Description

How will you show that—in addition to understanding a project's goals—you also know how to accomplish those goals? Propose a solution that outlines the project's needs and how you intend to meet them. This is not a line item breakdown of individual tasks but rather your strategy toward approaching the project and how you will bring it to fruition. Keep it short, sweet, and to the point.

job? Your primary goals should be to answer the what, where, why, when and how questions a project poses, and prove you thoroughly understand its needs and you are the right person for the job. Any information that will support this cause is fair game but be careful not to overload your prospect with useless information. Be detailed but do not be boring. Often including a simple Web site link with appropriate samples will be far more effective, for example, than including pages and pages of case studies or longwinded company history or background.

Each project comes with its own set of unique challenges, but the following questions provide rough guidelines for building a solid proposal. The order in which you include the following information should best reflect how you think it will be received.

FIGURE 3-11
STATE HOW YOU WILL ACCOMPLISH THE PROJECT'S GOALS AS CLEARLY AS POSSIBLE WITHOUT BEING TOO WORDY.

Project Goal

How will you concisely convey in as few words as possible the project's precise goal? After a cover page that contains all your pertinent contact info, project title, date, etc., begin the actual body of your proposal with a brief statement outlining the project's goals. This should be a terse and succinct paragraph that shows you have a clear understanding of what the project entails. Think of the goal statement as your project's boilerplate or thesis statement. It should coerce the reader into wanting more information.

Market and Competitive Analysis

How will you show that you understand why the project is necessary and where it fits into the bigger picture? Assess a prospective project's needs and describe in detail how it fits into the overall market. Create a competitive analysis statement that outlines what

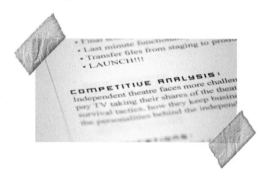

FIGURE 3-12
A COMPETITIVE ANALYSIS WILL SHOW THAT YOU UNDERSTAND THE CLIENT, THEIR MARKET, AND HOW TO BEAT THEIR COMPETITION.

kind of competition the project will face once released. Close with a statement describing approaches you will take to address rival projects and improve yours to exceed the competition's efforts. If you show you have done your homework in understanding a project's overall context, this could increase your chances of being awarded the job over someone who has not included this information.

Qualifications

Why are you the right fit for the job in question? Create a statement that includes relevant past projects, awards, market experience, and any bio information on key project personnel. Sell your skills to the best of your ability, but remember to be concise. If a prospect has questions or wants more information to help sell you as the right choice, he or she will most certainly ask or search it out.

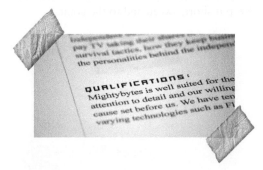

FIGURE 3-13
SHOW SPECIFICALLY WHY YOU ARE BEST-SUITED FOR THE JOB UNDER A QUALIFICATIONS HEADING.

Breakdown of Tasks

What will you do to bring this project to life? Give specifics of exactly what you propose to accomplish during the course of the project. Include as many tasks as you think the project will entail, from initial meetings and documentation through art direction, design production, programming, testing/debugging, project management, etc., and provide a

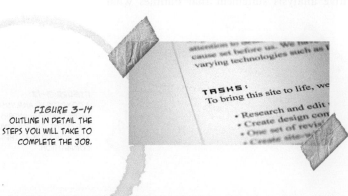

FIGURE 3-14
OUTLINE IN DETAIL THE STEPS YOU WILL TAKE TO COMPLETE THE JOB.

FIGURE 3-15
ASSOCIATE FIGURES OR A RANGE OF FIGURES FOR EACH OUTLINED TASK.

description of each and how they relate to the project's needs.

Budget Estimate

How much will all your services cost? Break down the project's finances as they relate to the tasks. Associate a figure with each task or include a range to cover a number of tasks. Be as specific as you can. If you think a Web site will have 12 pages or a Flash project will have 12 screens of information, estimate specifically for 12 screens or pages. If the project goes above or below that count, you have firm footing with which to renegotiate your contract. And keep in mind that these things *always* take more time than you think.

Expenses

Will you incur expenses during the job's life cycle? Will you need to license stock photography or video footage? Will there be shipping or supply costs? Must you acquire new software to complete the job? If so, be certain to outline as many of your expenses as possible. You may not know what the specific amount will be this early in the project cycle. However, make sure to include language under your contractual terms that you will be reimbursed for all expenses.

Timeline

When will you be able to complete the project? Even if the project has not been completely defined yet, including a rough timeline to completion of associated tasks can be helpful to identify a proposed launch or release date, or at the very least give you something to strive for. Remember to give yourself a wide

FIGURE 3-16
MAKE SURE YOU INCLUDE LANGUAGE IN YOUR PROPOSAL FOR
REIMBURSEMENT IF YOU THINK EXPENSES WILL BE INCURRED DUR-
ING THE PROJECT

FIGURE 3-17
IF APPLICABLE, INCLUDE A TIMELINE TO COMPLETION FOR
THE PROJECT.

berth in terms of deadlines if possible to allow for unforeseen production hiccups or extra revisions.

Promotion and Maintenance Strategy

How will you address the project once it has been completed? Including information for project promotion and maintenance shows you are strategic and forward-thinking rather than focusing only on the project's production.

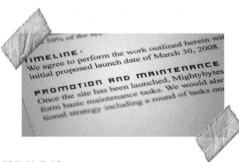

FIGURE 3-18
INCLUDING SUGGESTIONS FOR PROMOTION AND MAINTENANCE
AFTER A PROJECT IS FINISHED SHOWS THAT YOU ARE FORWARD-
THINKING.

Although this is not a mandatory facet of any proposal, including it as a "value-added" service could mean the difference between you being awarded the contract or not. At the very least you may suggest an option the prospect may not have considered and he or she will appreciate that. You can increase both the audience and shelf life of your project if you include a solid promotional campaign and maintenance plan with your proposal. Getting the word out about your project will increase its visibility and, if applicable, sales while simultaneously increasing your own visibility. Devising a maintenance plan that allows for content updates, bug fixes, and general improvements to your content will increase its value over time and keep its content fresh and viable. It may be rather difficult to apply dollar amounts to these tasks at this point, but be certain to leave yourself open for a discussion of terms.

Training

Will the project require that you train any parties on proper use of the tool you will develop? If so, be certain to include passages in your proposal that outline the details of what this could entail, how much it will cost, etc.

FIGURE 3-19
WILL YOU BE REQUIRED TO
TRAIN INDIVIDUALS TO ADMIN-
ISTER THEIR PROJECT ONCE IT
IS COMPLETE? IF SO, INCLUDE
A STATEMENT SAYING AS MUCH
IN YOUR PROPOSAL.

Contractual Terms

What are the proposed terms under which you will take the job? Will you maintain ownership of the source code or will the client? Will you be paid a "kill fee" if the project is canceled half way through production? Will you reserve the right to use the project's end result for promotion and to acquire more clients? How will the project payment structure play out? Be sure to include all contractual details for the project, especially in terms of

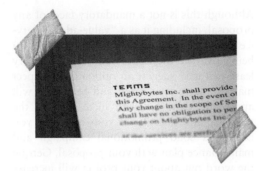

FIGURE 3-20
BE SURE TO INCLUDE ANY
IMPORTANT LEGAL TERMS IN
YOUR PROPOSAL AS WELL.

finances and scope change. A sample contract is included on the CD-ROM that accompanies this book.

Signoff Sheet

At the end of the proposal, include a signoff page that includes a statement of work and has room for signature, date, etc. This page should state that you have been awarded the contract and are authorized to begin work on the project based on the date signed. You may want to allot space at the bottom of each proposal page for initials. Once you have been awarded the project, duplicate the executed contract for yourself and the client.

Payment Structure

How you structure payments for a project is between you and the person making the financial decisions on the project. Whether you bill for 50 percent of a project's total estimated fee up front with the balance due upon completion, one-third payments at the project's beginning, middle and end, or hourly billing once every couple weeks, be sure to state these terms in your proposal. It helps to be flexible in this area as financial considerations on the client end could

change significantly from project to project. Just make sure to make whatever arrangement you agree upon part of your proposal.

Scope Document

In effect, your proposal serves as a first draft scope document. Within its pages you have defined all project details, timelines and costs, and in addition to some sort of financial deposit, you will require a signoff as approval of its content. Upon being awarded a project, its scope can and usually will change over time, however. Having an effective strategy in place to address and document scope change should be a key part of your workflow.

Change Request Forms

Language in your proposal that refers to a change request form can be a helpful means to address scope change or "feature creep" once you are working on a project. Essentially, a change request form outlines any tasks and associated costs considered "out-of-scope" from the original proposal and requires a client signoff before work can commence on those tasks. If the additional work will delay the project deadline, relevant language should be included in the form.

Fundamental changes to your project's scope will affect both its bottom line and the timeline in which you can implement a completed deliverable. It is important to track changes in your project's definition and cross-reference those with the details of your proposal to effectively communicate whether any tasks will take more time or cost more money than initially discussed. Be certain this is clearly understood by any involved parties.

FIGURE 3-21
MAKE SURE YOU GET A SIGNED
APPROVAL TO BEGIN WORK ON
THE PROJECT BEFORE ACTU-
ALLY DOING SO.

CONCLUSION

Creating proposals that will win projects every time requires a finely balanced mixture of experience, vision, detail, and clarity. And even then there is no guarantee. As great as your portfolio and as concise as your proposal may be, there is always the risk that a better fit for the job is also in the running. The best you can hope for is to put your all into the proposal, make your portfolio as attractive as possible, and keep your fingers crossed. The biggest asset to regularly being awarded jobs is often an existing relationship with the client. If you can establish that, you have already risen above a large percentage of your competitors.

EXERCISES:

Create a proposal for the project described in the RFP on the supplemental CD-ROM.

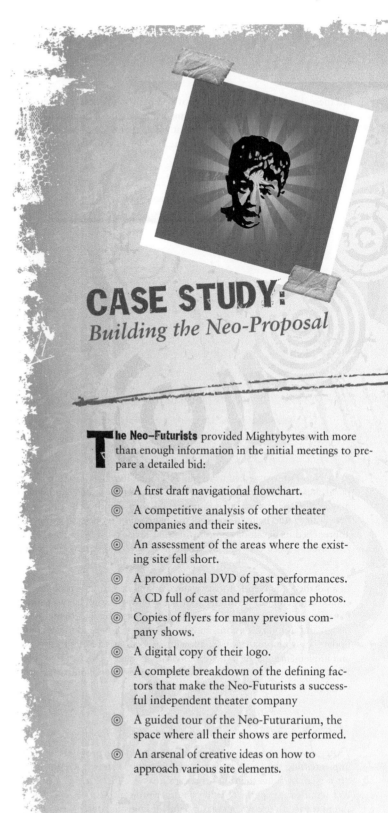

CASE STUDY:
Building the Neo-Proposal

The Neo–Futurists provided Mightybytes with more than enough information in the initial meetings to prepare a detailed bid:

- ◎ A first draft navigational flowchart.
- ◎ A competitive analysis of other theater companies and their sites.
- ◎ An assessment of the areas where the existing site fell short.
- ◎ A promotional DVD of past performances.
- ◎ A CD full of cast and performance photos.
- ◎ Copies of flyers for many previous company shows.
- ◎ A digital copy of their logo.
- ◎ A complete breakdown of the defining factors that make the Neo-Futurists a successful independent theater company
- ◎ A guided tour of the Neo-Futurarium, the space where all their shows are performed.
- ◎ An arsenal of creative ideas on how to approach various site elements.

All these details and documents provided the tools necessary to create a detailed and thorough proposal. Armed with stacks of notes and rough sketches on scratch paper, the folks at Mightybytes set about undertaking the task of compiling these materials into a cohesive proposal.

"The Neo-Futurists asked us to build as much functionality into our proposal as possible knowing full well that many of those bells and whistles may need to be implemented in phases," Kristala said. "The proposal's first draft would be used as a tool to obtain grant money, so we approached its development knowing that revisions were inevitable. We also wanted to be very succinct about how we could deploy the project in phases."

In a nutshell, the Neo-Futurists wanted an online business tool that could better connect it with its audiences. This still sounds awkward to me...Tim The company wanted to accomplish this by improving the site's design and usability, creating an infrastructure that would make content updates easy and manageable, allowing users to buy tickets to shows, and implementing a customer relationship management tool that would allow the company to sort donors, ticket buyers, merchandise buyers, etc., by different criteria for targeted marketing.

Joomla CMS

"After just a few discussions, we chose to build our proposal around implementing the Joomla content management system," Kristala said. "It was an obvious solution for several reasons. First, it was a tool we had significant experience using on other projects. Our clients also found it easy to use when creating and adding site content. Its extensible architecture allows developers to add components and site functionality over time, which coincided with our discussions of a multi-phased site

deployment for the Neo-Futurists. And finally, as an open source tool it certainly fits within a low-cost pricing structure."

With a universally agreed upon development solution in mind, Mightybytes created a proposal that outlined each step of the full site deployment and broke those steps down in groups with separate pricing structures for each.

Phase 1 included the following:

◎ Final technical requirements based on profiling a site's typical user.

◎ Art direction and design production for the site's visual overhaul.

◎ Design production, template creation, and Joomla installation.

◎ Programming and production of site style sheets, sitewide navigation system, random elements, PHP includes, etc.

◎ Testing and debugging.

Phase 2 primarily addressed creation and deployment of an online ticket-buying system. It included the following elements:

◎ e-commerce shopping cart development.

◎ Creation of front-end ticket and donation forms.

◎ Configuring shopping cart and forms integration.

◎ Site SSL certificate implementation and configuration.

◎ Testing and debugging transaction engine.

Phase 3 deployment entailed creating and implementing a customer relationship management (CRM) tool the entire company could use to stay in touch with its audience and facilitate targeted marketing campaigns. It included the following tasks:

- ◎ Research to define relationships between various Neo-Futurists audience factions and how to appropriately reach them.
- ◎ Installation of a Joomla CRM module that will work with research-based needs.
- ◎ Database development and configuration of Joomla module to facilitate needs.
- ◎ Creation of e-newsletter template for use in targeted mailing.
- ◎ Testing and debugging CRM system.

Mightybytes also offered several promotional and maintenance strategies with the initial proposal as well as a number of additional features to add engaging elements, such as games and animations, throughout the site. The proposal language made it clear these enhancements would be at least a Phase 2 or Phase 3 deployment but that the company was thinking about the site long term.

During the initial meetings Mightybytes asked the Neo-Futurists about the company's current hosting provider and if it would be amenable to switching to a suggested provider Mightybytes had extensive experience working with. Thus, Mightybytes included hosting solutions as part of its proposal.

"We have a hosting provider that we have grown quite fond of due to their excellent pricing, availability and support structure, and the wide variety of services they offer," Kristala said. "Of course it's not a requirement to work with us, but if our clients require hosting in addition to content development services we can pretty much guarantee a smooth experience when they are involved."

"The right hosting solution makes all the difference when successfully deploying a Web site that relies so heavily on server-side components, as in the case of the Neo-Futurists' Joomla site," Kristala said. "Developers need reliable hosting providers to help ensure that a site's launch goes well."

Once completed, the first draft proposal provided a comprehensive long-term plan for a complete ground-up overhaul of the Neo-Futurists' online identity, although Mightybytes purposely left out several key elements that a typical comprehensive site plan might contain.

"Writing is obviously one of the Neo-Futurists' strong suits, so we knew they would want to have complete control over the site's written content," Kristala said. "While we offer that service and will certainly make ourselves available to consult with them regarding how best to bring their written content to life, we didn't feel it was necessary to include that service in our proposal."

The Neo-Futurists' writing strengths coincided with the choice of Joomla as a development tool.

"As a system that separates design from written content, Joomla offers us the flexibility to give our clients freedom to control their own content," Kristala said. "Once the template is complete and the initial site shell and structure has been deployed we can turn the Neos loose on filling the shell with content after only a brief training session."

Allowing the Neo-Futurists to create and manage the site's content gave Mightybytes an opportunity to keep pricing down, something the Neo-Futurists appreciated.

"I find when working with collaborators, whether in artistic or business endeavors, the important thing is to be really up front and honest about the resources you have and the goals you want to achieve," Sharon said. "And if everyone speaks candidly with trust it always works out for the best. Mightybytes understands that as soon as we have the money to implement the next phase we will get in touch with them. In the meantime we will focus on completing Phase 1 to everyone's exacting standards."

After several subsequent discussions, the Neo-Futurists agreed to move forward with Mightybytes as its developer for a several-phased approach. With a revised contract sign-off and a deposit check from the Neos, Mightybytes hit the ground running to begin implementing Phase 1 of *http://www.neofuturists.org*.

TOOLS

Sample documents included on the CD-ROM that comes with this book:

◎ Sample RFP
◎ Sample proposal for a fictional project
◎ Sample contracts
◎ Sample Change Request Form

Files can be found in the supplemental disc labeled with the corresponding chapter number and title.

INTERACTIVE PRODUCER ALESIA TYREE TALKS ABOUT WHAT SHE LOOKS FOR IN A GOOD PROPOSAL.

PROfile:

Alesia Tyree, McDougal Littell
Elements of a Good Proposal

As an interactive producer with educational publisher McDougal Littell, Alesia Tyree often plays a critical decision-making role when proposals from prospective vendors cross her desk. She says she looks at several key factors when reviewing proposals for various projects.

"Don't try to buy the business," she said first and foremost, referring to the practice of vendors undercutting their fees in an effort to win contracts. "If your price point is so much lower than that of other vendors vying for the same job, a client will know you are trying to buy the business and no one will be happy in the end. The vendor may end up harboring some resentment if, or when, the project goes over budget and if the project does go well the client will inevitably expect bids for future estimates to come in just as low for other projects as they become available."

There are many things that impress Tyree when reviewing proposals but a clear understanding of how to get a project done is at the top of her list.

"We look for vendors who can demonstrate that they clearly understand what we ask of them and show us in detail what it will take to complete a project," she said. "It's definitely not just about the numbers. It's about comprehending the tasks at hand and having the resources to accomplish them."

A big part of gaining that understanding, Tyree says, comes from asking questions about the project.

"Vendors who query us about content in an RFP show that they want to understand the project and what is expected of them," she said.

She also places a high value on the vendor's creative expertise and approach to a project.

"Reviewing a new vendor prospect's portfolio is essential when considering them for a project," she said. "If their work is consistently impressive and shows the successful completion of projects similar in scope and range to what we are looking for or a firm grasp on our industry, that is definitely a step in the right direction."

Tyree says she also values vendor recommendations from industry people she knows.

"If a vendor referral comes from a trusted source I would be much more inclined to consider them for a project over someone I have never worked with or heard of before," she said.

(Continued)

(PROfile: Continued)

In addition to a creative approach and solid understanding of the project, Tyree notes that a vendor's proposed budget ultimately plays a role in her decision making.

"I almost always have a budget figure in mind when sending out RFPs, but don't typically reveal these numbers to the vendors because I want an accurate and realistic budget from them," she said. "If the figures in a proposal are higher than we have budgeted for internally and I want to work with the vendor, I will tell them that the price needs to be lower and we can go from there.

Tyree agrees that the number on the bottom line is important, but it should be realistic.

"Figures that are so obviously out of the ballpark will no doubt be just as detrimental to the possibility of a vendor winning business from us as numbers that are too low," she said. "We are ultimately looking for design and technology partners with whom we can build relationships based on frank discussions on every aspect of a project, including timelines, production techniques, and of course money. When we find vendors with whom we can build that rapport we typically stick with them."

Alesia Tyree is a senior project director at McDougal Littell, a division of the Houghton Mifflin Company.

www.mcdougallittell.com

CHAPTER 4

Defining Project Specs

Objectives

IN THIS CHAPTER YOU WILL LEARN:

1. WHAT PROJECT SPECS ARE AND WHY THEY ARE SO IMPORTANT.
2. HOW TO DEFINE TARGET USERS.
3. HOW TO CREATE A TECHNOLOGY PROFILE.
4. HOW PROJECT SPECS AFFECT THE PRODUCTION PROCESS.
5. THE IMPORTANCE OF GETTING A SIGN-OFF.
6. WHAT CAN GO WRONG WITH IMPROPERLY DEFINED PROJECTS.

The next step in the production process is important: It is time to define who will use your content and how they will use it. First, outline a target user profile and compile a set of technology specifications to guide you through the remaining steps in producing the project. Once established, these specifications will serve as a benchmark against which all functionality and design usability is compared for the final content.

DEFINE BEFORE YOU DESIGN

After you have decided what you want to create you might be inclined to dive right into the design process—sketch interfaces, create design comps, bring your "vision" to life—and then head into production. It does seem like a natural next step. And if you are creating the project for a client, one of the first questions she will undoubtedly ask is, "When can I see something?" So why not jump headlong into designing visuals for the project once we know what we want to create?

The answer is clear: You run the risk of really messing up the project, and it is not an efficient use of time. Although you often get your best work done in the creative process when you run with your whims, falling prey to the pitfall of creating visuals for the project before you have defined it is the quickest way to finding yourself in digital deep water. The number of things that can go wrong increases exponentially the further along in the production process you get without proper forethought.

There are somewhat serious consequences to the oversight of designing prior to defining. For example, if a client paid you to develop

the content on his or her Web site, but the user of the site is unable to experience that content (i.e., she cannot get information on the client's product, access a certain section of the site), the client will be dissatisfied with your services. If a user is unable to experience your content why build it in the first place?

The key to avoiding time-consuming and possibly devastating problems is to outline—in as much detail as possible—the specifications of what you want to create, and then follow those specs while still allowing your creativity to flourish. This is not to say that if a visual solution occurs to you in the middle of the night you should ignore it. Instead, jot it down, sketch it out, etc. and file it away for later use. Who knows? You may have nailed a project's design without realizing it. The important thing here is to focus on project definition so that you are armed with all the necessary information when you *do* enter the design process.

Creating a list of specifications is important. It provides a critical framework around which to begin assessing content, writing a script, compiling media assets, creating artwork and rapid prototypes, etc., through the entire production process. Whether you are developing a small interactive project independently or a large one in a team environment, creating proper specifications will help to define the project's development environment, the target user, and the target user's technology profile. If you are in a team environment, this information will help you and your fellow team members develop individual aspects of the project, while—as a team—you are working toward the same product. If you are developing the project individually, this phase will provide you with a document to reference should you come across a developmental stumbling block (i.e., how large to make the

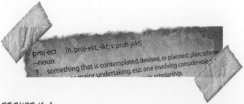

proj·ect   [n. proj-ekt, -ikt; v. pruh-jekt]
—noun
1.   something that is contemplated, devised, or planned; plan; scheme...
...major undertaking, esp. one involving considerable...
...in scholarship.

FIGURE 4-1
DEFINING YOUR PROJECT BEFORE YOU BEGIN PRODUCTION ON IT CAN GO A LONG WAY IN PREVENTING MISCOMMUNICATION DURING DEVELOPMENT.

video, how many sounds can play at once, etc.). Either way, developing a spec provides a consensus as to what is being developed and how it will be accomplished.

Another important aspect of interactive project development is that the spec will help you set up a testing environment in which to check the project's viability based on how it performs under the conditions outlined in your specifications. In other words, if you decide your project must perform on a Pentium II Windows 98 computer with a 250 MHz processor and 64 MB of RAM, then it is in your best interest to have access to a machine reflecting those specifications on which to test and run the project as it is being developed. This will help you catch development snags and performance flaws early in the production process, when it is inevitably easier to fix them.

Of course it is impossible to foresee every possible development snag. Unforeseen problems can lurk around every corner and can delay or postpone the project timeline or even cancel it. However, if you create appropriate specs for the project, you have done as much as you can to prepare for the unexpected.

Defining a Spec

A spec can consist of several elements: a target user profile, a technology specification, system requirements, a definition of the testing environment, and a list of the factors that affect development. Each section will vary in length depending on complexity of the project

FIGURE 4-2
CREATING APPROPRIATE SPECS FOR YOUR PROJECT ON THE FRONT END CAN ALLEVIATE MANY HEADACHES DURING PRODUCTION.

JUDI LAPINSOHN SAYS STRATEGIC FOCUS GROUPS CAN BE THE BEST WAY TO DEFINE THE KIND OF CONTENT YOUR AUDIENCE WILL REACT FAVORABLY TO.

PROfile:

Judi Lapinsohn
The Importance of Strategic Focus Groups when Assessing Content

Judi Lapinsohn, president of Judi Lapinsohn and Associates, an Evanston, Illinois-based qualitative research firm, says never underestimate the power of the data you can glean from a good focus group.

"A series of strategic focus groups can be the best way to identify key information about user preferences," she said. "Armed with that knowledge, developers can create the most user targeted Web and interactive content."

Lapinsohn continually stresses the importance of getting to know specifically what customers want from a Web site or interactive project.

"User needs and desires should drive content creation," she said. "So it is crucial to undergo focused research at the front end of a project and ask the right questions of different involved user groups. What do users want or need from your content? What are the processes by which they acquire information? Where else do they go to get the same type of information? What other types of information might they want? How do they want it to be organized? Answers to all these questions are important because different customer segments will want different things. For example, existing

(Continued)

customers may want to know their order history while prospective customers will probably want to easily find product applications and pricing."

Lapinsohn also points out that the focus groups she moderates typically do not define a target audience.

"We usually have a pretty clear idea who the audience is going into a focus group," she said. "While that audience information may be refined, this research is meant to define content for the target audience rather than the target audience itself."

Lapinsohn's specialty is qualitative rather than quantitative research.

"Quantitative research answers the *what* question providing statistics, such as *x percent* say one thing is important whereas *y percent* say another thing is important." she said. "Qualitative research answers not only the *what* questions, but the *why* questions as well, so it is appropriate to use when trying to refine content ideas. And, those answers are incredibly relevant to developers as they create interactive content, because it gives them valuable insight into specific user behaviors and perceptions."

Most of Lapinsohn's Web site groups typically consist of six to eight people. Generally, target subjects are those who fit a site's general demographic and tend to feel and think the same way about the relevant topic. The number of focus groups or interviews conducted largely depends on the number of customer segments, but she advises running no fewer than two groups and plan on doing more. The research plan includes a screening questionnaire and discussion guide, and the results of the groups are presented in a detailed report for the client.

In the case of a Web or interactive project, information gleaned from Lapinsohn's report helps her clients move forward with development. She says that although she does not typically interact with the developer directly, smart clients will involve developers in the entire research process. Developers might observe the focus groups in the backroom, watch tapes, read the report, etc., in order to identify how best to advance their project, be it continuing the research process, starting over, or creating a prototype and testing that with users.

"The most important part of a focus group is not so much what people want but *why* they want it," Lapinsohn said. "A good developer can use these answers as an opportunity to address any number of site functionality issues."

She may also recommend other qualitative research practices depending on the project needs: one-on-one interviews offer more personal experience feedback for the client, something that can be particularly worthwhile when dealing with sensitive subject matter. Phone interviews can help gather a wide range of opinions from participants all over the country, and phone focus groups, similar to conference calls, allow a group to work on the same part of a program or site in unison. Ethnographies, wherein subjects are observed in their own homes or in the workplace, can be helpful. Additionally, she says, online research tracking services like keynote.com—*http://www.keynote.com*—can be helpful to diagnose Web site performance problems at multiple levels.

No matter how you approach developing interactive and Web content, conducting focused research on how your content will be received by your target users can be an extremely helpful development asset.

"It's much easier and less expensive to find out what your users want and need before you begin development, so you can create a well-informed, targeted Web site or interactive project the first time," Lapinsohn said.

Judi Lapinsohn is the owner of Judi Lapinsohn and Associates.

www.judilap.com

FIGURE 4-3
GET TO KNOW THE USERS WHO WILL EXPERIENCE YOUR CONTENT
AND MAKE DECISIONS ACCORDINGLY.

and the number of known said factors. The goal is to create a spec that covers as many aspects of project production as possible and can be agreed upon by all parties involved. Most importantly, all said parties must agree and sign off on the final spec.

Target User Profile

Profiling the project's target user will help you define *specifically* who you are developing for, especially what kind of computer or device the user may have on which to experience your content. This information will help guide you through the design and development processes to ensure what you create can be experienced by those you create it for.

But what if your project is geared toward a broad, loosely defined user base and you are unable to define specifically who the average user will be and how she is going to experience your interactive media piece?

There are always going to be unknown factors regarding your audience. That is one of the many inevitable aspects of developing interactive media. Sometimes you will not know who is going to pick up, purchase, download, or log-in to your content and start using it. Your audience will simply be too broad to pinpoint in as much detail as you would like. As long as you set up expectations properly by making said user aware of what it takes to successfully run your content then the onus is no longer on you. But you have to know what those requirements are before you can impart them on others.

Remember, when you have defined the target user, do not pigeonhole yourself into a development corner by limiting your audience to said user. Instead, consider said user as the lowest common denominator around which your content will perform acceptably, and then use that information to develop accordingly. That is the non-negotiable part. If you cannot figure out exactly who the target user is, you have to figure out what an acceptable level of performance will be for the project and set a cut-off point, so a user with a less-than-adequate machine or device will know whether she needs to upgrade her hardware, software, plug-in, etc., to experience the media properly.

It is important to cast a wide net in terms of who might use the project. Put as much thought as you can into all possible users and try to define who will comprise the majority of those users. Will they be business users in an office environment? Will they be students in a college media lab? Will they be cell phone users subscribing to a Web service? Children pulling an LCD game from the bottom of a cereal box? Stay-at-home parents? Seniors? Create a list and then decipher who from that list will be the most likely users. Place them in order from most likely to least, even adding targeted percentages if you think you have a solid enough grip on who your users will be.

It is extremely important to put a lot of thought into this and the next step (the technology profile, discussed in the next section). Defining your user base gives you the opportunity to make an educated guess as to what kind of device or computer the target user will use to access the content. Once you have that information, you can make informed decisions regarding an entire range of interactive media development options that will increase the performance and usability of the content. Ultimately, the decisions you make at this juncture will directly affect those you make throughout the rest of the design and development process.

Technology Profile

With target user the definition of the target user in hand, you are ready take the first steps toward defining what kind of computer or media playback device said user has for running the content.

Users in the digital age of visual computing are generally an impatient lot. They will not wait long for content to download, waste time exploring content if the interface is not intuitive and the information they need is not available within a mouse click or two, and they certainly will not even bother viewing the content if playback of audio, video, animation, or other media elements are jerky, stutter, or for whatever reason, refuse to load. Thus, it falls on the developer's shoulders to make sure their experience is as flawless as possible.

Unfortunately, there is often a large gap between a developer's vision and what will perform acceptably on the widest number of machines or devices within a user base. This situation, if not managed properly, can at best lead to a poor reputation as a developer and at worst law suits, court cases, and devastating financial results. Depending on the nature of the project, the stakes could be very high. The key to success: Reach the widest possible audience without sacrificing too much of your vision and product performance. Another sizable step toward making that happen is to define the technology used to access the content.

The goal—when defining a technology profile—is to be as detailed as possible regarding the devices that will be used to access the content. Not only do you need to define *what* the lowest common denominator machine or device is that will run the project, but you also need to consider as many options for that device as possible. In other words, if you decide that your content will be most commonly accessed by stay-at-home mothers using a standard personal computer, you should give considerable thought to defining exactly what the phrase "standard personal computer" means in regard to stay-at-home mothers when developing the content. Would the typical computer a stay-at-home mother might use differ significantly from one a senior citizen or student might use? And if so, in what ways? Amount of installed RAM, processor speed, operating system, Internet connection speed and browser support are just a few of the things to consider when defining options for accessing the content.

To create a technology profile, first review your list of target users, focusing primarily on the group that comprises the largest segment. To the best of your ability, define what the average user within this segment might use to access the content, then define the specifics of that device for the average user. Do the same for other prospective segments, paying attention to device and performance options each segment may have when accessing the content.

Remember, we are talking lowest common denominator here. Stay-at-home mothers, for example, may have access to a wide range of personal computers with completely different specifications based on factors such as household income, number of children, geographical location, ethnicity, etc. Your goal is to define what development options make sense to reach the widest number of them.

So Many Questions . . .

In the following sections we have provided lists of sample questions to consider when creating a technology profile for your average target user. It is important to ask yourself each question as it relates to the type of content you are developing and who will use it, then come up with the best answer possible. You may not have specific answers to every question, but the goal is to answer as many in as much detail as possible.

FIGURE 4-4
ASK A LOT OF QUESTIONS WHEN TRYING TO DECIPHER THE TARGET USER'S BEHAVIOR AND TECHNOLOGY PROFILE.

Personal Computer–based Applications

If your content is going to be accessed by computer users, consider the following questions:

- ◎ What computing platform will the majority of users view the content on?

- ◎ What operating system version will be used?

- ◎ What processor speed will the typical machine have?

- ◎ How much RAM will the typical machine have installed?

- ◎ What kind of monitor will the content be viewed on?

- ◎ What is the monitor's size, resolution and color depth?

- ◎ Will the average user need a plug-in or third-party software to view the content and if so, how will that plug-in or software be distributed?

- ◎ Will the content require a technical support infrastructure once it has been released/launched?

Internet–enabled Applications

If your content requires an Internet connection, consider the following questions:

- ◎ What browsers will the content support?

- ◎ Which versions of those browsers will be supported?

- ◎ What is the speed of the target user's Internet connection?

- ◎ Will the average user need a browser plug-in or third-party software to view the content and if so, how will that plug-in or software be distributed?

- ◎ How will loading content be addressed for users with a slower connection?

Device–specific Applications

In addition to the previous questions, careful attention should be given to development considerations for applications that will run

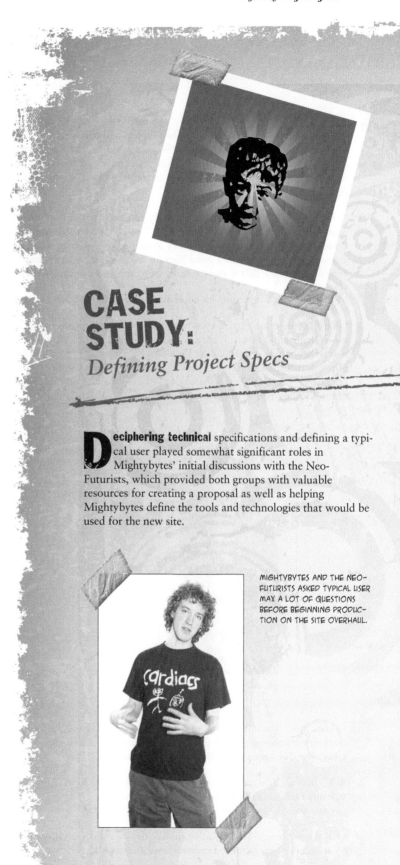

CASE STUDY:
Defining Project Specs

Deciphering technical specifications and defining a typical user played somewhat significant roles in Mightybytes' initial discussions with the Neo-Futurists, which provided both groups with valuable resources for creating a proposal as well as helping Mightybytes define the tools and technologies that would be used for the new site.

MIGHTYBYTES AND THE NEO-FUTURISTS ASKED TYPICAL USER MAX A LOT OF QUESTIONS BEFORE BEGINNING PRODUCTION ON THE SITE OVERHAUL.

"We talked to the Neos about who their typical audience was and that's how we found Max," Kristala said. "We asked Max about the computer he uses, what he looks for in a good Web site, and a bunch of other pertinent questions that might be relevant to considerations for the Neo-Futurists' site."

"I like sites that make all the content easily accessible without splash pages or lengthy Flash intros," Max said. "I usually prefer that as much content as possible be just a click away from the home page for easy access. I guess I prefer that a good Web site takes a somewhat utilitarian approach, but one that is also executed with care, enthusiasm, and style."

Max was queried regarding his computer usage as well.

"I have a variety of Mac, Windows and Linux-based computers that I use at home and at work," he said. "At home I use Firefox on an AthlonXP-based system running Windows XP. At work I use a Red Hat Linux thin client also running Firefox, and sometimes a G4 iBook running either Firefox or Safari. Assuming I'm not on a tiny monitor I tend to use 1152 by 864 as my monitor resolution."

WITHOUT MAX'S INPUT, THERE WOULD HAVE BEEN MANY UNANSWERED QUESTIONS THAT WOULD HAVE TIED UP VALUABLE DEVELOPMENT TIME, KRISTALA SAID.

"Max's input was important, but it wasn't the only defining factor in creating recommended specs for the Neo-Futurists' site though," Kristala said. "We also went with cold, hard statistics as well."

W3 Schools, a free online portal resource for Web developers, publishes monthly browser and computing statistics online at: *http://www.w3schools.com/browsers/browsers_stats.asp*.

Mightybytes turned to this site when making several key decisions regarding the Neo-Futurists' technical specifications.

"We regularly turn to the W3 Schools' site for references on how the global Internet market shifts on a monthly basis," Kristala said. "It provides us with a reputable source to use when creating specs for our projects."

At development time for the Neo-Futurists site, Internet Explorer 6 on a Windows XP operating system with a computer monitor resolution of 1024-by-768 pixels and 65,000 colors held the dominant global market share. If Mightybytes wanted to reach the widest possible audience, these would be the expectations to meet.

Of course statistics can be misleading. Just because the global average denotes one spec that does not mean it is relevant for a project's specific audience. In the case of the Neo-Futurists, it was important not to alienate users outside the dominant spec.

"Since we knew many of the Neo-Futurists' audience was made up of creative people, we wanted to be certain to include the Mac market in our specs, too," Kristala said. "Firefox and Safari would need to be given considerable development time as well. Internet Explorer 7 on Windows deals with Flash and some JavaScript content differently than other browsers, which posed yet another consistency challenge. While the act of creating the content won't be different, the act of embedding it will need to be universally supported by all browsers."

Web Accessibility Guidelines

The W3C guidelines and quick tips for creating accessibility-friendly Web sites include the following suggestions:

- ◎ **Images and Animations:** Use the *alt* attribute to describe the function of each visual.

- ◎ **Image Maps:** Use the client-side *map* element and text for hotspots.

- ◎ **Multimedia:** Provide captioning and transcripts of audio and descriptions of video.

- ◎ **Hypertext Links:** Use text that makes sense when read out of context. For example, avoid "click here."

- ◎ **Page Organization:** Use headings, lists, and consistent structure. Use CSS for layout and style where possible.

- ◎ **Graphs and Charts:** Summarize or use the *longdesc* attribute.

- ◎ **Scripts, applets and plug-ins:** Provide alternative content in case active features are inaccessible or unsupported.

- ◎ **Frames:** Use the *noframes* element and meaningful titles.

- ◎ **Tables:** Make line-by-line reading sensible. Summarize.

Mightybytes turned to the World Wide Web Consortium's (W3C) Web Content Accessibility Guidelines (WCAG) Overview at *http://www.w3.org/WAI/intro/wcag.php* for information on how the site's content may be experienced by people with disabilities.

"As a general rule when developing sites we try to use as many accessibility-compliant elements—such as image and animation alt tags, CSS formatting, no frames, and so on—in our sites as possible," Kristala said. "Our goal is always to allow as many people to view our content as possible, but of course we also keep our target audience in mind as well."

The final tech requirements, like most documents associated with a typical Web project, were revised several times before meeting everyone's approval.

"Mightybytes gave us project specs very early in the development process," Sharon Greene said. "They outlined all the technology requirements for our project and helped us understand realistic expectations for how the site will be viewed and experienced once complete."

THE FACT THAT MIGHTYBYTES ASKED SO MANY QUESTIONS UP FRONT REALLY HELPED US TO UNDERSTAND MANY ASPECTS OF THE DEVELOPMENT PROCESS THAT WERE UNKNOWN TO US GOING INTO THIS PROJECT, NEO-FUTURIST SHARON GREENE SAID.

on specific devices, such as cell phones, DVD players, and game consoles.

- ◎ Can standard graphic and authoring programs be used to develop content for this platform and if so, are there development restrictions, plug-ins, or specific alterations to consider?

◎ What authoring environment, programming languages, and applications are required to develop content specific to this device?

◎ Will people with disabilities access your content and if so, what compliance standards must you adhere to? What accessibility-compliant devices will be used to experience your content and what considerations must be taken into account when creating for these devices?

FIGURE 4-6
ONCE YOU HAVE DEFINED TECH SPECS AND USER PROFILES, REVIEW THE INFORMATION WITH ALL APPROPRIATE PARTIES TO GET THEIR BUY-IN.

Lock and Load

Once you have documented answers to those questions a picture should begin to emerge as to who the majority of users will be for the content and what type of computer or device the majority will use to view it. Use this information to create a one-target spec that accurately reflects the lowest common denominator for the content, then incorporate said information into the document you created that defines your target user.

An example tech spec might insist that the following conditions be met:

◎ Windows 2000, SR2 or higher

◎ Mac OS 10.1 or higher

◎ 450 MHz processor or higher

◎ 256 MB of RAM or higher

◎ 24-bit monitor, 1024 × 768 resolution

◎ 16-bit sound card

◎ Internet Explorer 5.0 or higher

◎ Macromedia Flash plug-in 6.0 or higher

◎ Broadband connection at 384Kbps or higher

Once you have defined the spec—which should outline the lowest level machine to effectively run the content without performance issues—and it has been accepted by all parties involved, machines running less than the specifications outlined herein are not the developer's responsibility. The onus then lies on the user to upgrade his or her hardware or software in order to experience the content as it was meant to be experienced.

Sign-off

If you are in a team environment or working with a client, clear your specs with those involved in the decision-making process and ask for their input. If possible, get signatures or initials on a document stating that they agree to the terms outlined in the spec. This is important because if you develop content keeping the spec in mind and test often based on that spec, you ostensibly should not have any developmental stumbling blocks based on pure performance alone. You may have to go back and fix some broken code or change the color on a few graphics, but once fixed, the content should run free of worries or playback glitches on machines defined in the spec.

FIGURE 4-5
AS YOU FURTHER DEFINE TYPICAL USER BEHAVIORS A PICTURE OF JUST WHO THEY ARE SHOULD BEGIN TO TAKE SHAPE.

FIGURE 4-7
SPEC SIGNOFF: MAKE SURE YOU GET APPROVAL FOR YOUR SPECS
UP FRONT TO ALLEVIATE ANY CONFUSION LATER IN THE
DEVELOPMENT PROCESS.

APPLYING YOUR SPECS

Once you have defined a technology profile
based on target users, incorporated its content
into the full project spec, and acquired a sign-
off from all appropriate parties, what do you
do with all this research? How do you put this
information to the test?

As mentioned earlier, the specifications outlined in this chapter should really be used as
a foundation for the remaining steps in
developing your project. Everything from
graphic development decisions and programming interactivity to choosing video, audio,
or animation formats should be run through
the litmus test of how those decisions will
affect performance on your target machines.
Two areas where this information is especially helpful are in publishing your content's
system requirements and defining a testing
environment.

System Requirements

Once you have defined the spec, you should
let your users view it. One way to do this is to
publish system requirements on the external
packaging or home page of the content. This
way, users can find out what it takes to run
your interactive content.

If you look at the packaging for any disc-
based interactive title it invariably includes a
section on the front or back dedicated to
defining system requirements for running the
title. The requirements usually define the

HOSTING PROVIDER
JASON SAUNDERS, OF
HTTP://.WWW.CHARLOTTEZWEB.COM,
WARNS THAT SITE HOSTING IS OFTEN
TAKEN FOR GRANTED AND CAN VERY
EASILY TURN A PROJECT SOUR IF IT IS
NOT HANDLED WITH PROPER CARE.

PRO*file:*

Jason Saunders, Charlottezweb.com
Choosing the Right Hosting Provider

Defining hosting options—if relevant to your
project—should be done early in the production process as possible. When searching for
a provider to host your content, look for someone
who offers a variety of easy-to-use services and is
eager to become your ally when developing Web
projects. Sure, cost-effectiveness is important,
but available tech support and a wide array of
easy-to-configure utilities and server enhancements
go a long way in making your job as a developer
much easier.

A difficult or unresponsive hosting provider can be
one of the quickest ways to ruin a relationship
between you and your client. If something goes
wrong on the server and you do not have the access
privileges to fix it or cannot get hold of the person
who does, you will be in an awkward predicament.
Should the problem take the form of an unresponsive or broken Web site, you can be certain that as
the developer you are the first person a client will
turn to when something goes wrong.

"As a designer or developer, your clients turn to
you for guidance not only on their site's creation
and maintenance, but also if they have any
problems as well," said Jason Saunders,
hosting provider for charlottezweb.com

(Continued)

(PROfile: Continued)

(http://www.Charlottezweb.com). "If they are tech savvy and handle their domain/hosting independently, you may not need to worry about server-side problems. I have personally found, however, that most of my clients are fairly reliant upon my advice. With that in mind, the need to deliver what you promise to them is key. Hosting is something taken for granted when everything goes well but can very quickly turn a project sour when there are problems."

If you do not want to be a systems administrator, you owe it to your client to partner with someone who is willing to handle those responsibilities and will be available to help should something go wrong.

Saunders' past experience as a developer has made him sympathetic to the plight of working with inadequate hosting providers. He tapped into that experience when setting his company up and creating services for his clients.

"I started out on the design-side and ultimately got my first dedicated server as a direct result of not being happy with the hosting accounts I had for my clients with various other providers," he said. "I make sure in running my own hosting business that I am flexible and readily available to my clients at a moment's notice. Of course there's always the possibility that a request might come in the middle of the night and not be

addressed until the following day, but that's certainly not something I hide when answering questions for potential customers. I am extremely straightforward with what I can and cannot offer."

Saunders employs a variety of server-side utilities to help his clients easily administer their sites and make the jobs easier for the developers.

"Charlottezweb utilizes cPanel with some custom additions so clients can set up and manage many account features on their own through an administrative interface that facilitates control over backups, e-mail accounts, databases, statistics, subdomains, shopping carts, and so on," he said. "Couple that with a willingness to install custom configurations that are safe for a shared environment and I think we offer a pretty well-rounded set of services geared toward developers and the general public alike."

Saunders finds working with designers and developers makes his job easier.

"Without a doubt, when I have current developers who purchase accounts for their clients, it makes my job easier because these users are typically a tech-savvy group, which means far fewer support tickets to respond to than would be the case for someone completely new to hosting," he said. "That's a definite reason for me to continue to provide the best level of support I can for my multi-account holders to keep them happy with my service."

When developing technical specifications for your clients, be sure to include some kind of statement that breaks down the services and support a project's hosting provider offers. If at all possible, try to find a hosting provider that both you and your client can grow with over time. If a client is gung-ho about using her existing provider, be sure to thoroughly research the provider's hosting and support options *before* committing to the project. Finding out that a hosting provider does not support a key piece of technology required to make your site work halfway through development can be an ugly surprise.

Jason Saunders is the owner of hosting company Charlottezweb.com.

www.charlottezweb.com

CHARLOTTEZWEB.COM'S CPANEL IMPLEMENTATION OFFERS ENHANCED FUNCTIONALITY FOR THE CLIENTS THAT USERS CAN CONFIGURE ON THEIR OWN. THE COMPANY CUSTOMIZES ITS USERS' CPANEL INTERFACES USING HTTP://CSKINS.COM.

supported operating system(s), RAM and processor speed requirements, and any third-party software—such as QuickTime, RealMedia, Flash, Shockwave, etc.—to run the title.

Many Web sites will publish tech specs on their default home page as well. These usually read something to the tune of, "This site is best viewed with Internet Explorer version X.0 and a monitor resolution of at least 1024 × 768 (or 800 × 600, etc.)," or "You must have the Flash plug-in version X.0 and a broadband connection in order to view the content of this site." These messages usually are written in small type across the bottom of the page or in an unobtrusive corner.

This information is important because it lets your users know what kind of experience to expect when viewing the content. It is also a safeguard against your phone ringing off the hook due to unhappy users having a less-than-gratifying experience because they are still running a 486 computer with a 28.8K modem. If the requirements are properly displayed on your packaging or as your online content loads, they can be very helpful in ensuring that your content reaches the desired audience intact.

Testing

One of the most important questions to answer no matter the details of the project is how will you recreate an environment for proper testing and debugging based on what you have learned by creating the spec? Frequent testing that reflects lowest common denominator specifications outlined in your technology profile is a big step toward ensuring your content will successfully reach its widest possible audience and perform acceptably once there. A detailed breakdown of the testing process is outlined later in this book in Chapter 13, but for the purpose of this chapter's objectives, we have defined several options to consider when deciding how best to test your project. This may seem a bit premature, but these options are included here because it is important to consider how the testing process will affect timeline and budget, something you need to think about long before you actually start testing your content.

Large-Scale Testing

When it comes to testing, arguably the best-case scenario for your project is to consider hiring a dedicated testing and quality assurance (QA) company. The advantages of this are multifold. Not only will it free your time up to focus on development, but it will also secure a resource whose *only* focus is to run your content through the wringer and try to break it.

FIGURE 4-8
PUBLISHING SYSTEM REQUIREMENTS ON YOUR PROJECT ONCE IT IS COMPLETE IS AN EASY WAY TO LET USERS KNOW HOW BEST TO EXPERIENCE YOUR CONTENT.

QA companies contain large banks of computers and devices that reflect virtually any kind of playback configuration you can imagine, and you can rest assured that on the rare chance they do not have a machine or device that reflects your specific needs, they will get one (or reconfigure an existing one). The staff is solely dedicated to providing you with detailed feedback outlining every minute hiccup in playback, every button rollover that does not work, or every dead link, browser error, installation problem, etc., based on the spec you provide. It is possibly one of the best ways to ensure the fidelity of your content when it goes out to the masses.

It is also, unfortunately, one of the most expensive options. Many projects may not have the budget necessary to procure large-scale testing with a dedicated facility. It is important to discuss this upfront with your client and agree upon whether the testing will be handled internally or externally.

Guerilla Testing

If your budget does not warrant outsourcing the testing process to an external, specialized entity (and let us face it, many do not), and if you cannot afford to purchase an entire bank of machines or devices reflecting all your targeted users, there are other options for effectively testing your content. Your needs have not changed: You still have to test the content on machines reflecting your spec. You just need to be more resourceful in getting those needs met.

That said, libraries, cafés with Internet terminals, friends with laptops, school media labs, or even your estranged Aunt Betty's house are all perfect places to test your content if they have the machines or devices you are looking for. When it comes to guerilla testing, any place that suits your needs is fair game providing you can get permission to use it.

Regardless of the path you choose, the point with testing is that it takes time and really should be based on your spec. Also, you will eventually need to compile a budget or estimate for your project. It is important to consider the testing process and how it relates to the project spec when doing so.

A CAUTIONARY TALE

If you are wondering just what can go wrong if specs for your project are not properly defined, consider the following story.

A client approaches an inexperienced developer with what initially sounds like a great project: tons of animation, sound effects, video clips, numerous things happening on the screen at once, huge "eye candy" factor. When it comes to project specs, the client tells the developer that the content needs to be delivered on a CD-ROM. After agreeing to what the developer considers a rather meager budget considering the amount of work ahead, progress begins on the project and the

FIGURE 4-9
TESTING ON MACHINES THAT MEET YOUR PROJECT'S SPECS IS CRITICAL TO ITS SUCCESS.

FIGURE 4-10
MANY DISAGREEMENTS CAN ARISE IF YOUR PROJECT'S SPECS ARE NOT CLEARLY DEFINED.

next several months are spent juggling deadlines, animating graphics, editing video, syncing sound effects, etc. The developer runs the content on every machine available and once acceptable performance is achieved, delivers a final product to the client. At this point he has been working on the project for five months, two months longer than initially anticipated.

Several days later the client calls, complaining that she cannot view the content using AOL on her home computer, a six-year-old Macintosh.

"But you never said this thing was supposed to run on a Mac," the developer, now exasperated, snaps into the phone. "Let alone a six-year-old Mac with AOL installed. Don't you think this is something you should have told me five months ago?"

"You didn't ask," the client snaps back.

After a lengthy, tension-filled discussion of options, tempers flare and the two parties find themselves at an impasse in negotiations. The developer is angry and refuses to do any further work without more pay. Due to the client's extensive revisions the developer has already spent five months working around the clock and, per his calculations, has not brought in much more than minimum wage. The client is angry and refuses to extend the budget because the deliverable has not met his or her expectations. Both sides feel cheated, both sides hang up the phone, and the next thing the developer knows, he is slapped with a lawsuit for the project's entire budget plus damages because now the date-to-market has been pushed back, costing the client "thousands of dollars."

In this situation, neither party bothered to define *specifically* what was expected of the other and both parties paid dearly because of it. Unfortunately, this story has unfolded itself many, many times over in the world of interactive media development. Do not let it happen to you!

CONCLUSION

As you can see, no matter which side you fall on, the consequences of improper forethought when developing interactive content can be dire. An educated client who really knows how to communicate and can speak your language is the best possible client, but let us face it, very few clients looking for interactive media content actually fall into that category. As an interactive designer or developer, you are often viewed by clients as the expert and as such are responsible for keeping expectations on both sides realistic and attainable. Properly defining the spec of each project and getting every party involved to sign off on that spec is a critical part of the development process.

EXERCISES:

Consider the following audiences. What kind of decisions would you make regarding a development environment and technological specifications? Create a project spec—including a target user profile and technical specification—for each.

- Stay-at-home moms who want up-to-the-minute tips on childcare.
- Educational games that parents can install for children ages three to ten.
- An online recipe service for people who do not like to cook.
- Technology news feeds for executives in the telecommunications industry.
- Cell phone users who want maps and directions to specific locations.
- Animated online greeting cards targeted toward seniors.

SUPPLEMENTAL MATERIALS

Sample documents are included on the CD-ROM that comes with this book:

- Target User Profile
- Technology Spec
- Sample Project Spec

Files can be found in the folder labeled with the corresponding chapter number and title.

CHAPTER 5

Content Assessment and Treatment

Objectives

IN THIS CHAPTER YOU WILL LEARN:

1. HOW TO DEFINE CONTENT FOR YOUR PROJECT.
2. HOW TO CREATE A CONTENT DEVELOPMENT SCHEDULE.
3. HOW TO DEFINE TEAM MEMBERS (IF APPLICABLE).
4. HOW TO DEVELOP THE PROJECT'S VOICE AND PERSONALITY.
5. HOW TO CREATE A TREATMENT/CONTENT OUTLINE FOR YOUR CONTENT.
6. OUTLINE OPTIONS FOR PEER REVIEW.

CONTENT IS KING

At this point, you have brainstormed an idea for your project, profiled your user base, and defined technology that will be used to access and experience the project. Now you need to decide what content will engage your end users and figure out how you will create that content.

FIGURE 5-1
DEFINING WHAT CONTENT WILL BEST ENGAGE YOUR USERS IS A KEY STEP TOWARD DEVELOPING IT.

What Makes a Good Story?

An end user's needs should never stray far from your sights when assessing content for your project. Ultimately, it is the user who you will create and develop for, so his or her needs should be taken into consideration at every step in the creation process. Also, when creating interactive media the end result is often to inspire a user to do something: register to vote, become a member, sign a petition, request

FIGURE 5-2
AN END USER'S NEEDS SHOULD NEVER STRAY FAR FROM YOUR SIGHTS WHEN ASSESSING CONTENT FOR YOUR PROJECT

information, subscribe to a newsletter, share a story, download software, click the "Buy Now" button, etc. You owe it to your audience to make its experience engaging enough to warrant the desired response. The key to making this happen starts with good storytelling.

Where Will the Content Come From?

Depending on your role in the production process and how comfortable you feel with developing content versus wrangling code or designing graphics, you may want to consider working with a copy- or scriptwriter. This is the point at which your story begins to come to life. Remember, the nuances in how the story is told—how effectively key points are conveyed and the logic with which the story unfolds—will make all the difference in its reception.

Whether conveying how a new cell phone works, outlining Revolutionary War battle tactics, or unraveling the mysteries of nuclear fusion, you are ultimately telling a story. If you do not have confidence in your ability to accomplish that task, you should consider reinforcements. If you are in a team environment, a dedicated copywriter and/or content development expert is usually a given, even if that person doubles up on other duties. Freelance artists or small project studios, however, will sometimes attempt to wear all the hats a project calls for without possessing the required expertise. Unfortunately, product quality is typically what suffers.

If, however, you are the only person who could do justice to your story, then undertake this task without restraint. Just be sure your content comes across as concisely on the page as you envision it in your head. You may want to consider running completed drafts by another party for an objective opinion on how the information in your head translates to the page, and eventually to the screen. Even reading your treatment aloud can help ascertain the clarity of its key points and its narrative flow. If it does not sound natural, then chances are the finished product will not sound natural either.

If you have decided to work with a writer, your ideas for the story and its many details must be conveyed to him or her in a succinct manner. It is all about the details. Include as many of them as you can. Engage in an in-depth discussion of schedules and availability with the writer as well.

FIGURE 5-3
TALKING THROUGH YOUR CONCEPT WILL HELP DEFINE HOW BEST TO TELL YOUR STORY.

How Will the Content Be Defined?

At this point, you should define the content of the project and how a user will experience it. This is different than the previous chapter, where you defined technology requirements for your users to ensure smooth playback of the content. Now you must focus on how users will experience the story as opposed to how their computers will handle the content. What is the message you want to convey and how do you want that message delivered?

FIGURE 5-4
FOCUS NOW ON HOW USERS WILL EXPERIENCE THE WRITTEN ELEMENTS OF YOUR CONTENT RATHER THAN HOW THEIR COMPUTERS WILL PERFORM DURING PLAYBACK.

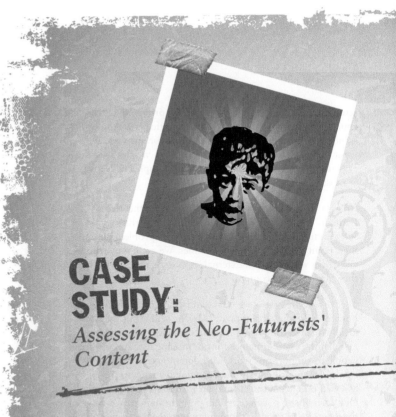

CASE STUDY:
Assessing the Neo-Futurists' Content

To best assess content for the new company site, the Neo-Futurists worked with current site content and received external feedback about what needed to change.

"The first thing we did was ask someone from outside the organization to scan for jargon that may be nonsensical to them," Sharon Greene said. "We discovered that as an organization we had developed an entire language of insider jokes that meant a lot to us but meant nothing to anyone else. In keeping with the site's goal of expanding our audience, we decided it was important to clarify some of that language for the general public while still maintaining our signature voice."

That signature voice is a big part of what makes the Neo-Futurists theater company what it is. *Too Much Light Makes the Baby Go Blind* is rife with irreverent and sometimes non-sensical statements on everything from politics and the war in Iraq to the Super Bowl, Valentine's Day, and masturbation. The company's quick-witted and thought-provoking approach to this wide array of topics is part of why the show consistently has been sold out weekend after weekend for nearly twenty years. The content is timely, in your face, and most importantly, funny. Always funny.

"We want to make sure moving forward that the site maintains a clear, consistent voice that represents the company," Greene said. "Our biggest challenge when assessing content was to strike a balance between copy that was casual but not sloppy, irreverent but not mean, copy that utilized run-on sentences and made-up words while still providing clear, concise answers to commonly asked questions. We understand that our users will come to the site for answers. We want to make sure the answers to any of their questions are easy to understand and not more than a couple clicks away at most."

Kristala from Mightybytes, said, "Given that the Neo-Futurists can pull off a weekly show featuring thirty plays in sixty minutes, we're sure they will have no problem getting their point across in a concise manner. We are happy to provide them with as much external support as necessary while they develop their content."

"Because we're artists we admittedly don't often think about how to make the most money," Greene said. "But the site ideally must accomplish a handful of things: sell tickets and merchandise, gather names for our mailing list, and inspire people to support our work with donations. None of that can be accomplished without engaging content, so we assessed ours from the ground up with those things in mind. Our current site puts a premium on information. We want this new site to take that information to the next level and put the premium on user action."

"OUR VOICE IS A BIG PART OF WHAT MAKES US WHO WE ARE," SHARON GREENE SAID. "IT IS IMPORTANT THAT IT COMES ACROSS WELL ON OUR WEB SITE."

Usually, in a team environment, this involves a face-to-face meeting and making several key decisions. If you are on your own, it may involve writing a few detailed sentences at the beginning of your treatment (which we will get to in a bit). Either way, when defining project content you should focus on a number of questions.

First, what kind of voice will best suit the target audience? Will the copy be light and breezy with injections of humor? Will it be detailed and technical? Or does the content require your voice to be direct and empowering, meant to incite a call-to-action, even if that action is the mere click of a button or input of an e-mail address? Will the story be told from first (I), second (you), or third (they) person perspective?

Second, the order in which key sections of the story will be told should be defined in terms of how best to engage the user. Should the story be told in a linear manner, restricting the user's ability to navigate to other sections in order to make the most sense of the story? Or should all information be accessible within a mouse click or two, and if so, how will the content be written in such a way as to make the most sense if it is accessed randomly?

Finally, are there other factors that will affect how the story is told? We briefly touched on technology spec for accessibility-compliant devices in order for people with disabilities to experience the project. If that scenario is relevant to your content, you should now decide how accessibility compliance standards will affect its creation. The same goes for content delivered in multiple languages, content for mobile devices, etc. Any factors that will affect how your content is delivered need to be taken into consideration as early as possible.

FIGURE 5-5
DEFINING USERS: DOES YOUR CONTENT NEED TO BE ACCESSED BY PEOPLE WITH DISABILITIES, MOBILE DEVICES, OR IN MULTIPLE LANGUAGES? IF SO, HOW WILL THAT AFFECT HOW YOU TELL YOUR STORY?

Your Content Development Schedule

Once you have defined content elements, you must address the challenge of how and when the content will be created. Rare is the project that does not adhere to a timeline. Even if you do not have a final deadline for the project, you should assign yourself one in order to plan a production schedule around it. This will give you the framework needed to accomplish your goals.

FIGURE 5-6
KEEPING YOUR SCHEDULE FLEXIBLE ENOUGH TO ALLOW FOR UNFORSEEN CHANGES CAN MAKE ALL THE DIFFERENCE IN YOUR PROJECT'S SUCCESS.

Inevitably, you will decide how much time to allot to research, script writing, and content development while taking into consideration the final deadline for the entire project. Setting up realistic expectations and practical timelines with enough flexibility to allow for unforeseen production hiccups are paramount to moving forward with the project.

When it comes to scheduling, often it is best to work deadlines and benchmarks out in terms of how they relate to the final deliverable date, so start there and work backward. There is no rule as to how long it takes to develop a treatment and subsequent script for an interactive media project. That is going to depend on the story you have to tell and on the schedules of those you will work with. Every project is different. Ultimately, writing the content is only a small portion of the entire process, so take that into consideration.

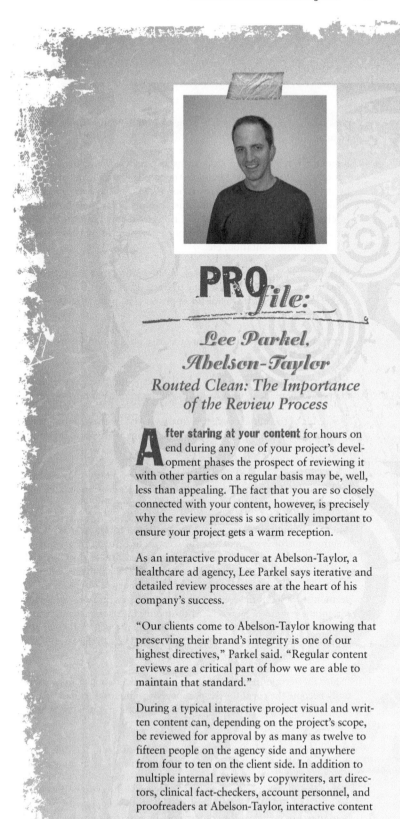

PROfile:

Lee Parkel, Abelson-Taylor
Routed Clean: The Importance of the Review Process

After staring at your content for hours on end during any one of your project's development phases the prospect of reviewing it with other parties on a regular basis may be, well, less than appealing. The fact that you are so closely connected with your content, however, is precisely why the review process is so critically important to ensure your project gets a warm reception.

As an interactive producer at Abelson-Taylor, a healthcare ad agency, Lee Parkel says iterative and detailed review processes are at the heart of his company's success.

"Our clients come to Abelson-Taylor knowing that preserving their brand's integrity is one of our highest directives," Parkel said. "Regular content reviews are a critical part of how we are able to maintain that standard."

During a typical interactive project visual and written content can, depending on the project's scope, be reviewed for approval by as many as twelve to fifteen people on the agency side and anywhere from four to ten on the client side. In addition to multiple internal reviews by copywriters, art directors, clinical fact-checkers, account personnel, and proofreaders at Abelson-Taylor, interactive content

(Continued)

(PROfile: Continued)

goes through multiple rounds of reviews with the company's marketing team and the client.

Regulatory, medical, and legal teams also review the content to ensure it meets legal standards. Many of Abelson-Taylor's clients are regulated by the Food and Drug Administration (FDA), so there are specific guidelines regarding what claims they can make for their products. Abelson-Taylor must be mindful of this fact throughout the production process to alleviate the possibility of legal repercussions over false claims, misrepresentation, etc.

Each time copy, storyboards, design comps, prototypes or other deliverables are presented for review they pass the desks of various decision makers within Abelson-Taylor for approval. The process starts with the copywriter and art director.

"Copywriters and art directors are the base units of our creative team," Parkel said.

"They come up with a project's initial concept and develop the idea to the point where it can be presented to an internal team of reviewers."

The result of the initial concept is first reviewed by the group's creative director, then the individual client's brand team at Abelson-Taylor for approval.

"No content moves to the next development step until it routes clean," said Parkel, referring to the practice of review teams signing their initials of approval on internally routed project documents.

After the brand team signs off on the content, a formal review with the creative director is set up. Once the creative director's revisions have been made, clinical fact-checkers then add references to the copy and the content is routed past the brand account team, which makes comments and revisions based on its understanding of the client's expectations. The account team sends the content back to the copywriter and art director for another round of revisions. At this point, the client account team at Abelson-Taylor reviews the content, makes revisions based on what it thinks the client wants, and sends the content back to the art director and copywriter for another round of revisions.

"Since the account team has the most direct client contact they essentially become the client for the purposes of an internal review," Parkel said. "This helps us anticipate a client's reactions and make any final changes before reviewing the content with the client."

After another round of proofreading and sign-off from the brand team, the approved content will go before the client for his or her review.

"Once the client's marketing team has reviewed the content the entire process starts all over again," Parkel said. "If the client changes anything that affects referencing, the content goes back to the fact-checker. If the design is affected, it goes back to the art director, and so on. All content is then proofread and reviewed again on our side until it routes clean."

Occasionally, there may be another client-side marketing review. Otherwise, the content goes directly into a client-side medical and legal review. This review, which could last a week or two, ensures the content meets legal standards set by the FDA. When the review is completed, the client's marketing team reviews the content for consistency.

"At that point we make additional revisions based on feedback from both the client's marketing team and the medical-legal review," Parkel said. "Then the content undergoes a regulatory review to make sure the results of our revisions still adhere to medical and legal standards."

Once the content finally routes clean at Abelson-Taylor and meets client approval, it is prepared for production or launch, depending on the deliverable.

"It is important to note that any one of these reviews can happen multiple times, which can be especially challenging," Parkel said. "The timelines for our projects are typically pretty stringent. All of the media elements are developed concurrently with each other because of FDA approval dates. Any campaign can involve a number of print, television, Internet or interactive components, all of which need to be ready at the same time. When you add the strict medical and legal requirements that all our content must adhere to, you can see why it is absolutely essential that we have a very detailed review process that operates like a well-oiled machine."

Lee Parkel is an interactive producer for Abelson-Taylor.

www.abelsontaylor.com.

If applicable, clear schedules and proposed delivery dates with all others involved, so they understand what is expected of them. If you are on your own and have not done this before, make your best guess. Eventually, you will want to plug all deadlines and benchmarks into the rough timeline you created in Chapter 2 and revise as necessary.

Try to be as realistic as possible. As mentioned before, an interactive media project will always take longer to develop than you think. Understand that no matter how hard you or those involved with the project make concentrated efforts to stay on track, something will come up and push your schedule back, sometimes by as little as a few hours or as much as a couple months. Personal illness, computer crashes, client-driven revisions, people quitting, financial difficulties, communication errors—the list of potential pitfalls goes on and on. The most successful projects are run by people who understand this concept and make decisions accordingly. As development continues you will need to refine the schedule you create here, so remember to build in enough inherent flexibility to allow for changes.

The Treatment/Content Outline

Once all scheduling and role assignation is behind you, it is time to develop a written creative treatment of the project's goals and outline how the story will be conveyed. This can be accomplished in outline form, narrative form, or a combination of both, depending on what writing style best suits your content. Sometimes a bulleted list of key points is the best option. Other times it might be necessary to write a section of your treatment in story form to truly convey its tone, emotional depth, character nuances, setting details, and political or social context.

Ultimately, the length of your treatment manuscript will depend on the level of detail your story must convey, but the goal is to create a document that offers a wide view of the entire project in a succinct manner. Remember, this is neither a script nor a flowchart. Each section should be outlined in a few sentences, so it is important that those sentences be wisely chosen.

Your Organizer

Gone are the days of flipping through Page-A-Day Calendars, stacking sticky note upon sticky note. The better you are at managing your schedule, the better your project will turn out. Although many managers still rely on countless handwritten notes either in a notebook or their daily planner, there is the danger of losing something in the shuffle. Luckily project management does not have to be so slipshod with online and software programs that organize your tasks and help you to see the big picture.

Basecamp, a project collaboration tool offered by 37signals, is a Web-based program that allows you to manage to-do lists, collaborate with others, schedule, share files, and track time. It also gives the project manager control over who has access to certain files. Basecamp can be customized with a company logo and can be viewed by clients who want to see how the program is progressing. The program is available for a 30-day trial at *http://www.basecamphq.com/*.

If you are a chart-oriented person, MinuteMan Systems offers a Windows-only application called MinuteMan, which allows you to view your project a number of ways. Different options allow you to manage the workflow, timeline, and resources in a few keystrokes. Numerous reports can be generated that allow you to track resources, spending, tasks, and staffing assignments. MinuteMan would be an excellent program for larger projects. Files can also be shared with co-workers and clients. A 21-day free trial is available at *http://www.minuteman-systems.com/*.

Numerous project management programs can also be reviewed and downloaded at *http://www.freedownloadscenter.com/Best/free-scheduling.html*.

Begin by revisiting the broad project definition statement you wrote in your proposal. Does it need to be revised in any way, knowing what you now know about your users and their technology profile? Has your idea changed? Does it need to be broadened or otherwise further refined to fit your audience or technology restrictions? If so, revise the initial statement and define the categories and sub-categories required to tell your story. Once that has been accomplished, define the content in each category or sub-category using either outlined bullet points or narrative-style prose, depending on which you feel works best for the message being conveyed. Further revise the content until you have a document that will allow anyone who reads it to understand your intentions.

Like the technology assessment and user profile, a completed treatment serves as a stepping-stone toward the next steps in the project: defining the project's architecture in a visual manner and creating a flowchart that conveys how a user will navigate within the content. It will also serve as the basis by which the writer will develop a fully fleshed-out version of the story's script.

FIGURE 5-7
ONCE YOU HAVE COMPLETED A THOROUGH ASSESSMENT OF YOUR CONTENT, HAVE SOMEONE ELSE LOOK IT OVER FOR CONSISTENCY AND EFFECTIVENESS OF ITS MESSAGE.

Peer Review

Once you have completed a draft of your treatment, an objective viewpoint will help maintain its effectiveness at communicating key concepts. You want to be sure the story

Finding Writers

There are probably as many writers available as you have tasks to complete for the project. Writers are hiding in every nook and cranny, as well as every coffee shop and bookstore, with twitching fingers poised on the keyboard to work for you.

The cheapest and most available resources are colleges, technical colleges, or writing schools. Many colleges have job boards or know their students well enough that the name of a student will be readily available to them. General writers can be found in English or Communication departments. If you are working with specific content, say on traveling in Spain, then call the Foreign Language Department. Typically, the biggest downfall with student writers is their lack of experience. You might get them cheap, but it may mean extra work for you in reviewing manuscripts or training them for the specific assignment. Do not be afraid to ask for a senior or recent graduate.

Other inexpensive resources are online job sites such as Monster.com (*http://www.monster.com*), Yahoo! HotJobs (*http://www.hotjobs.com*) or even posting a Craig's List ad (*http://www.craigslistonline.com*). Writer's Weekly, an online ezine for writers found at *http://writersweekly.com*, also has a space allotted for those looking for creative freelancers.

Freelance writers are another resource readily available. Try searching online for freelancers in your specific city. Many freelancers host their own Web sites and can be found in the phone book, or by posting an ad at a local library. Professional writers or organizations can be found in trade magazines or writing magazines. Writer's unions, such as National Writers Union (NWU) and the American Society of Journalists and Authors (NSJA), can also be used to find writers that are willing to work.

If all else fails, ask a friend. Everybody knows a writer or a friend of a friend that writes. Think of the type of writer you need for the project and after a day or two of looking your writing worries should be over.

you want to tell is one your audience can easily comprehend and that makes sense in terms of structure, language, and clarity. On some projects peer review is required.

Recruiting someone who has either not been involved in the project or who is an expert on its subject matter to review your treatment will help you gain a fresh perspective on how best to convey your story. He may also point out language, spelling, grammar, or structural inconsistencies that have gone unnoticed.

In some cases, such as scientific, medical, and educational content, peer review is often mandatory for ensuring a project's pedagogical and legal integrity. Lawsuits are likely the last thing on your mind when the project's content has not been developed yet, but if it is the least bit slanderous, contains inaccuracies that have not been fact-checked, or is missing pertinent information, there could be unforeseen legal ramifications to your endeavors.

Another set of eyes is rarely a bad thing, and sometimes it is legally mandatory. If you want to ensure your content's message is clear and get a fresh perspective on how it is being conveyed, then recruit some help.

CONCLUSION

As you move forward developing your project, keep in mind that it is the project content that will most effectively attract users and keep them engaged. It must be concise, succinct, and developed with the users' needs in mind. This will drive how the content is developed and take you one step closer to the project's successful deployment.

EXERCISES:

Write treatments for several ideas and discuss which ones are viable to pursue as projects. Review another student's treatment for content inconsistencies.

CHAPTER 6

Information Architecture and Navigation Chart

Objectives

IN THIS CHAPTER YOU WILL LEARN:

1. HOW TO OUTLINE INFORMATION FLOW FOR YOUR PROJECT BASED ON CONTENT ASSESSMENT.

2. HOW TO DEFINE PROJECT NAMING CONVENTIONS FOR FILES AND DIRECTORY STRUCTURES.

3. HOW TO CREATE NAVIGABLE CONTENT SEGMENTS.

4. HOW TO DEFINE RELATIONSHIPS BETWEEN CONTENT SEGMENTS.

5. HOW TO LOOSELY DEFINE MEDIA ELEMENTS AS ESTABLISHED BY CONTENT SEGMENTS.

6. HOW TO CREATE A VISUAL CHART OUTLINING YOUR PROJECT'S CONTENT.

CONTENT STRUCTURES

Defining how your content will afford a truly interactive user experience will help you ready your project for production. You have already created a loose structure for your content through the process of writing its treatment. Your goal for the next step is to segment the content into small, manageable sections and define the relationship between various elements in each. This will help users chart their way through the content, and allow you to create a visual chart that outlines the information flow and navigation options for the entire project.

FIGURE 6-1
CHARTING A USER'S PATH THROUGH YOUR CONTENT PRIOR TO
DEVELOPMENT CAN MAKE ALL THE DIFFERENCE IN THEIR
EXPERIENCE.

Information Architecture

When defining your project's information architecture, the primary goal is to help users through your content. In this phase you will not only define the content's primary segments and what pieces of your interactive puzzle are going to fall in each section, but also you will define the relationship between content in different sections. You will want to outline the complete structure of your project in a visually concise and intuitive manner and create a reference blueprint for your project's remaining steps. In the simplest terms, you will define the buttons your users click to get from screen to screen in the project.

The Breadcrumb Trail

To simplify complex data structures and confusing navigation options, many developers include a "breadcrumb trail" on their pages to help users get their bearings when clicking through a site. Typically, a breadcrumb trail is a series of links that shows a user's navigation history, allowing him or her to return to a previously visited page with one click or helping him or her figure out which section of a site he or she is currently exploring.

There are three types of Web breadcrumbs: path, location, and attribute. Path breadcrumbs are created dynamically and show the direct route a user has taken to get to a specific page. Location breadcrumbs are static and show where the page is located within the many levels of the site no matter how the user arrived there. Attribute breadcrumbs give the stats about where the page fits in relation to the other pages, such as in what categories a specific product falls.

A breadcrumb trail can be an automatic response within your site if the site was set up in a hierarchical structure. A simple online search will turn up many code examples that make it easy to create a trail, but automatic generation of breadcrumb trails is typically set up and configured when the site is developed.

Unfortunately, there is not a bevy of off-the-shelf software tools available to help you create breadcrumb trails, short of hand-coding them. The Internet is full of forums, articles, and advice, however, about the engineering of such a task.

FIGURE 6-2
CREATING A NAVIGATIONAL 'BREADCRUMB TRAIL' FOR
YOUR WEB SITE WILL HELP USERS FIGURE OUT WHERE THEY
HAVE BEEN.

Cross-referencing your content is a bit more complex than just clicking buttons, however. Defining relationships between content in different sections of the project needs to make sense to your users. If you really want to make the users' experience an intuitive one, in addition to providing them with multiple options to navigate from section to section, you should provide them with an easy way to move throughout the content screens in a nonlinear fashion. This will increase the project's usability as well.

Let us say you are creating an online interactive portfolio for your work. One section will feature samples of projects you have completed. Another section may outline your strongest areas of competence, your expertise, services, or the market segments and industries you specialize in. Perhaps healthcare is an industry in which you have a significant amount of experience. When stating this fact on an "About Me" page, it might be a wise idea to cross-reference specific samples within your portfolio pages as they specifically apply to healthcare projects. It is these kinds of relationships you want to convey when developing a navigational flowchart for your project.

Define Media Elements

In addition to content, you should define the specific media elements used in your project as well. Perhaps in one section of your project you need to demonstrate a specific procedure. Will that procedure be best served by a video clip, series of photo images with narration, 3D animation with music, or just text? These are important questions to answer because they will directly affect how engaging your content is, as well as how much time is necessary to create the elements. Let us say you decide a video clip is the best route but then realize you

do not have the funds necessary to produce the video. What is an acceptable alternative?

Eventually, you should define media elements for each screen of your project and apply cohesive naming conventions to them. This list will become your asset inventory, an essential production tool.

Define Naming Conventions

You need to define naming conventions not only for folders on the computers that will house your media content as it is being developed, but also for the files. Text files, images, scripts, flowcharts, design comps, contracts, video clips, even layers within graphic files should all follow some kind of consistent naming convention that is defined and agreed upon by all parties involved. How you define that naming convention is up to you. Just make sure the system you create is clear to everyone involved on the project.

FIGURE 6-4
PROPERLY NAMING EVERYTHING RIGHT DOWN TO THE LAYERS IN A PHOTOSHOP DOCUMENT WILL HELP KEEP YOU ORGANIZED.

The primary purpose of naming conventions is to alleviate confusion when working with production files, of which there are many for a typical interactive project. This is crucial when working in a team environment, but even if you are working independently, naming conventions can assist in guiding you

FIGURE 6-3
DEFINE THE MEDIA ELEMENTS WITHIN YOUR PROJECT AS YOU STEP THROUGH ITS CONTENT.

through the maze of files associated with your project, help you stay organized, and save time when searching for specific elements.

When working with others, multiple parties can access a project's files at any given time, make changes, overwrite important documents, and wreak general havoc with your project directory if they do not know what they are doing. Naming conventions can help alleviate confusion as to where files can be found, when they were last updated, what the most recent version is, if they have been backed up, what information screen they apply to, what section they are in, etc. Any number of critical pieces of information can be conveyed through file naming structures and there are no set rules as to how you should go about naming your files. The key is to get as much information from a filename as possible without making it hundreds of characters long.

Creating proper naming conventions and directory structures goes hand in hand with the development of a navigational flowchart for any project. Small projects get the same treatment as larger projects in this respect, albeit on a less detailed level. Sometimes a flowchart can be as simple as a hand-drawn illustration, then scanned and filed into a project's documents folder for future reference. Other times a flowchart is several weeks in the making and requires multiple levels of approvals and revisions. On each occasion,

FIGURE 6-5
THIS FILE NAME MAY APPEAR CRYPTIC AND CONFUSING, BUT IT'S REALLY QUITE SIMPLE. FOLLOW ALONG AND YOU TOO CAN BE NAVIGATING THROUGH YOUR FILES WITH EASE.

Sample Naming Conventions:

Let us say we are creating a series of six high school level educational modules on world history in both English and Spanish. The modules will be created in Flash for Web delivery and each will contain about fifteen to twenty information screens with several audio and video clips. By the time we reach the production phase, we will need to keep track of hundreds upon hundreds of files in various stages of development. The first step toward staying organized is to define appropriate naming conventions and stick to them.

That said, let us break down our naming convention into its base components:

"WH05"

In this case, the first four characters of our name narrow our file down in the broadest sense: the module it belongs to. Those first characters tell us this file is associated with world history module five and can be filed accordingly.

"S03_SC02"

This portion of the name tells us what section and screen number the file is associated with, in this case section three, screen two.

"E"

As this is a bilingual project, the "E" tells us this file is in English.

"090407"

This part tells us when the file was last saved.

".aif"

The extension on the file tells us this is an audio file and thus would likely be found in an audio directory of some sort. Again, there are no set rules for defining naming conventions. Define a system that works for you and stick to it. Remember, when naming files that go on servers never use spaces in the names.

the project's naming conventions are typically defined during the course of one or more conversations with the client based on the complexity of the project and applied immediately to the navigation chart. From that point forward all files associated with the project adhere to the agreed upon naming conventions. Those files are then housed within a central repository that also adheres to those conventions and is accessible to the parties involved with the project.

FIGURE 6-6
KEEP YOUR FILES ORGANIZED IN FOLDERS BOTH ON THE COMPUTER AND OFF.

Revisit Your Tech Spec

If you add media elements—such as audio or video clips—as you define the content of the project, and you have previously not considered those elements in past steps, you should decide whether they may affect the project's existing technology specifications. Will you need to use Windows Media Player to play your videos? Will the project now require use of the Flash plug-in? Once these technologies have been defined, revise your technical specifications accordingly, considering too that

these new requirements must be compatible with everything in your tech spec. If you have added Windows Media files to your project, how will these be addressed for Mac users? Is the version of Windows Media you are targeting compatible with the version of Windows in your tech spec? These things must be taken into consideration before an accurate content assessment can be completed. If your tech spec changes, route it among the appropriate parties and get another sign-off, if necessary.

Define Directory Structures

A clean, organized directory structure is just as important as proper naming conventions. After all, what is the point of giving your files organized names if you are just going to leave them on your desktop? Sure, search tools have come a long way, but it would be easier to drop those files into the correct folder from the beginning.

As with naming conventions, how you set up directories is personal preference and works only if the parties involved understand and agree to the structure. In general, it is a good idea to keep administrative documents separate from art files, and videos separate from audio files. Original files should be kept in a directory safe from accidental alteration and all files should be archived in some manner on a daily basis.

FIGURE 6-7
ORGANIZED DIRECTORIES ON YOUR COMPUTER ARE JUST AS IMPORTANT AS NAMING CONVENTIONS.

Asset Management Tools

Asset management programs, such as Extensis' Portfolio or Adobe's Bridge and Version Cue, can help you edit, manage, and control key bits of information about all files associated with your project. The primary advantage of such tools is that they can help you integrate all project files associated with a project—from Word documents and spreadsheets to photos, art files, and other media elements—with your production process as well as handle version management for these files. All information, including any metadata, is stored in a database and can be placed on a server for quick reference by anyone, making them especially helpful on large-scale projects where entire teams of writers, designers,

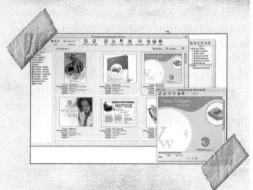

FIGURE 6-9
EXTENSIS PORTFOLIO FEATURES SYSTEM-LEVEL INTEGRATION FOR MANAGING YOUR ASSETS.

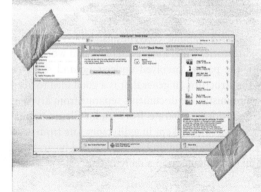

FIGURE 6-8
BRIDGE, PART OF ADOBE'S CREATIVE SUITE, CAN HELP YOU KEEP YOUR FILES CENTRALLY ORGANIZED.

developers, and project managers work in tandem to bring a project to life.

Adobe Bridge, a component of the Adobe Creative Suite, can help keep your files centrally organized and features XMP metadata tagging and search functions. Users can manipulate a number of images at the same time and save them as collections for later use. Royalty-free stock photos can also be browsed and purchased without leaving the application. Bridge Center, the program's starting point, offers access to your most recent files and helpful advice on how to use various features. Used in tandem with Adobe's Version Cue (also part of the Creative Suite), Bridge

can help with file sharing, version management and track your workflow and files as they progress through the production and approval process. Its biggest payoff comes in the time you will save managing these files without it. Free trials of the program are available from the Adobe Web site: *http://www.adobe.com*.

Portfolio 8, by Extensis, offers some of the same sorting and cataloging capabilities as Adobe Bridge. The program offers a number of tutorials and catalogs to help the software work to your specific needs. Files are easily organized and catalogued and projects are organized like playlists in Apple's iTunes, making ease-of-use a big benefit. Scratchpad galleries are temporary workspaces in which you can modify single or multiple files before incorporating them into the project. It also features system-level integration with the application and software tools you typically use to create and develop a project, unlike Bridge, which is designed to work with Adobe's Creative Suite of tools.

If cost is no option, Apple offers an XServe G5 server as the perfect complement to Extensis Portfolio for enterprise-wide creative asset management using a combination of hardware and software. Company-wide integration will run well into the five-figure range. A free twenty minute seminar on this partnership is available from the Apple Web site: *http://www.apple.com/*.

Content Management Systems

If you are working on a Web-enabled project, a content management system (CMS) can ease the burden of costly and time-consuming content updates and significantly extend a project's shelf life. These server-side, database-driven applications make content updates quick and easy. With some targeted training, clients can usually take over the task of editing and updating their content, a prospect that empowers them as an active member of the production process.

Learning to deploy a CMS can involve a steep learning curve, depending on which product you choose and it typically must be decided before development begins whether this is a viable option. There are many different flavors of CMSs available and all vary in price and technology. Some, such as Joomla, Drupal, or OpenCMS, are open source and free, which can be the way to go for projects with limited budgets. However, free products offer little in terms of live tech support. Unless you know someone who regularly uses the product, you are pretty much limited to poring over forum posts and online support documents to get help if you get stuck.

Others, such as Microsoft's Office Sharepoint Server, Vignette, or Power CMS, offer enterprise-wide solutions that can reach well into the five figure cost arena but which also include some kind of support contract for when you reach a developmental snafu.

Some CMS tools, such as Joomla, require the creation of a custom template into which site content is flowed and formatted. The general page layout is managed by a design template, plenty of which are available online for download. Otherwise, you can create your own using Joomla's custom PHP tags. The PHP template is then imported into the CMS, while the style and visual appearance of specific elements on each page is controlled by one or more cascading stylesheets (CSS), HTML, etc. The content itself, such as graphics, images, and site copy, are all housed within the CMS database.

FIGURE 6-10
CONTENT MANAGEMENT SYSTEMS SUCH AS JOOMLA CAN
HELP KEEP A WEB SITE'S CONTENT UP-TO-DATE.

FIGURE 6-11
AFTER YOU HAVE DEFINED YOUR PROJECT'S CONTENT STRUC-
TURES, CREATE A CHART TO HELP EVERYONE VISUALIZE THE RELA-
TIONSHIP BETWEEN CONTENT SECTIONS.

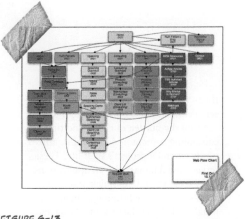

FIGURE 6-13
HOPSCOTCH THROUGH YOUR DIGITAL MEDIA PROJECT BY USING
YOUR FLOWCHART AS A REFERENCE POINT FROM WHICH ALL THE
MEDIA ELEMENTS WILL EVENTUALLY SPRING.

CREATING YOUR FLOWCHART

After you have defined content structures, naming conventions, and assets, create a visual representation of the project to help envision its scope and the relationship between content sections. This will give the programmers and designers an idea of what is expected of them, or, if you are working alone, it will help you get an idea of what lies ahead.

The first version of this chart may best be served by sketching it out on paper. Depending upon your work style, you may prefer to use an illustration program or visualization tools like Omnigraffle or Visio to create the navigation chart. The end result should be in a digital format you or anyone you work with can reference, print, and, if necessary, alter.

As with your treatment and content assessment, the goal is to create a bird's eye view of the project, only this time you will employ visual elements to create the project's roadmap, rather than using words and sentences.

Conditional Logic vs. Information Screens

All interactive media projects prominently feature conditional logic on every screen. Will a user click a certain button and if so, what happens? A conditional logic chart can be helpful when trying to define every step in an interaction process. It also might be a nice supplement if there is an area of the project that is unusually complex. Programmers can find conditional logic charts very helpful when building applications. Designers probably will not. When trying to produce a navigational flowchart that offers a bird's eye view of the project as a whole (and will likely end up in a designer's hands before it goes to a programmer), you might consider creating a hierarchy diagram flowchart based on individual screens of information as they will appear to a user rather than outlining the individual processes on each.

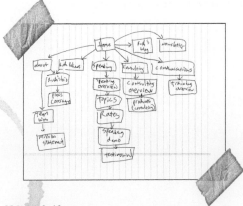

FIGURE 6-12
A FIRST-DRAFT FLOWCHART WILL OFFER A BIRD'S EYE VIEW OF
YOUR PROJECT'S CONTENT.

Types of Charts

Architecture diagrams help give the project structure. As the project takes shape, you can adjust the diagrams to reflect changes. Different projects require different types of diagrams. Web or interactive applications may best be served by decision or process flowcharts, whereas a simple Web brochure may require a hierarchy diagram. Following are several types of interactive applications and their related diagram types.

Hierarchy Diagrams

Interactive brochures present information to visitors. Content is usually clustered within menus and sub menus. The following layout diagram is helpful because it shows the actual layout of site menus. However, notice you can only see content of the "shop" tab. A hierarchy diagram can solve this problem.

The following hierarchy diagram was created with a standard word processing table tool. Although this diagram shows all the menu items on the site, it does not give any indication of the site layout.

You might want to include both a sample layout diagram and a hierarchy diagram to give your team the clearest understanding of the site's information architecture. An interactive rapid prototype with working menus can be

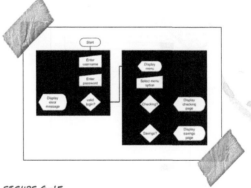

FIGURE 6-15
A SIMPLE DECISION/PROCESS DIAGRAM.

helpful to accompany these diagrams. The menus items can simply lead to placeholder pages. Allowing individuals to click through actual menus will lead to the clearest understanding of the site structure. This can be accomplished quickly and easily with simple HTML pages and hypertext links.

Decision/Process Flowcharts

Unlike brochure sites, interactive applications allow users to input information and make choices which affect the generation and display of application content. To convey the decisions and inputs available, standard decision/process flowcharts are created.

Decision/Process diagram

Of course, Web applications may have hierarchical menu structures that surround site functionality. In those cases, you would use a combination of decision/process flowcharts and hierarchy diagrams.

Computer-Based Learning: Tables and Outlines

Simple computer-based learning applications are generally a series of consecutive screens. Learning Points (LPs) are presented and followed by assessment questions. For this type of project, a condensed table/outline combination can give your team a quick overview of the content on each screen.

Interactive learning *simulations* are not linear. Users will get "off path" as they make mistakes throughout the simulation. To represent these more complex learning sites, use a decision/process flowchart.

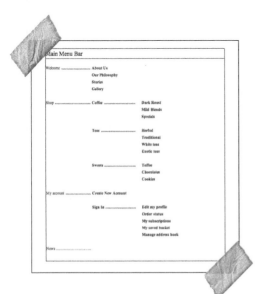

FIGURE 6-14
A SIMPLE HIERARCHY DIAGRAM CREATED IN WORD.

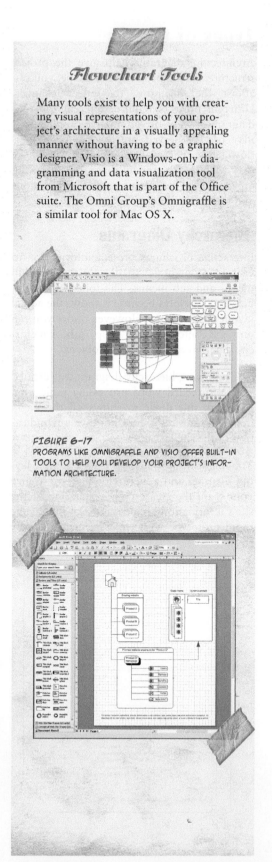

FIGURE 6-16
TABLES AND OUTLINES FOR A COMPUTER-BASED LEARNING PROJECT.

Create Wire-frames

Sometimes using those antiquated tools of yesteryear known as pencil and paper can be helpful when defining media elements on your project's primary screens. There is no room for fancy here: The whole purpose of creating project interface sketches is to help define media elements for each screen and provide the first visual reference of what each screen will include. Sure, some concepts of layout and design may creep into these sketches, which will help down the line when you are creating design comps, but for now, their primary purpose is to define the elements on various screens in the project.

First, pick several information screens that represent a cross-section of the project: a main menu, a second, third, and even fourth-level information screen, a credits screen or privacy policy, etc. The choice is yours. Once you have chosen several key screens, using your treatment and other documents as reference, begin sketching out all the media elements that belong on each screen. Using simple shapes such as squares, rectangles and circles can represent content items.

Think through each screen in as much detail as you can muster. Does a company logo need to be included on every screen? Find a place to put it and sketch a thumbnail in an area of the paper where you think it belongs. Do users

Flowchart Tools

Many tools exist to help you with creating visual representations of your project's architecture in a visually appealing manner without having to be a graphic designer. Visio is a Windows-only diagramming and data visualization tool from Microsoft that is part of the Office suite. The Omni Group's Omnigraffle is a similar tool for Mac OS X.

FIGURE 6-17
PROGRAMS LIKE OMNIGRAFFLE AND VISIO OFFER BUILT-IN TOOLS TO HELP YOU DEVELOP YOUR PROJECT'S INFORMATION ARCHITECTURE.

FIGURE 6-18
SKETCHING OUT WIREFRAME IDEAS ON PAPER CAN BE A GOOD
FIRST STEP TOWARD VISUALIZING YOUR PROJECT'S INTERFACE.

CASE STUDY:
Information Architecture

The Neo Flow

The Neo-Futurists provided Mightybytes with a rough flowchart at the project's outset, an asset that was incredibly helpful when trying to assess scope and how the flow of information might play out on the site.

"We had many discussions with the Neo-Futurists on how best to approach primary and secondary navigation systems," Kristala said. "The Neo-Futurists' ideas for site content were cohesive as a whole, but we jointly revised their information architecture several times in attempts to make it more intuitive to an end user who may or may not be familiar with the company."

Mightybytes' first attempt at revising the navigational flowchart was met with enthusiasm but did not quite hit the mark. Its hierarchal view of content did not offer intuitive solutions to cross-referencing content and certain important content elements that needed to be "front-and-center" were buried a level or two down.

"Mightybytes had a great eye for how to organize the information," Sharon Greene said. "But we still needed to re-prioritize several screens of key information and trim the primary navigation options down a bit. Mightybytes helped us understand how choosing to give our users a few clear categories to organize all our information was essential. We had to prioritize. In a meeting with members of both teams in the room we cut the main navigation buttons down significantly. Going through that exercise caused our company

need access to the previous screen they landed on? What about getting to the header screen of that section? Do they need to get to the home page/main menu? Try to come up with as many navigation scenarios as possible and include media elements, boxes, buttons, and form fields to represent each. Inevitably, you will miss key elements in this process, but that is OK. This is a first-pass endeavor meant only to jog your memory of previously discussed screen component, so you can get them on paper. It is not meant to be pretty either. If your sketches are not covered with scribbles and eraser marks then you are not thinking hard enough.

Define Possible Future Content Structures

As you develop the project's content, think about its future. What will the requirements be once the project is finished? Does it need to be flexible to facilitate regular content updates once it has been distributed? If so, will you make those changes? Planning appropriately will extend the shelf life of the project and ensure its longevity.

leadership to have a really productive conversation. What did we really need the site to do? Where did we believe the company would be growing in the future? Clearly, our Web site played a key role in the answers to those questions."

As part of the information architecture documentation provided to the Neo-Futurists, Mightybytes also included scratch images of how other sites implemented PayPal as a shopping cart yet were still able to keep some primary branding elements, such as logo and color palette.

"Although the online ticket booth was a Phase 2 implementation," Kristala said. "We wanted to be very clear about how we planned to integrate the site's existing PayPal setup with our Phase 1 design overhaul."

Mightybytes also worked with the Neo-Futurists to revise some nomenclature used in its navigation. The button reading "Our Shows," for instance, became "Current Shows" and then eventually "Tickets and Shows" to best reflect the fact that ticket purchasing options should be readily apparent on the home page.

"Our existing site was rife with jargon that may be recognizable to someone familiar with our aesthetic and the shows we produce," Greene said. "But since our primary goal was to expand our audience we also wanted to be certain the information flow was completely intuitive."

Both parties eventually agreed upon a flowchart that, although less standard than a hierarchal content view, better showed the relationships between section categories and how external data—such as blogs, podcasts, ticket purchasing, and donations—fit into the site's structure.

With the site's structure clarified, Mightybytes began creating design comps while the Neo-Futurists busied itself with the site's written content.

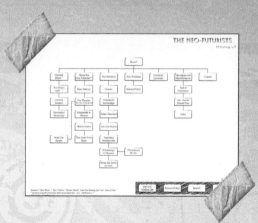

THE SECOND DRAFT FLOWCHART WAS CLOSER BUT STILL NOT QUITE THERE YET.

"CHOOSING TO GIVE OUR USERS A FEW CATEGORIES IN WHICH TO ORGANIZE ALL OUR INFORMATION WAS ESSENTIAL," SHARON GREENE SAID.

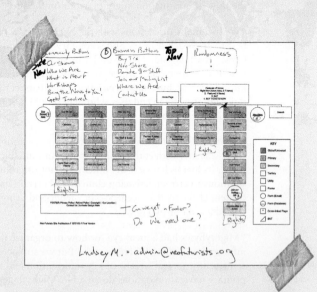

MIGHTYBYTES' FIRST DRAFT FLOWCHART WAS MET WITH ENTHUSIASM BUT DIDN'T QUITE HIT THE MARK.

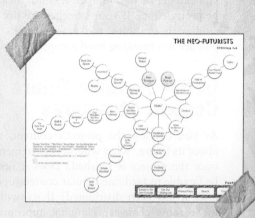

JUST RIGHT: THE THIRD FLOWCHART DRAFT FINALLY MET WITH APPROVAL FROM ALL PARTIES.

FIGURE 6-19
A FINAL DRAFT WIREFRAME.

CONCLUSION

Once your architecture has been completed, run it by all appropriate parties for approval. You many need to revise it before everyone is in agreement, but once finished it will become the blueprint around which you will build the rest of the content.

EXERCISES:

Create a conditional logic chart, brochure diagram, and hierarchy diagram. Download trial versions of Omnigraffle or Visio to create a flowchart. Create a flowchart the old fashioned way, with pen and paper.

SUPPLEMENTAL MATERIALS

Sample documents are included on the CD-ROM that comes with this book:

◎   Sample navigation charts

Files can be found in the folder labeled with the corresponding chapter number and title.

CHAPTER 7

Creating a Script and Asset List

Objectives

IN THIS CHAPTER YOU WILL LEARN:

1. WHEN IT IS APPROPRIATE TO USE A MORE TRADITIONAL SCRIPT FORMAT.

2. HOW TO TRANSFORM YOUR NAVIGATIONAL FLOWCHART AND TREATMENT INTO A WORKING SCRIPT.

3. HOW TO FORMAT YOUR SCRIPT SO IT OUTLINES ALL MEDIA ASSETS AND INTERACTIVITY.

4. HOW AND WHERE TO USE NAMING CONVENTIONS IN YOUR SCRIPT.

5. HOW TO CROSS-REFERENCE YOUR CONTENT FOR CONSISTENCY.

6. HOW TO CREATE A SUPPLEMENTAL ASSET LIST.

TELL YOUR STORY

Now that you have outlined your project's information flow, use your treatment to create a full-blown blueprint for bringing your ideas to life. Your script and accompanying asset list will be invaluable documents to anyone involved with producing the project. In fact, it is likely both documents may become the most viewed items in your arsenal of tools during the development process. In a team environment, designers will reference them to create interfaces, animators will utilize them to decipher where elements exist and how they should move across the screen, audio and video producers will utilize them to record voiceover or video narration, programmers will create the project's interactivity based on how it is described in the script, the project manager will reference both documents when creating progress reports, etc. If you are working on your own, your script and asset list will become invaluable organizational reference tools with which to create the final product. Either way, you should put as much detail as possible into both documents.

Head to Head: Script vs. Flowchart

Although a navigational flowchart can be a useful tool across all types of interactive media projects, not all will require that you write a script as well. A detailed script will be most helpful on projects that require some sort of linear narrative and make extensive use of animation, audio, and video elements. Examples of these types of projects include computer-based training modules, product demonstrations, educational titles, and online games.

Typically—but not always—these projects are developed using tools like Flash and/or an audio or video editing application (depending on the amount of each element needed). When distributed online, projects of this nature tend to focus on a specific topic that requires a narrative discourse and are often part of a larger, more comprehensive Web site. For instance, a healthcare Web site may offer a series of video or animation-driven training modules doctors can sign up for to attain continuing medical education accreditation. Or a company that produces printers might feature online animated interactive modules on the care and maintenance of its products.

Although a flowchart is still a helpful tool to outline interactivity, creating a script for these types of projects allows developers

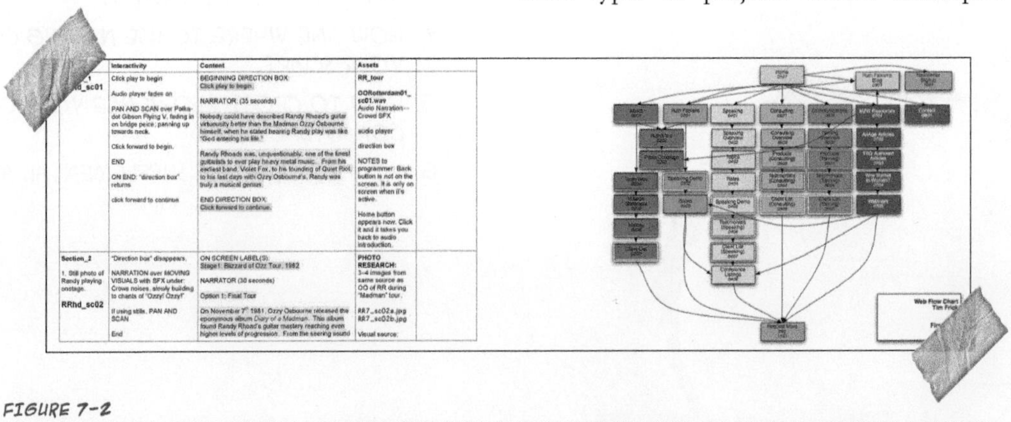

FIGURE 7-1
YOUR SCRIPT AND ASSET LIST MAY BE THE MOST REFERENCED TOOLS IN YOUR ARSENAL.

FIGURE 7-2
SOME PROJECTS WILL BE BEST SERVED BY A DETAILED SCRIPT WHILE OTHERS WILL BE BEST SERVED BY SOME COPY DOCS AND A DETAILED FLOWCHART.

FIGURE 7-3
YOUR WEB SITE MAY NOT REQUIRE A FULLY DEVELOPED SCRIPT.
HOWEVER, YOU STILL NEED TO WRITE CONTENT FOR IT. ADOPTING
FILE AND FOLDER NAMING CONVENTIONS CAN HELP YOU KEEP THE
CONTENT ORGANIZED.

more freedom to outline specific project details. It also provides a structural framework for recording a project's audiovisual elements: narration, interviews, demonstrative scenarios, and dramatic reenactments.

In the case of a typical text and graphics-driven Web site, your "script" would likely comprise the content you devise for each individual site page based on the project's navigational flowchart. In that case, a series of individual text documents named to match the conventions of your project and filed accordingly may better suit your need than a formatted narrative script would.

The Script

When you develop a script for an interactive project, you should think beyond typical scriptwriting conventions. An interactive script should include all the elements a typical linear

FIGURE 7-4
A TYPICAL INTERACTIVE SCRIPT SHOULD CONTAIN ALL THE ELE-
MENTS A LINEAR NARRATIVE SCRIPT CONTAINS AND THEN SOME.

script contains—dialogue, exposition, narration, promotional copy—plus everything necessary to fully realize the project's interactivity and computer-based nature. Your script should include specific naming conventions for all files associated with the project as well as detailed descriptions of how buttons and other interactive elements will function. A breakdown of audiovisual elements, text, and graphics should also be included. Explicit details on each element will form an integral part of your asset list. Along with said list, the final script becomes a fully realized plan for implementing your project that anyone can follow.

Before you begin the scriptwriting process, reference your treatment and navigational flowchart. At this juncture, they should be detailed and well executed documents (and approved by the appropriate parties), so expanding them should be an intuitive process. After you have thoroughly reviewed each in detail, ask yourself several important questions:

◎ How will you develop the narrative style necessary to get your information across in the appropriate manner?

◎ How will you expand the treatment content into detailed script pages that contain all necessary information?

◎ How will you organize the expanded content and apply naming conventions to files you do not have or have not yet created?

Using your navigation chart as a reference, begin writing content for the first screen the user will see. Focus on how the story will unfold and on the elements needed to tell that story. If your document is not formatted to accommodate everything you need, format it accordingly or use one of the provided templates on this book's supplemental disc.

When creating your script, include as many details on content structures as you can. Your script should break down what graphics and text will appear on each screen and include cues for voiceover, music, animation, hyperlinks, video clips, and interactive elements. Content sections should be separated from each other by subscribing to cohesive naming conventions.

Anatomy of a Script

The information in your script should be formatted so elements on each screen can be isolated by anyone associated with the project. It should also be formatted to provide a sort of "inventory-at-a-glance" view of the project. Once you have formatted the first set of rows and columns, save the file in an appropriate directory with a name that adheres to your project naming conventions and will be easy for others to find and understand. Keep in mind that the script will become a constantly evolving document based on changes in project requirements, so version management will become an issue to watch out for. Make sure you have a system set up so important documents do not get accidentally overwritten.

Your script should contain references to any relevant project document or asset.

Some of those references include:

◎ **Screen Number:** Relevant screen number based on your naming conventions.

◎ **Text:** Any copy that is featured on the current screen.

◎ **Asset Name:** Name of assets associated with the current screen.

◎ **Asset Type:** Column that breaks media elements down by type and format.

◎ **Interactivity:** Direction that describes that asset's interactivity.

The project's specific needs should delineate how you build the script. If the project contains significant amounts of audio and animation but no video you may need to adjust the script's template. Just remember to keep it simple and organized while still including all relevant categories and information necessary for production.

	Interactivity	Content	Assets	
...ion_1 RRhd_sc01	Click play to begin Audio player fades on PAN AND SCAN over Polka-dot Gibson Flying V, fading in on bridge peice; panning up towards neck. Click forward to begin. END ON END: "direction box" returns click forward to continue	BEGINNING DIRECTION BOX: Click play to begin. NARRATOR: (35 seconds) Nobody could have described Randy Rhoad's guitar virtuousity better than the Madman Ozzy Osbourne himself, when he stated hearing Randy play was like "God entering his life." Randy Rhoads was, unquestionably, one of the finest guitarists to ever play heavy metal music. From his earliest band, Violet Fox, to his founding of Quiet Riot, to his last days with Ozzy Osbourne's, Randy was truly a musical genius. END DIRECTION BOX: Click forward to continue.	**RR_tour** OORotterdam01_sc01.wav Audio Narration—Crowd SFX audio player direction box NOTES to programmer: Back button is not on the screen. It is only on screen when it's active. Home button appears now. Click it and it takes you back to audio introduction.	
Section_2 1. Still photo of Randy playing onstage. RRhd_sc02	"Direction box" disappears. NARRATION over MOVING VISUALS with SFX under: Crows noises, slowly building to chants of "Ozzy! Ozzy!" If using stills, PAN AND SCAN End	ON SCREEN LABEL(S): Stage1: Blizzard of Ozz Tour, 1982 NARRATOR (30 seconds) Option 1: Final Tour On November 7th 1981, Ozzy Osbourne released the eponymous album Diary of a Madman. This album found Randy Rhoad's guitar mastery reaching even higher levels of progression. From the seering sound	PHOTO RESEARCH: 3–4 images from same source as OO of RR during "Madman" tour. RR7_sc02a.jpg RR7_sc02b.jpg Visual source:	

FIGURE 7-5
SCREEN DETAILS: INCLUDE SECTION AND ASSET NAMES AS WELL AS ANY DESCRIPTIVE INFORMATION FOR EVERY SCREEN IN YOUR PROJECT.

FIGURE 7-6
CHECK YOUR SCRIPT'S CONTENT AGAINST THE PROJECT'S FLOWCHART
FOR CONSISTENCY.

The difference between descriptive text and voiceover narration should be apparent. If you need to color code text to delineate between script elements, then do so. The final documents should be easy to understand by anyone without prior knowledge of the project.

Consistency Check

Once you have completed a rough draft of your script, cross-reference its content with that of your flowchart and make sure they match. Make sure the naming conventions you have applied to elements within the script are consistent with the actual files on your hard drive. Check the language for consistency. Does it sound coherent from section to section? How about from screen to screen? Have you used language on one screen that sounds inappropriate compared to the rest of the script's voice? Does the same personality shine throughout the document or does it make a noticeable shift? The goal is to build content that, while spread across multiple sections, works as a single unit, offering uniformity in voice, style and content integrity. If you notice inconsistent passages revise them. Remember, your script should make sense to anyone who reads it for the first time. It might also be helpful to review the content with another party before moving on to the creation of an asset list.

CASE STUDY:
Script and Asset List

Scripting the Theater

The Neo–Futurists' Web site did not require that a narrative script be developed. Instead, the company faced the challenge of creating many pages of written content that followed its site map. Maintaining consistency in voice and style throughout the site would prove to be a challenge.

"Obviously, the easiest way to get a clear and consistent voice across the board is to have a single person do all of the writing," Sharon Greene said. "Sometimes, however, that's just not possible. In our case, because resources are a scarce commodity at the Neo-Futurarium, we assigned certain content pages to different company members until all pages on the new site were spoken for."

Once all the content was submitted, the Neo-Futurists assigned two staff members to edit everything for consistency.

"Keeping uniformity between a number of markedly different voices was a challenge," Greene said. "But all the company members are well-versed in the Neo-Futurists' approach to prose, which helped a bit."

Since the Neo-Futurists are keepers of the prose, a site content management system played a key role in development discussions. The structural framework of the site had been defined, so once a prototype of the content management system was deployed, the Neos were set loose to input a first round of content. This allowed both parties the flexibility to develop the site's design, architecture, and written content concurrently with one another.

PAGE CONTENT FOR THE NEO-FUTURISTS' SITE WAS SPLIT UP AMONGST STAFF AND ENSEMBLE MEMBERS.

THE ASSET LIST

While writing your script, specific ideas for images, text, video, and graphics will arise. Although a script is the first place to describe such ideas, it is not necessarily the best platform in which to include all the information you need about these media elements to actually produce the script, such as:

- File names associated with each script section
- Format, size, and resolution of required assets
- Where to procure the assets if you do not have them
- Status of permissions on licensed assets
- Status of procurement
- Production notes

As the inventory of all the elements you need to create the project, an asset list can be an incredibly valuable tool for many types of interactive media projects. It provides a comprehensive breakdown of required assets for all screens of the project. On Web projects it works in tandem with the flowchart to give you a master checklist of assets for creating the site. On Flash or rich media projects it works in tandem with the script to provide an inventory-at-a-glance view of the project. The asset list can be as simple or complicated as you want or as is required by the project.

FIGURE 7-7
NICE ASSETS: USE AN ASSET LIST TO MANAGE KEY ASPECTS OF ALL ELEMENTS IN YOUR PROJECT, SUCH AS WHETHER OR NOT YOU HAVE ACQUIRED RIGHTS TO USE A CERTAIN IMAGE OR WHERE AUDIO FILES EXIST ON YOUR HARD DRIVE.

Sometimes a simple spreadsheet will do. Other projects may require a database-driven online application to manage assets, versions, etc. If you are using an asset management tool, such as Extensis Portfolio, most information required for the project will be stored in the program's database for instant retrieval by any involved party. Just remember that no matter how you approach it, your asset list needs to include all the necessary information to manage your project's files. This is especially crucial if the project needs to be seamlessly handed from one team to another during various production phases.

FIGURE 7-8
ASSET MANAGEMENT APPLICATIONS LIKE EXTENSIS PORTFOLIO INCLUDE BUILT-IN TOOLS TO HELP KEEP TRACK OF ALL YOUR FILES DURING THE PRODUCTION CYCLE OF A PROJECT.

CONCLUSION

Once you have defined the project's script or content needs, distribute both the finished script and asset list to any necessary parties for feedback and revise until you have a document that meets all project requirements and everyone's satisfaction. Make certain a sign-off on these documents is part of the approval process.

PROfile:

Judy Cammelot, Devore Software
Developing Scripts for Interactive Projects

Judy **Cammelot**, a project manager and instructional designer for computer-based e-learning and multimedia projects, works with interactive media scripts on a daily basis. Devore Software specializes in creating technical programming solutions for its clients. Custom educational software modules are a significant part of the products it develops.

Although most of her work is for instructional Web sites, Cammelot says many similarities exist between developing educational content for browser delivery versus Flash projects intended for commercial applications.

"It is the instructional component that typically drives how a project's content is built," she said. "Whether it is a standard Web site or content developed in Flash, the instructional approach defines what activities a project will contain and whether or not the content will be presented in a linear fashion or as a non-sequential interactive experience."

Cammelot's team does initial research to define the project and who on the client side has expert knowledge on the subject matter. They then glean as much information as possible from the subject

(Continued)

(PROfile: Continued)

matter experts (SMEs) to create an effective approach for presenting the content.

"Our clients' subject matter experts are the source for our educational interactive content, but they don't typically know how to break their expertise down into appropriate instructional activities or sequence them effectively," she said. "That's where we come in."

Cammelot analyzes SME content from an instructional design perspective, breaking topics into manageable chunks and devising course segments that make sense educationally. The SMEs are often directly involved with the content's development, sometimes observing the course structure as it is built and providing input throughout the process.

"Oftentimes, the content definition process involves one or more long sessions in a room filled with instructional designers who work with the SMEs to draw out the content's critical elements," Cammelot said. "We then come away from those initial interviews with the information necessary to develop a content outline and eventually a script."

She says these steps are similar for technical, audience, job and motivational analysis and are analogous to those used in defining business rules that guide other Web site development efforts.

"Our deliverables at this phase in a project will typically include a content outline, performance objectives, and an evaluation plan for the project along with instructional objectives, project structure, and a suggested screen flow," she said.

Once the content has been defined, assessed, and approved, actual script development begins.

Cammelot makes certain the project's educational component is at the forefront of her scriptwriting process by considering a variety of approaches that support that priority.

"It is important to remember when you begin scripting and building in interactivity," she said. "This interactivity will allow users to demonstrate knowledge acquisition or apply that knowledge to a new situation. Ideally the instruction will allow students to seek out new information that will lead to key learning benchmarks or 'teachable moments' when information begins to sink in. Also, using a case-based approach when writing a script fosters learning with the context of how knowledge will be used in a real-world situation, which is critical to a project's success."

Cammelot also says simulations will enable learning to take place in a protected environment without the negative consequences of improperly applying new concepts in a real-world or on-the-job scenario, so they play a prominent role in many of the scripts she develops.

A typical script will go through several rounds of revisions with the client and subject matter experts to ensure it accomplishes the goals set up at the project's outset.

"Once the script has been approved," she said, "we begin adding key asset information and continue with this iterative development process."

During production, Cammelot uses just one master document, typically created in Microsoft Excel or Word, that serves as both script and asset inventory list.

"We will start off with a basic written script and then add columns or sections to it for assets as the content evolves and production continues," she said. "Depending on who needs to review its content I may hide certain columns or save out versions that include only specific sections that are relevant for the recipient."

Cammelot says the script becomes a critically important component during production.

"It specifies requirements for all media elements on a project and directs all production efforts," she said. "We make certain to keep it up-to-date and as detailed as possible to ensure the project's integrity."

Judy Cammelot is a project manager and instructional designer for Devore Software.

www.devoresoftware.com

EXERCISES:

Create a script for the rich media portions of the project. Create an asset list of media elements necessary to produce the project.

TOOLS

Sample documents are included on the CD-ROM that comes with this book:

◎ Sample Script Template

◎ Sample Asset List Template

Files can be found in the folder labeled with the corresponding chapter number and title.

CHAPTER 8

Art Direction and Interface Design

Objectives

IN THIS CHAPTER YOU WILL LEARN:

1. EXERCISES AND RESOURCES FOR KICK STARTING THE DESIGN PROCESS.
2. HOW TO CONCEPTUALIZE YOUR DESIGN COMPS.
3. HOW TO WORK WITH EXISTING DESIGN STANDARDS.
4. WHAT TO INCLUDE IN DESIGN COMPS.
5. HOW DESIGN TEMPLATES CAN BE USEFUL.
6. WHAT TO INCLUDE IN A DESIGN RATIONALE DOCUMENT.
7. HOW TO PRESENT TO A CLIENT.

DEFINED, DESIGNED

Based on your tech spec, you should know the pixel dimensions your designs must accommodate as well as any other pertinent pre-production information necessary to start the creation process.

Conceptualization

During this phase you give the project its visual personality. Successful design implementation should build upon all communication thus far and refine the project's aesthetic properties in detail. Good designers create layouts that work on multiple levels, conceptually, thematically, even metaphorically while also outlining functionality that is intuitive and easy for a user to grasp. Colors, graphics, logos, and typography must work in unison to tell the story, complementing each other so one element detracts from another only if it is the designer's distinct intent to do so.

But how do you find out what type of visual elements would best suit your project? You have already done a bit of cursory brainstorming with involved parties on the project but if you have been following the steps in this book, that was likely "bigger picture" brainstorming on overall project concepts and detailed discussions on the logistics of how best to complete the project. Though you have previously discussed creative concepts, now is the time to approach the nitty-gritty decisions of what button goes where, how many colors will be used, and what visuals

FIGURE 8-2
MANY ELEMENTS WILL PLAY A PART IN CONCEPTUALIZING DESIGN COMPS FOR YOUR CLIENT.

will thematically express the project's personality. You must face the task of taking all the information that has been communicated to you thus far and transforming it into a visual project identity that exceeds expectations.

Before you even pick up Photoshop's Pen tool, create a DIV tag in Dreamweaver, or use Illustrator to draw a stroked box, it is a good idea to do a little creative conceptualization. There may have been a notion in the back of your head on how the project should look since day one, but good design rarely relies on visual appeal alone. By organizing the random thoughts in your head and rationalizing their pros and cons in a detailed manner, you should be able to flesh out your ideas into thorough creative concepts that effectively communicate your project's objective and thus be an easy sell when presented to key decision makers.

To prepare for the brainstorming process, pore over all the data you possess that will affect the designs. You should be clear on the content of your tech spec, user profiles, flowchart, scope doc and other technical documentation, but at this stage it is perhaps more important to set those aside for the moment and concentrate on creative treatments for the project. Review the initial project treatment and cross-reference it with your initial design

FIGURE 8-1
YOUR DOCUMENTATION THUS FAR SHOULD HAVE PAVED THE WAY FOR YOU TO BEGIN THE DESIGN PROCESS.

FIGURE 8-3
SKETCHING OUT IDEAS WITH GOOD OLD-FASHIONED PENCIL AND PAPER CAN SOMETIMES HELP WHEN CONCEPTUALIZING IDEAS.

The Almighty Brand

In most corporate communications scenarios, the design solutions you devise will often need to comply with a client's existing corporate identity standards and design guidelines. In other words, you will be required to incorporate specific color palettes, font sets, or client-supplied graphic elements into your designs. This may not be true in regard to projects like game design or those where the client's intent is to divorce the project's visual identity from that of the company producing it. However, depending on who your client is, you will likely have to comply with his or her standards on one level or another.

Many companies, especially larger ones, employ dedicated teams whose purpose is to enforce their "brand guidelines" with guard dog tenacity. They review every communications project, approve every vendor, and at times even force internal and external designers and other visual media creators to go through "brand training" sessions. These sessions can be as brief as a couple hours or as long as several days and will undoubtedly include homework assignments with spiral-bound identity standards manuals that are exhaustive in scope.

ideas. Are they in sync? Do you see anything in the treatment that may be incongruous with ideas you are considering for initial screen designs?

Reread your written content. Even if you wrote it yourself and can nearly recite it from memory, reread it, this time concentrating on what visuals might best serve each concept being conveyed and what metaphors you might employ to better convey those ideas. Make notes in the margins, or jot down ideas in a sketchbook. Do whatever feels necessary to get you into the right creative head space to begin designing your project's visual elements.

Review any existing art elements you will be expected to work with. In many cases, designers are provided with existing assets—logos, fonts, photos, graphic elements, etc.—and are expected to incorporate those elements into their designs. Ultimately, this will affect how you create your comps. Many companies have existing identity standards that outline what you can and cannot do with their logo or other identity elements, which will also significantly affect your design process. It is best to know what these restrictions may be and how they could affect your work before conceptualizing a design strategy.

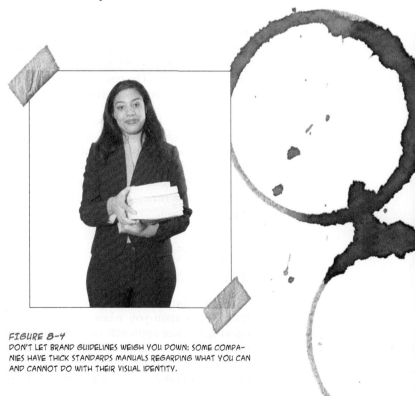

FIGURE 8-4
DON'T LET BRAND GUIDELINES WEIGH YOU DOWN; SOME COMPANIES HAVE THICK STANDARDS MANUALS REGARDING WHAT YOU CAN AND CANNOT DO WITH THEIR VISUAL IDENTITY.

The Brand Manager

One of the primary roles of a brand manager is to enforce company logo usage guidelines. Before you invert the colors on your client's logo or add a drop shadow to it, you should check with your client to make sure you do not violate any of the "rules" when it comes to creative treatments of his or her logo. Most companies have strict standards regarding what you can or cannot do to the symbol that represents their identity. Some will restrict the color palette you can use. Others will not allow any graphic elements within a defined amount of space from the logo. Sometimes you can get away with adding a slight bevel or a lighting effect, but if the company has a dedicated brand team, you can almost be guaranteed that if you violate the company's identity standards you will be asked to change your design, which could affect your timeline and budget. The brand manager is the primary company enforcer of these rules.

Inversely, other companies may simply request that you always keep their logo and tagline together on every screen or use a specific shade of blue. The rest of the design is all you with few creative restrictions.

Either way, it is the responsibility of the designer to adhere to these standards when devising layouts, so in an initial meeting with the client it is a good practice to ask first if a set of design/identity guidelines exists and second if you can review them as reference for a future discussion.

Conceptualization Take Two

Once you know the identity restrictions that may be put upon you when creating screen layouts, you can approach your designs with the benefit of foresight and continue the conceptualization process. Often it is helpful to think on a grander scale when approaching

your designs. Look beyond the product you are promoting or the service being offered by your project. Consider the story being told, the industry to which it belongs, and what competitors are doing. Think metaphorically. Are there images that might support your concept without being too obvious? And, of course, always consider the users. What concepts might they best relate to? What can you do visually to convey your point to users without insulting their intelligence? Your design must speak *to* them, not go over their heads or belittle them.

When brainstorming, ask yourself the following questions:

- What is the general mood of the story being told?
- How will your design best reflect that mood?
- What color schemes are most often used in the industry you are targeting?
- Will purposely changing those colors help you stand out or detract from your message?
- Can you use a visual metaphor to get a point across?

Try to think of as many questions as possible regarding what an effective design solution might entail and jot down the answers for later reference. Use your answers as a stepping stone to begin formulating the design strategy.

External Inspirational Resources

Although your treatment and script can be good creative stepping stones, and tech documents will serve as often referenced inventory checklists to ensure you have not neglected crucial interface elements, they may not be very effective at kick starting the creative process. You may need to cast a wider net to do that. While always keeping in mind the script and narrative elements that define your story, sometimes it is also helpful to look outside the realm of the project to find the resources you need to create effective interface designs.

Online showcases are great resources for creative inspiration. A quick Web search of

FIGURE 8-5
LOOK OUT: SOMETIMES YOU MAY NEED TO TURN TO EXTERNAL RESOURCES FOR CONCEPTUAL INSPIRATION.

relevant keywords can bring up projects similar to your own, whereas numerous online design showcases exist to offer inspiration in the form of award-winning projects in a huge range of industries, applications, vertical markets, etc.

Published design annuals can also be an effective resource for inspiration, albeit a more expensive one. The art or design aisle of most bookstores will carry books showcasing the talents of individual designers, projects in a specific area (i.e., commercial Web sites or corporate identity), or "'best of" publications that highlight outstanding design solutions over a given period of time. These books are great for visualizing screen designs of other interactive projects. However, unless they come with a CD-ROM of links to the original projects, you will not really be able to get firsthand experience on how the interactivity works, what any animation looks like, etc. Although nothing quite compares to the good old-fashioned feel of heavyweight pages between your fingers, these publications are generally expensive, often costing $100 or more for a single book, and they likely will not provide the best source for creative inspiration on an interactive project since they typically offer little more interactivity than flipping pages.

Design or communications magazines provide a more cost-effective printed resource for design inspiration. These publications regularly print the winners of ongoing design contests and will give you a solid idea of your competition as well as the standards to which your work will likely be held. The added bonus of such magazines is that in addition to showing off projects by other designers, they provide insight into current design trends and up-to-the-moment tips and tricks on how to get the most out of your design tools. Many of these publications, such as *HOW*, will also provide resources on how to run a more effective design business, where to find cost-effective stock illustrations and photography, how to write effective proposals, and how to build a more creative workspace.

Competitive Analysis

Although you have already done a preliminary competitive analysis for the project proposal, revisit your client's competitors, viewing their sites and collateral, only this time from purely a design perspective. Your intent should be to exceed competitors' efforts in both form and function, so thoroughly perusing their content will serve as a helpful asset in creating your own designs. Take screen grabs of competitors' Web sites and print them for a side-by-side comparison. If applicable, request brochures or promotional CD/DVDs. Take notes on what you see and how it could be improved upon and/or applied to your work. Ask an objective third party for his or her opinion on what works and what does not in each design.

Kick it Old School

Sometimes the benefits of a good old-fashioned pencil and sketchpad cannot be underrated. They can be helpful tools for outlining possible layout options simply and quickly. You might have taken this approach when you created wire-frame sketches, but now you can take the same approach without another person's expectations getting in the way. On your own you perhaps will discover better solutions than in a collaborative environment. If staring at a computer screen for hours on end does more to hinder your process than help it, at the end of the day you still have to get the job done. Scribbling down ideas on a piece of paper could help your creative process.

Straight to the Source

The quickest and sometimes most effective way to approach project design comps is to ask your client what he or she likes. You will have plenty of face time with the client by this

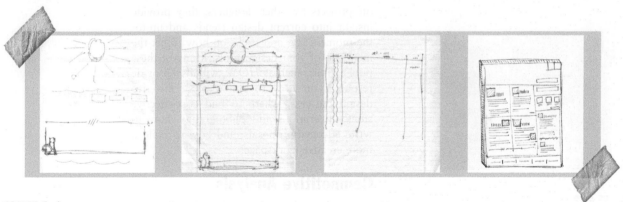

FIGURE 8-6
HAVE THE WIREFRAMES YOU DEVELOPED BROUGHT UP ADDITIONAL INTERFACE CONCERNS?

point, so ask him or her during one of your meetings or phone conversations. Although clients often profess to not having the right words to describe their needs (the old "I'll know it when I see it" routine), most have a solid idea what they are looking for, whether they have shared it with you. It is your job to interpret their needs in a useful way. Often a thorough survey of what they like (or do not like) can go a long way in helping you figure out the conceptual framework around which to build the designs.

Creating Design Comps

After you have outlined concepts around which to create your designs, it is time to bring a few exemplary screens to life. The interface comps you create should represent a

cross section of the project's hierarchal structure based on all the documents you have created thus far. Choose screens from your flowchart that represent typical examples of user interaction throughout your project. If you are unsure of where to begin, the project's home page, main menu or primary information screen is a safe bet. It will likely contain the most examples of required design elements and, as the first screen a user will see, carries with it the highest expectations on the client side.

Choosing a second-level page or screen that features most common navigation and design elements is a good idea. Most likely this layout can be used as a template into which the remaining sub-level content can be dumped and styled, especially helpful if your project features a content management system (CMS) that separates design from content. Even if most screens in the project will be populated with static information, it is good practice when creating comps to treat one or more screens as design templates from which to springboard into subsequent information screens.

Personality Plus

Remember that in addition to aesthetically communicating the project's key message, your comps should visually represent its voice and personality. It is one thing to verify inclusion of all necessary interface elements, titles, copy, etc., but if your comps miss the mark aesthetically, you will likely burn hours and hours on extensive rounds of revisions. Is the

FIGURE 8-7
TALK IT OUT: SOMETIMES THE SIMPLEST WAY TO GET IDEAS IS TO SIMPLY ASK.

Design Templates

No matter the scope of the project, design templates can be a helpful tool to save time and money. We know the purpose a project must serve can and will change over time. Markets fluctuate, content expands, and needs change. The more flexible you can make a project to accommodate these changing needs, the more impressed key decision makers will be and the longer a project will remain current. Anything you can do to extend a project's shelf life will ingratiate you to its purveyors and inevitably provide you with repeat business. This too is a formula for conservation success, as the time you save by using templates can be devoted elsewhere to other details that will enhance and improve the project's design, functionality, and usability.

general theme of the project kitschy or retro or is it more somber and conservative? Whatever the answer, make certain your visuals support this theme. Also, if you can devise a design concept that works metaphorically or on multiple levels, it will likely gain a more enthusiastic reception.

The importance of understanding good design concepts and how to translate those concepts to the screen cannot be underestimated when it comes to communicating an effective message. Once you have completed a first draft of the design comps, ask yourself if you have answered questions such as does the navigation system represent all options outlined in the flowchart and does it seem intuitive for the user? Have you conveyed the appropriate messages in your tagline, graphic elements, etc.? Commercial design is first and foremost a communication tool, so if your interface layout is not properly bringing forth the ideas you wish to convey in a succinct manner, then you should rethink it.

PROfile:

Christina Weisbard
The Creative Process and Working with Clients

Freelance Web designer Christina Weisbard has been designing sites since the mid-1990s. Within that time she has developed a solid approach to art direction and design production on projects. Weisbard follows a process used by many other designers, a result of years of frontline experience. It is the small nuances she has added that makes her approach to designing Web sites her own.

Her biggest questions during an initial client interview typically deal with timing issues: What is the project deadline? How many hours should be spent on design? How much time should be spent on research? Etc. These answers help her decipher how best to approach the project from initial conceptualization through to final deliverable.

In developing a project's competitive analysis, Weisbard puts the information obtained from an initial interview to good use. A typical first discussion will center on how a client sees his or her company among the competition. Weisbard lets the client talk freely about his or her ideas and product to gain perspective when creating her initial design comps.

"During this time I try not to pollute the process and will typically do my competitive research after the initial meeting in order to try and think more like my client thinks," Weisbard said.

(Continued)

(PROfile: Continued)

The first meeting does not end there.

"I grab everything they have," she said, referring to the print products, graphics, brochures, promotional mailers, business cards, stationery, etc., that she uses to help conceptualize her designs. "I also like to know the things they like, the things they hate, and also eventually share the things I like and dislike for them as well, so I ask a lot of questions up front."

The goal is to find an aspect she and the client can agree on.

Other discussion points in the first meeting are technology needs and budget concerns. As the technology aspects of the project come to light, Weisbard makes sure the technical requirements are discussed, allowing her to set the project timeline in motion—building a third of the time for the creative process, a third for development, and a third for technical time.

"I don't leave the table until all the expectations are out in the open," Weisbard said. "It's important that everyone knows what their roles are and how the project has been defined."

Weiibard takes a marathon runner's approach to art direction, sometimes hammering out designs for as many as fourteen hours in one sitting. During this time she employs all reference materials obtained and begins devising different ways to utilize them.

"I like to deal with all the ideas at once without losing momentum," she said.

First impressions are key to Weisbard during this time. She searches through the screen grabs and print materials gathered during her research, looking for useful elements such as colors, the ratio of one element in relation to others, shapes, and text-image relationships that work well on the page, as well as what is and is not working. All these pieces lead her in a direction from which to design.

"I'll start working in a few design directions, copying and pasting sections of my inspiration materials into a few Photoshop files, until I like the way my chunks are laying out and mentally assigning information to those chunks and using color, type, imagery to push elements back or bring them forward to the user's attention," she said.

Although this process is a very important means to an end for both Weisbard and her client, it is also what gives her creative inspiration.

"It's a pretty visceral process," she said. "Playing, making small things huge, making blue things yellow. I try to look at all my chunks of information in a new way."

The result of a marathon design session may yield anywhere from five to seven comps, only a couple of which may ever make it before the client.

"While I typically only present a couple designs to the client, it's helpful to have more options available should I need them," Weisbard said.

When it comes to revisions Weisbard makes a very clear distinction between design and content revisions.

"Depending on my relationship with the client, I will usually contract for two rounds of revisions to nail down a site's design," she said. "I then make it very clear that the design phase is over and the content development phase has begun. Content revisions, such as copy changes and so on are typically easier to implement, so I tend to be more flexible in that area."

If a project's scope changes during this process, Weisbard's approach is simple.

"When a big change arises during development, I casually point out that the tasks in discussion are not part of the original project scope," she said. "Then I ask whether or not we should discuss extending the budget or keeping the project within the original specification."

If the client is unsure how to approach such a situation, Weisbard offers the alternate option of segmenting the site launch in two or more phases. The first launch includes all the important and primary details of the original project while the second includes the out-of-scope tasks discussed during the original project's development.

"My first goal is always to make sure my clients get what they need," she said. "By listening attentively while we define a project and keeping in regular communication with them throughout the process, I usually have no problems accomplishing that."

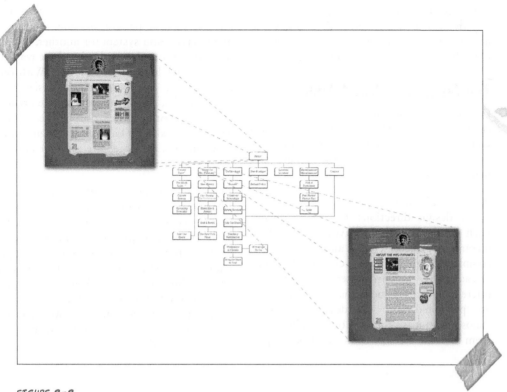

FIGURE 8-8
WHEN CREATING DESIGN COMPS CHOOSE SEVERAL KEY SCREENS TO REPRESENT A CROSS-SECTION OF NAVIGATION AND INTERFACE CHOICES.

If you think the layout is doing its job and translates all the necessary concepts, perhaps you should move on to the next design comp. Or better yet, get a good night's sleep and start fresh the next day. Once you have completed the initial design push, let the output of your creative energies gestate for a while in the back of your mind. Most likely, an additional design improvement or functionality feature will come to you after

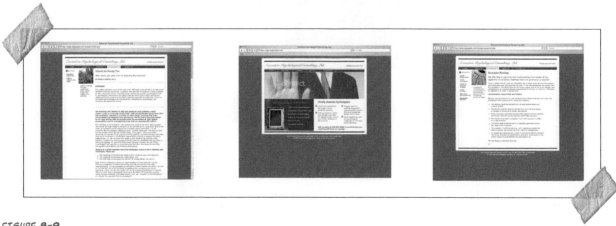

FIGURE 8-9
LAYOUTS THAT WORK STRATEGICALLY ON MULTIPLE LEVELS WILL BETTER HELP COMMUNICATE YOUR MESSAGE. EXECPSYCH.COM EMPLOYS VARIOUS IMAGES OF TREES, VINES, ROOTS AND TO GREAT METAPHORICAL EFFECT TO IMPLY CONCEPTS OF FAMILY LINEAGE, SUCCESSION PLANNING, AND SO ON.

reopening the file a day or two later, thus improving your work and making a case for not procrastinating on the design process until the night before the comps are due.

Too Much of a Good Thing

How many design comps you present to your client is up to you. However, the more choices you offer a client, the more opportunities he or she has for questioning the designs and making revisions to them.

At Mightybytes, we typically present two different design directions for client review. Each direction includes layouts for several hierarchal project screens and showcases a completely different approach from the other. Occasionally, a third alternative may be offered, but rarely more than that. If clients are presented with six design comps to choose from it is often too overwhelming for them to make a single choice that best repre-

sents their interface design needs. They may like the color palette of one comp, the menu/navigation system for another, the textured background on a third and the way you treated their logo on yet another. With only two comps, this becomes an easier task. Occasionally, the client requests we create a hybrid of both designs during the revision process, a task that can be challenging if the two concepts presented are on opposite ends of the design spectrum.

This is not to say you should restrict your creative process to only two design comps. If the muse so strikes you and you have time in the budget, create three, four, or even ten, knowing that at most only a few will be presented to the client. Often the right solution will not hit you until well into the creative process. Once you have selections you are happy with, choose the best two. You can always save the extras for future projects. That being said, the biggest design challenge

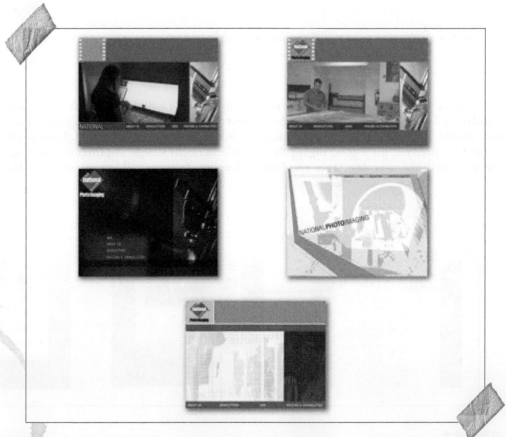

FIGURE 8-10
DESIGN CHOICES: YOU MAY CREATE FOUR OR FIVE DESIGN COMPS WHEN DEVISING THE RIGHT SOLUTION FOR YOUR PROJECT BUT IT MIGHT BE BEST TO ONLY OFFER TWO OR THREE IN THE FINAL PRESENTATION.

usually lies in balancing the amount of time you have estimated for creating comps with the amount of time it takes you to come up with the best solution. Revisions to your comps only complicate this process.

Creating a Design Rationale Document

Once you have completed your designs and chosen those you wish to present, it can be helpful to accompany them with a design rationale document, in which you pitch the philosophy behind each design choice. Creating said document may not always be required—especially if you have a longstanding relationship with your boss, client, or the person funding your project and it is easy to communicate with them—but it can be helpful in scenarios where you need to explain the deciding factors that were key to completing your designs.

In its simplest terms, a design rationale document is an explanation of why you made the choices you did, and it will ultimately help in "selling" your design strategy solution. It can be as brief as several lines of explanatory text beside each comp in a PDF or on a Web page. A more ambitious document will take the client step by step through your thought process and can assist in his or her decision making by outlining in detail what each design comp entails, how you arrived at key design decisions, how those decisions works thematically or metaphorically, and how the comp fits in with the overall picture of the project, your client's industry, the competition, etc. It also

FIGURE 8-11
PRESENTING YOUR DESIGNS IN PERSON GIVES YOU THE OPPORTUNITY TO FIELD QUESTIONS REGARDING YOUR RATIONALE IN A SPONTANEOUS MANNER.

offers a great opportunity for you to shed some light on how you envision interactive elements on the screen working, what button rollover states or drop-down menu systems will look like, etc.

If you are presenting the design comps in person you may want to print your design rationale (in color, of course) on larger boards with simple notes that can serve as a springboard to presenting the design strategy.

What to include in a Design Rationale Document

When creating a design rationale document you are essentially giving the reader insight to your thought process, so if you ran on instinct when putting the comps together, now is the time to think about what that instinct entailed. Try answering the following questions for each comp you present:

- How does the imagery used support your overall thematic concept?
- Why did you choose specific color schemes?
- Why do your font choices most effectively communicate your ideas?
- Why does a specific comp outshine the competition?
- How do your comps fit within the overall brand scheme and identity guidelines?

If you have taken any notes during the design process, you should look them over. Any insight you can provide regarding your process or any thoughts you have that could help sell an idea should be included in the rationale document. Use a page layout program for either Web or print to include screen grabs of each design comp, organized by scheme, with accompanying text that sheds light on your process, preferences, strategy, etc.

Begin the first page of your document with an overarching statement on how you approached creating design comps for the project. Include any relevant details on the state of the industry, current design trends, thematic considerations, and anything else you think might be helpful in outlining your intent. It does not need to be the length of a term paper, just a few sentences or paragraphs that clearly define your approach.

Continue by focusing another statement of intent specifically on the first set of design comps, typically those you most favor. Again, keep the descriptive text brief and concise but with as many details as you think are necessary to sell the design.

Follow that with color swatches from the palette and examples of fonts you used in the comp. Include relevant RGB, Hex or even CMYK (if this project is being co-produced alongside a print project) color values and, if applicable, compare those—side-by-side—with any existing brand colors or identity guidelines. This will show the client that you are attentive to his or her standards and willing to comply with them. Repeat the process of showing how your font choices complement any existing collateral or guidelines, how they fit in with current design trends, etc.

Next, insert a screen grab of the home page or main menu screen below the fonts and color palette, followed by descriptive text that outlines how the menu system will work, what button rollover states look like, and any other information relevant to the design or showing how it will function.

Include any sub-level screens you have created for this design scheme along with pertinent descriptive text. Close with a statement explaining why you believe this solution will best fit the project's needs.

Repeat the process with any subsequent schemes you plan to present and export the document as either a series of Web pages, color printouts, or a format that is easy to

FIGURE 8-13
DOG 'N' PONY SHOW: PRESENTING YOUR IDEAS IN PERSON IS MORE EFFECTIVE THAN DISCUSSING THEM BY PHONE OR E-MAIL.

send via e-mail, such as PDF. Once completed, the design rationale document will be a useful tool that can be distributed to any necessary parties to help them understand your strategy.

Presenting the Designs

Presenting the designs in person will always be more effective than providing clients with a Web link or e-mailing them a PDF. By giving the "dog 'n' pony show" routine you are offered the opportunity to infuse the presentation with your personality and direct clients in a preferential direction. Inevitably, the client will have questions. If you are meeting in person, you can answer such questions immediately, a task that is difficult to accomplish over the phone or via e-mail.

The Waiting Game

Once you have presented your ideas, the waiting game begins. Give the client enough time to digest your presentation and its concepts to make an educated decision on your work, but not so much time that it jeopardizes the schedule in your proposal. If you have come this far, then the client has signed off on your proposed timeline and a deadline, however close or distant, ultimately looms. There is no set rule as to how much time is too much or not enough, but if by this point you have established a level of rapport with the client then it should be an easy task to check in with them a day or two after your presentation if for no other reason than to see if he or she needs anything else from you.

FIGURE 8-12
SENDING LINKS TO YOUR COMPS FOR REVIEW IS A QUICK WAY TO GET THEM IN FRONT OF THE RIGHT PEOPLE, BUT WHY NOT PRESENT THEM IN PERSON INSTEAD?

FIGURE 8-14
WAITING FOR FEEDBACK CAN BE A MIND-NUMBING PROCESS.

Comp Revisions

Typically, when clients contact you to discuss your presentation, they will have a list of revisions they would like you to implement, although it is possible they will ask you to create another round of comps if you have not nailed what they want in the first go-round. Address the requests accordingly, depending on the language used in your proposal. Complete the revisions or new comps discussed with your client and present the new files to him or her.

Final Approval

After all design and functionality haggling over your comps is finished and they have been revised to the necessary parties' spec, you should get a written sign-off on the completed comps. An e-mail to your client confirming he or she has reviewed the comps and that you have his or her blessing to move forward with prototyping and design production should suffice. With this action, the client confirms his or her desire for you to continue and thereby reduces the possibility he or she may go back on his or her word and make additional revisions to the comps once you have moved into production. Once you have begun programming and authoring the final files, it is likely you will need to flatten layers and reduce file size on your graphic files, compress video clips, etc. Making aesthetic revisions at that point becomes a much more laborious and time-consuming process that, if you can, it is best to avoid.

CASE STUDY:
Art Direction and Interface Design for the Neo-Futurists

After completing the architectural structure phase for *www.neofuturists.org*, Mightybytes began compiling resource materials to use as a springboard for creating design comps.

"From the project's outset our resource folder grew on a daily basis," Kristala Pouncy said. "After every meeting with the Neo-Futurists we had an internal discussion on how best

IT WAS PRETTY CLEAR TO US FROM OUR DISCUSSIONS WITH SHARON [GREENE] AND COMPANY THAT THEIR COMMITMENT TO IMPERIAL RED WAS INFALLIBLE,

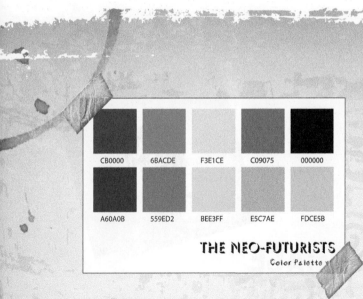

| CB0000 | 6BACDE | F3E1CE | C09075 | 000000 |
| A60A0B | 559ED2 | BEE3FF | E5C7AE | FDCE5B |

THE NEO-FUTURISTS
Color Palette

THE NEO-FUTURIST SITE COLOR PALETTE.

to approach their site's look and feel. We reviewed design magazines, pored over texture samples and in general just grabbed snippets of elements we liked from other sites, layouts, type treatments, and so on. We had plenty of hand-drawn sketches generated during our meetings as well as a clear idea from the Neo-Futurists regarding what they were looking for, so the direction in which to head design-wise was pretty intuitive."

Mightybytes' design approach for comps on the site was to start with the larger elements and work inward toward the smaller icons, buttons, etc. The first elements created were the background and content shell that would be common to every site page. Many considerations went into the final choices for color, texture, and design elements.

"It was pretty clear to us from our discussions with Sharon [Greene] and company that their commitment to imperial red was infallible," Pouncy

said. "So we chose to keep that element from the existing site as the background color, although we dirtied it up a bit with some texture. Since it is such a bright and arresting color we opted for more neutral tones to make up background for the actual site content. Adding distressed masking tape to the corners as a design element seemed to work in tandem with the Neo-Futurists' DIY philosophy."

Once the folks at Mightybytes were happy with the background and content shell designers concentrated on the site's top banner, where the navigation and most dominating visual elements would reside.

"We had numerous discussions over use of the baby head icon and how to treat it on the site," Pouncy said. "As the company's most recognizable visual element, we knew that it required significant weight on every page."

IMPERIAL RED: MIGHTYBYTES TRANSITIONED THE RED BACKGROUND ON THE NEOS' EXISTING SITE TO THE NEW SITE, UPDATING IT WITH TEXTURED ELEMENTS. NEUTRAL COLORS WERE USED FOR BACKGROUNDS THAT WOULD SIT BEHIND ACTUAL SITE CONTENT. OLD MASKING TAPE ROUNDED OUT THE LOOK.

THE NEO-FUTURISTS' MOST DEFINING VISUAL ELEMENT. THE NEO-FUTURARIUM PROMINENTLY FEATURES A WALL-SIZED MURAL OF THE BABY HEAD WITH GOLDEN LIGHT RAYS EMANATING FROM IT. AUDIENCE MEMBERS ARE GREETED BY THE IMAGE PRIOR TO EVERY SHOW AS THEY WAIT FOR DOORS TO OPEN. MIGHTYBYTES OPTED TO REFLECT THIS TREATMENT OF THE ICON FOR ONLINE USE.

"While it wasn't shown in our comps, our intent was to slowly rotate the light rays around the baby head in a manner that wasn't too visually jarring but that provided an element of motion for each site page," Pouncy said. "It ended up being one of the first elements we prototyped."

MIGHTYBYTES MADE CERTAIN TO GIVE THE NEO-FUTURISTS' BABY HEAD THE WEIGHT IT DESERVED ON THE SITE'S HOME AND SECONDARY PAGES.

Mightybytes then moved on to other individual elements on the home page, such as icons, buttons, and page footers.

"We had a laundry list of required elements to include on the home page from our information architecture discussions, so it was pretty clear what we needed to create," Pouncy said. "There were still a couple questions regarding icons for their blog and podcasts, which they had yet to implement, but for the most part our inventory of elements was obvious."

HAND-DRAWN SKETCHES WOULD SIT SIDE-BY-SIDE WITH ORNATE ELEMENTS, IMAGES OF OLD INDONESIAN TRIBAL MASKS, DINGBATS, SCRIBBLES, AND STAINS FOR A RANDOM COLLAGE LOOK.

Once the icons and navigation elements were created, Mightybytes' final challenge was to lay out all the elements onscreen in a manner that would make sense for home and secondary page design templates.

"As is typical in this process, we tried a number of different options and finally decided on the layout we presented to the client," Pouncy said.

THE FIRST ROUND OF DESIGN COMPS PRESENTED TO THE NEO-FUTURISTS.

The results were home and second-level page designs Mightybytes felt embraced the client's aesthetic and philosophy while simultaneously functioning as templates for Joomla and thus allowing for easy content updates once deployed.

"Under different circumstances we may have spent the time creating another round of comps," Pouncy said. "But we were so certain we had hit the mark with our first round of comps for the Neo-Futurists' site that we decided to present them without creating a second set. It was a risky move, given our tight timeline for completing the site, but it ended up being a smart one, as the files we presented were very well received."

"The team at Mightybytes gave us exactly what we were hoping for," Sharon Greene said of the comps. "The comps provided a look that keeps the ideas of randomness and lots of different voices coming together to make something unique, but balances that with the need for the site to be legible and functional. When we showed the first design comps to Max Crowe and other volunteers they responded really well, they said it still looked like us but now they could find stuff on the site."

"Sharon showed me the comps just after they were finished," Crowe said. "I think Mightybytes really nailed it. I can't offhand think of anything I'd suggest changing."

"We were ecstatic that our work was so enthusiastically embraced," Pouncy said. "After reviewing the comps for just a couple days, the Neo-Futurists came back to us with only a few revisions, really. It was a good feeling to know that we had done our job well."

TARGET USER MAX CROWE AGREED THAT MIGHTYBYTES HAD 'NAILED IT' WITH THE FIRST SET OF DESIGN COMPS PRESENTED.

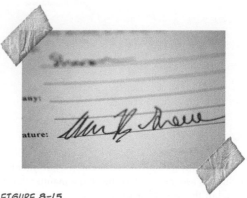

FIGURE 8-15
ONCE AGAIN, MAKE SURE YOU GET A SIGNOFF ON PAPER OR VIA E-MAIL ONCE YOUR COMPS HAVE BEEN APPROVED.

If you built a payment structure of thirds into your proposal, now might be a good time to send out that second invoice with verbiage included stating payment of the invoice denotes approval of all files up to that point.

CONCLUSION

Defining a project's visual identity is time consuming and requires a lot of forethought and its importance in a project's overall structure should not be underestimated. Start thinking about art direction early in the process and work with your client to discuss as many visual options as possible. This will go a long way once you sit down to actually create the project's interface.

EXERCISES:

Create two or more design comps for a sample project and accompany them with a design rationale.

TOOLS

Sample documents included on the CD-ROM that comes with this book:

◎   Sample design rationale documents

Files can be found in the folder labeled with the corresponding chapter number and title.

CHAPTER 9

Revisions, Approvals, Scope and Feature Creep

Objectives

IN THIS CHAPTER YOU WILL LEARN:

1. HOW TO APPROACH REVISIONS.
2. HOW TO DEFINE THE APPROVAL PROCESS.
3. WHEN TO GET IT IN WRITING.
4. HOW TO DEFINE WHEN A REQUEST IS "OUT-OF-SCOPE."
5. HOW TO ADDRESS FEATURE CREEP AND OUT-OF-SCOPE REVISIONS.

THE REVISION FACTOR

Revisions are a necessity when creating interactive media. Sometimes, you will not know if your design works until you see it implemented. Other times you might need to record new audio, revise content, or even add entire sections to the project before it can be tested and debugged. In the course of producing a project, it can be easy for you, your team, boss, or client to get lost in the excitement of adding functionality or design elements. In certain cases, adding functionality or additional design elements can be a very necessary thing.

These decisions have consequences, however, when it comes to making deadlines and staying within budget. Adding a new section to a Web site might improve its usability and increase site traffic, but will it allow you to make the deadline? Will this addition force you to acquire expertise from a third party? Who will pay for this expertise and will it stay within budget? Clients will be very excited over the prospect of improving their site. They will be even more excited if this improvement will be free and still allow them to make their deadline. It is up to you to get and keep a handle on this and communicate accordingly with the person holding the purse strings. Make sure they know the difference between bug fixes, content revisions, and feature or scope creep.

Unfortunately, many inexperienced designers and developers make the mistake of not sticking to the scope of the project when producing interactive media. By not maintaining control over the specifics of what you will create and the amount of remuneration you agree to create it for, you open yourself up to essentially working for free. Depending on how complex or time consuming the new functionality is, it is possible you could work without pay for weeks or months. This could result in disastrous consequences.

Sure, it can be very easy to let a couple requested changes slide: "Can you make that button red instead of green? Can you change the word 'their' to 'there'?" You know such changes will not take long and are going to keep the client happy, so you smile and nod your head while saying, "Sure, that's not a problem."

Well, in reality, unless the mistakes are your fault, it actually can be a problem. And—depending on when in the development process those requests are made—something as simple as a changing a button color can be more time consuming than you might think once you have flatten layered graphics or converted them from RGB to indexed color. Of course, there is no need to be difficult or disagreeable about it. Longstanding client relationships are, after all, the basis for a successful business. You simply need to make clear to those with whom you are working what is and is not included in your proposal.

Unless you have a longstanding relationship with your client agreeing to revisions outside the scope of the project can set a precedent for the scales to be tipped out of your favor. You think you are being flexible. You think you are being agreeable and that the client will appreciate that. And, to be certain, you are. But those tiny little favors easily add up. If you have a client who does not understand that each time he or she requests a change you are put in the awkward position of having to decide whether it is within the project's scope. And although these requests might make for a better product, all this scope creep can put you in the poorhouse.

Creepers at Bay

To prepare for such a situation, make the details of your proposal clear and build financial padding into it to cover such possibilities. Outline how many rounds of revisions are included with your price, how many interface design comps you will provide the client with, how change requests and out-of-scope revisions will be dealt with, and how many prototypes are included.

If you are asked to add content or functionality you would consider out of the project's scope, you should ask yourself:

- ◎ What are you contractually obligated to provide?
- ◎ How will it affect the project if you say "Yes" to these additions?

FIGURE 9-1
MAKE SURE YOU ARE EXPLICITLY CLEAR IN YOUR PROPOSAL
REGARDING HOW YOU WILL ADDRESS REVISIONS.

- ◎ How will it affect the project if you say "No" to these additions?
- ◎ Will the new features greatly improve the product?
- ◎ What kind of relationship do you want with the client in the long run?

Managing Expectations

Mastering the fine art of managing expectations is a more valuable skill than being a top-notch designer, crack programmer, or talented creative strategist. If you are able to set up realistic parameters you know you can meet and exceed those expectations, the scales are tipped in your favor and most times everyone is happy. This process starts with your initial meeting and ends when the project is completed.

Although you may know from the get-go that a project will take a specific amount of time and materials to create, it is always preferable to estimate high and come in *under* budget rather than having to ask for more money. Although it is not without its own set of caveats, the same principle applies when it comes to timing. If you know a project will take you six weeks to complete and you tell the client eight, imagine how delighted he or she will be when you turn it in early. However, do not hand over your deliverable *too* early, as it will give the client time to come up with excuses to revise the product.

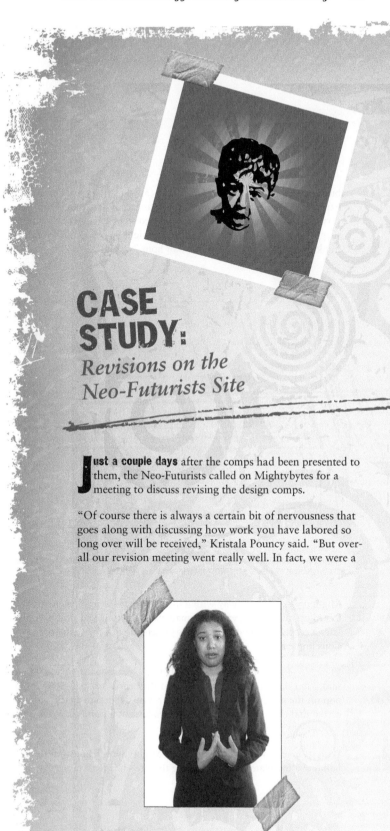

CASE STUDY:
Revisions on the Neo-Futurists Site

Just a couple days after the comps had been presented to them, the Neo-Futurists called on Mightybytes for a meeting to discuss revising the design comps.

"Of course there is always a certain bit of nervousness that goes along with discussing how work you have labored so long over will be received," Kristala Pouncy said. "But overall our revision meeting went really well. In fact, we were a

A CERTAIN AMOUNT OF NERVOUSNESS OVER HOW
YOUR WORK WILL BE ACCEPTED IS UNDERSTANDABLE.

bit surprised because the Neo-Futurists called us two days before we expected them to, so they were actually ahead of schedule. They were very clear about the few things that needed to be changed and offered suggestions regarding how the revisions might be treated. All total, I think the meeting barely lasted a half hour."

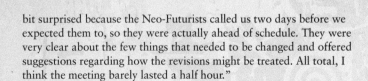
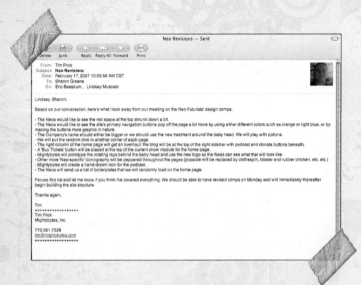

MIGHTYBYTES FOLLOWED THE REVISION MEETING WITH A LIST OF REVISIONS TO MAKE CERTAIN EVERYONE WAS IN AGREEMENT WITH WHAT NEEDED TO BE DONE.

Mightybytes walked away with a list of changes to implement and followed up the meeting with an e-mail clarifying expectations. Two days later a second round of comps was presented with the requested revisions implemented.

"The Neo-Futurists seemed fine with all the revisions we made," Pouncy said. "But they were a bit worried that the primary navigation wouldn't pop off the page enough. Rather than revise the design again, we suggested that they let us prototype the header banner and then discuss their concerns further."

With its marching orders in hand, the Mightybytes team went to work building a template and prototyping the site's header banner.

REVISED DESIGN COMPS BASED ON THE NEO-FUTURISTS' REQUESTS.

Revision Philosophy

Next to scope creep, design revisions are the most likely project phase to career your scope (and budget) out of control. As mentioned previously, it is important to adopt a practice for revisions from the get-go, let your client know what that practice is in your proposal, and then stick to it. Although it has been known to happen, a designer will rarely nail a screen design on the first try. Even if you have included every necessary design and navigation element in the layout, design is ultimately a subjective process—what works for one party may not work for another and the reasoning is rarely based on logic but often on a gut feeling that something "just isn't right." Additionally, if the comp's message is not being appropriately communicated then, really, the design is flawed at its base level and you should consider rethinking it.

So what is a good stance to take on revisions? That depends on your relationship with those making the decisions and how flexible you plan to be throughout production. Just as you want your project to be consistent across the board, so too should your work standards. It makes no sense to allow three sets of revisions in one production area but only one set in another area. Inform clients of the number of rounds you have allotted for revisions (i.e., in your proposal) and stick as close to that number as is possible. Sure, you want to be flexible to maintain good working relationships, but flexible can easily turn into exploited. Just remember it goes both ways. Mutual respect is what we are striving for.

FIGURE 9-3
HOW MANY ROUNDS OF REVISIONS WILL IT TAKE TO GET YOUR DESIGN RIGHT?

If a client returns for several rounds of revisions after what you proposed has been completed, politely remind him or her that the revisions—unless you have planned for such in the proposal—are above and beyond what was included in the estimate and that he or she will be billed accordingly. Of course, this is where things can get real sticky real fast. No one want to hear the words, "This is going to cost you more money." Also, most clients will fight to get what they want as long as it will not increase their expenditures. They have already accepted your proposal and likely do not relish in the idea of having to ask their superiors for more money, regardless of whether what they are asking for is *way* out of project scope. There is no single bigger relationship killer than the "I need more money" routine.

Like it or not, good business is all about building relationships. Ultimately, you have to weigh the remunerative benefits of charging more money against the risk of jeopardizing what could be a long-term relationship with your client. Would you like to work with this client in the future? Would it be more beneficial to work on several projects over the course of a year than to nickel-and-dime the client on this one?

If you know you will likely never work with the client again, then stick to your guns and hold him or her to the terms of your proposal on principle. Tell the client additional design

revisions will be billed hourly or at an additional agreed upon fee.

If, on the other hand, you would like to foster a long-term working relationship with the client, then perhaps it is not such a bad idea to let him or her slide with a few "extras" every now and again. However, be mindful that you could risk setting up a bad precedent, especially if it is your first time working with this client. Unfortunately, there are clients who exploit inexperienced developers. In such a situation, when you agree to out-of-scope revisions you inadvertently convey the message that it is OK to do so. Most likely, if you work with that client again, you will run into the same situation.

As long as the relationship does not become decidedly one-sided and exploitative, however, showing a little flexibility on your end can go a long way in nurturing a mutually beneficial long-term relationship.

Unrealistic Expectations

There is always the chance you will work with someone whose expectations are not realistic or whose understanding of technology and the work necessary to accomplish certain tasks reaches new levels of ignorance. The demands such clients make will reflect their lack of understanding and—if they are not listening to your suggestions—they are likely not paying attention to what is and is not part of the project scope.

FIGURE 9-4
THE BEST WAY TO DEAL WITH 'OUT-OF-SCOPE' REVISIONS IS ULTIMATELY UP TO YOU. JUST MAKE SURE YOU ADOPT A PHILOSOPHY AND STICK TO IT.

FIGURE 9-5
UNREALISTIC DEADLINES OR BUDGETS COUPLED WITH A CLIENT WHO MAY NOT UNDERSTAND THE DEVELOPMENT PROCESS CAN EASILY MEAN DIGITAL DISASTER FOR YOUR PROJECT.

In those cases, the best you can hope for is to quickly extricate yourself from the relationship without any disastrous consequences. Make certain you follow every guideline outlined in your proposal and provide the client with a project that fulfills every requirement with little room for misinterpretation. Then move on.

APPROVALS: WAITING FOR THE THUMBS UP

Revisions are the most iterative process in developing interactive media. They start very early in the development process and typically last until the very end. It seems there is always one last aesthetic tweak to make, one last functionality enhancement to implement until your deadline has arrived and you have no choice but to let a few things slide. Revisions can also eat up a project's budget and timeline faster than anything else, which can quickly make the difference between a successful, well-implemented project and certain disaster. Adopting revision standards from the beginning helps keep things on track.

Keeping track of those revisions—knowing which files have been approved and which files still require attention—brings its own set of challenges. Remember, get written sign-offs for work you present for review and keep track of those sign-offs.

Contract Addendums

The choice is yours as to whether you should bill out-of-scope time hourly or with a set rate. Either way, after you have discussed everything with your client, present a contract addendum/change request that outlines the out-of-scope requests, revised schedule (if applicable), and revision pricing structure for him or her to sign and return to you.

If you have decided on additional billing, do not work on the additional revisions until you have received the signed addendum or work change request. However respectable his or her intent, a client may verbally agree to out-of-scope tasks but then neglect to provide a signed addendum. At project's end, this gives the client the opportunity to dispute your invoice while depriving you of the ability to respond in kind. If you can at all avoid that situation, do so.

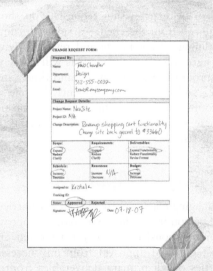

FIGURE 9-7
AN ADDENDUM TO YOUR CONTRACT MAY BE NECESSARY TO PERFORM OUT-OF-SCOPE REQUESTS.

FIGURE 9-6
IF POSSIBLE, TRY TO GET WRITTEN APPROVALS AFTER EVERY PHASE OF YOUR PROJECT TO KEEP PROGRESS MOVING FORWARD.

Defining the Approval Process

Present all files for review in a cohesive manner once they have been completed. If you want to automate the review process, there are hundreds of digital asset management tools available to help you track who has approved what file when. A simple Web search on "approval tracking software" or "asset management" brings up a large number of results for software packages ranging in price from free to thousands of dollars.

If you are adopting a more lo-fi approach, the process can be more challenging but still manageable, especially if your project has hundreds of screens. Post the files to your Web site, create a PDF document, or send them via e-mail and request a detailed response on each screen. Make sure to tell the client his or her response should include whether the file is approved or how many revisions are necessary until it is approved.

When fielding revision requests, you should require—from the client—a single document outlining all comments and revisions within an agreed upon timeline. This will allow you to progress in an organized and timely manner, addressing all comments in one fell swoop rather than in piecemeal fashion, where you will run the risk of missing key requests.

Managing Approvals

Managing client approvals can get harried if the person from whom you require approvals is not responsive. Try to get a written or at least e-mailed approval from any necessary parties on all primary deliverables from the script to the design comps and each prototype before you move forward. When asking for these approvals, be very clear as to what date you require approval by in order to maintain the schedule outlined in your proposal. If you do not receive approvals in a timely fashion and you think it will affect your ability to make an upcoming deadline, alert any necessary parties. If unresponsiveness becomes a repeating pattern, reconsider working with the client again.

If your project is long-term and or more complex, managing approvals and the flow of communication is complicated. Make sure a dedicated resource stays on top of all revisions and the approval of all files associated with the project. If you are a one-person shop it may mean staying in the office a few extra minutes each day cross referencing your written correspondence, but the results of those extra minutes will pay off. Once you have received a timely approval of all files, you can continue the project's momentum.

CONCLUSION

Creating an effective line of communication with your client that includes the ability to engage in frank discussions of money, timelines, expectations, etc., cannot be undervalued. You will need to decide the limits of your comfort level and when it is time to draw the line. Make sure you communicate where the line is drawn and be certain it is reflected in your proposal.

EXERCISES:

Keep written track of requested revisions during production of your project. Define 'Out-of-Scope' requests with a Change Request form and create a work addendum. Cross reference out-of-scope requests with your original proposal. Are you staying on track?

TOOLS

Sample documents included on the CD-ROM that comes with this book:

- ◎ Sample RFP
- ◎ Sample proposal for a fictional project
- ◎ Sample contracts

Files can be found in the folder labeled with the corresponding chapter number and title.

CHAPTER 10

Prototyping and Scope Creep Redux

Objectives

IN THIS CHAPTER YOU WILL LEARN:

1. WHAT PROTOTYPES ARE.

2. WHY YOU SHOULD BUILD THEM INTO YOUR PRODUCTION PROCESS.

3. WHEN TO PROTOTYPE.

4. RAPID PROTOTYPE.

5. REAL-WORLD SCENARIOS FOR PROTOTYPE DEPLOYMENT.

STOP, CLICK, AND ROLL(OVER)

Despite your best efforts to document all the specs and elements of a project, key decision makers often will not know how to react to a project unless they can interact with it. This is where a prototype comes in handy.

A prototype is a quickly compiled trial version of the project or a portion of it with several key functionality specifications implemented. The featured functionality of the prototype might be as simple as hypertext links, button rollover states or basic navigation click-throughs or as complex as a showcase of data tracking, or custom media player integration.

The functionality you build into the prototype or how many prototypes you intend to build over a project's production cycle is between you and the person whose approval you require to move forward. A prototype's primary purpose is to show *some* level of functionality implementation for review. This will give everyone a chance to discuss whether the project is on the right development track or if it should be re-evaluated.

FIGURE 10-1
PROTOTYPE IT: SOMETIMES YOUR CLIENTS MAY NOT BE ABLE TO VISUALIZE CERTAIN ELEMENTS OF YOUR PROJECT UNTIL THEY CAN ACTUALLY INTERACT WITH IT, AS WAS THE CASE WITH THIS PULL-DOWN MENU FROM TRENDSIGHT.COM.

Rapid Prototyping and Iterative Steps

Some interactive media production steps occur concurrently, while others are iterative. With an iterative process, you work through a series of steps, assess the outcome, modify the project, and then repeat the steps. When this process is done quickly at the outset of the project, it is considered Rapid Prototyping. The same process occurs during testing.

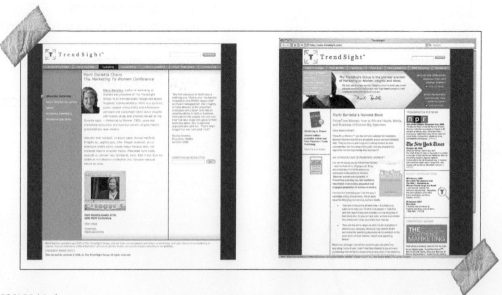

FIGURE 10-2
WHEN CREATING THE WEB PRESENCE FOR TRENDSIGHT.COM, MIGHTYBYTES PROTOTYPED SEVERAL NAVIGATION OPTIONS FOR THE SITE, DECIDING ON DROP-DOWN MENUS AFTER REVIEWS OF EACH OPTION.

When to Prototype

"Test early and test often" is a mantra you sometimes hear from seasoned developers, and creating prototypes is a rudimentary, yet essential, form of testing. In addition to helping you discover where the project's strengths and weaknesses lie, prototyping can be essential in helping you define the project. Some developers will create prototypes alongside the project definition process. These rapid prototypes often start as simple click-through applications made perhaps with hypertext links and little else. As the project is defined and interface elements are developed they are integrated into the prototype, which is then repeatedly reviewed and revised until it is a completed application or Web site.

One Little, Two Little, Three Little Prototypes

Depending on the complexity of a project, build time into your proposal for several rounds of prototypes. This is less true on simple projects, but if yours is a particularly involved project for which the interactivity cannot be so easily defined by discussions and documentation, as in the case of dynamic data-driven applications or multi-player games, the more times you can get an iteration of the project in front of the decision makers the better. In such cases you may need to build separate prototypes for key interactive functions, such as navigation, data input and tracking, game play, animation, or video playback. Each prototype will offer opportunities to discuss and perhaps revise the spec to ultimately improve the product.

The number of prototypes you create and how many times you revise them will depend on how many you have planned and budgeted for in the proposal and what feature functionality you have outlined for each. When you create them should be between you and the decision makers. Some developers create a prototype at the end of each project phase or round of revisions. Others build only one as a precursor to the final deliverable. Still others engage in the prototyping process as soon as they start a project.

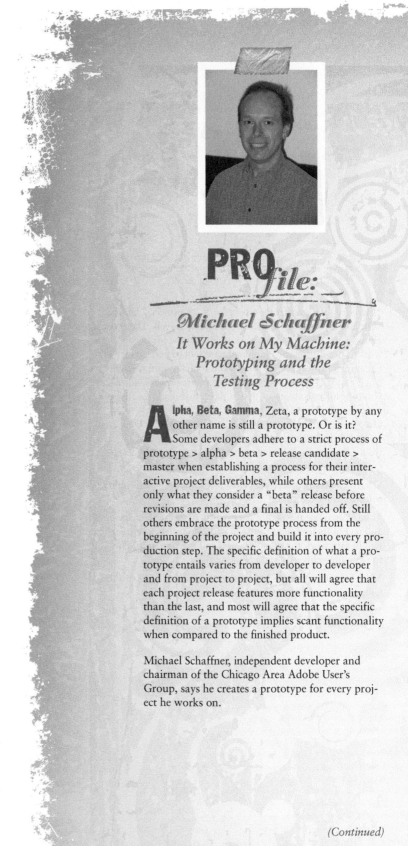

PROfile:

Michael Schaffner
It Works on My Machine: Prototyping and the Testing Process

Alpha, Beta, Gamma, Zeta, a prototype by any other name is still a prototype. Or is it? Some developers adhere to a strict process of prototype > alpha > beta > release candidate > master when establishing a process for their interactive project deliverables, while others present only what they consider a "beta" release before revisions are made and a final is handed off. Still others embrace the prototype process from the beginning of the project and build it into every production step. The specific definition of what a prototype entails varies from developer to developer and from project to project, but all will agree that each project release features more functionality than the last, and most will agree that the specific definition of a prototype implies scant functionality when compared to the finished product.

Michael Schaffner, independent developer and chairman of the Chicago Area Adobe User's Group, says he creates a prototype for every project he works on.

(Continued)

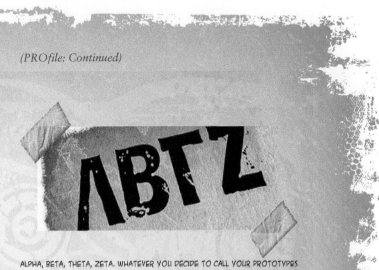

ALPHA, BETA, THETA, ZETA. WHATEVER YOU DECIDE TO CALL YOUR PROTOTYPES MAKE SURE THEY ARE AN INTEGRAL PART OF YOUR PRODUCTION PROCESS.

"I will try to a least create a beta for every project," he said. "On larger jobs I like to include an alpha, as well. The process allows you and your client to confirm that the ideas you worked out during the planning phase will be cohesive. Creating a prototype also allows you to make sure that you catch many issues or oversights early in the process, allowing you to resolve usability or design flaws that might be disastrous if caught too late. I often recall a job I did early in my career where right before the final project was to be delivered, we realized that there was no way to exit the application, as we forgot to include a quit button. Had we properly prototyped the project we probably figured that out."

Schaffner says prototyping helps him test new functionality prior to implementation, as well.

"I will often use the prototype process to test new techniques and technologies I plan to use in order to prove whether they will in fact work for the job, and if not give me ample time to seek alternative solutions," he said.

Mike Schaffner is a freelance programmer and head of the Chicago Area Adobe Users' Group.

So what, exactly, does one include in a prototype? That somewhat depends on its intent. If its purpose is to show basic interactive structure, then you can create your first prototype as quickly as you can throw together a few Web pages after initial discussions of how the project should work. Remember, it will be extremely rough and appropriate parties should be alerted to that fact. If you want to give detail on how an entire section of the project will work or if you want to show the overall project structure, you should wait until you have rough screen layouts completed, either for an individual section or the entire project.

FIGURE 10-3
PROTOTYPING SEVERAL PROJECT ELEMENTS CAN GIVE EVERYONE INVOLVED SOLID IDEAS ON HOW THE FINAL DELIVERABLE WILL WORK.

Feature Creep

When you create prototypes you could run into scope creep, the inevitable addition of functionality and features that may not be in the proposal. If you are rapid prototyping you might embrace this because you began creating prototypes at the outset of the project to help define it (and subsequently built padding into the budget to proceed accordingly). Even if you have only planned for a single prototype toward the end of the project, you should have built some flexibility into your proposal and budget to allow for this.

FIGURE 10-4
HOW USERS INTERACT WITH YOUR PROTOTYPES MAY PROVE THE
NEED FOR ADDITIONAL UNBUDGETED DEVELOPMENT.

Users will interact with the prototype and ideas on how to improve its functionality will arise. Often, the added features that crop up from said users could ultimately result in a far superior product, something every developer should strive for. However, if the new functionality is considered "out-of-scope" of the proposal, you owe it to yourself and other involved parties to alert them to the fact and begin discussing how best to address the expanded project definition. You might end up presenting them with a written change request that outlines how much implementing the new ideas will cost and how long it will take. Or you might end up curtailing the ideas for the first version of the project with the understanding they will be included in a future version. This is all going to depend on how well-defined the project is, how much budget and timeline flexibility you have built in, and how you communicate with the decision makers.

PROfile:

Christopher Salvo
The Benefits of Rapid Prototyping

Christopher Salvo, from The Hensal Group (http://www.hensalgroup.com), embraces prototyping from the outset of any project and believes it gives his company a competitive advantage.

"Rapid prototypes are very helpful during the pre-production or early design phase," he said. "Our first rapid prototyping efforts typically result in what we call an 'ugly,' a tangible, interactive mock-up that helps assure all team members are on the same page. We call them uglies because they are project skeletons with content and media place-holders and little to no design. The coding is rough and limited and lets everyone quickly interact with a project that, until now has been sketched out on paper and discussed in design sessions."

Salvo says adopting a rapid prototyping strategy has helped the communication process with his clients.

"On most projects we discover that different people involved actually had other ideas about the project's performance than were communicated verbally or through written documentation, even though everyone seemed to agree on the specs initially," he said.

(Continued)

(PROfile: Continued)

Salvo does not worry when a prototype brings up undiscovered issues or changes on a project.

"When that happens," he said, "we simply modify the prototype and quickly create another to help further define the specs."

Keeping his approach flexible allows Salvo and his co-workers to work on multiple project tasks simultaneously and thus significantly reduce development, something their clients appreciate.

How many prototypes you create for a project and what you name them (alpha, beta, rapid, etc.) is up to you. As long as they show key functionality in action throughout production and serve as a springboard for discussion on how that functionality fits into the spec.

THE HENSAL GROUP'S HOME PAGE.

Christopher Salvo is a partner in The Hensal Group.

CONCLUSION

Depending on where you are at in the production process and whether this is your first prototype, your third, or your last, once all parties have viewed the files and commented accordingly you should have a concrete idea where to head next. As with any files you present, get a written confirmation regarding the route the project will go moving forward.

EXERCISES:

Create a navigation prototype from included graphics. Create a rapid prototype using HTML pages and your flowchart as a guide.

PROfile:

Dave Clarke
Prototyping Games in Flash

The Marketing Store, a branding and communications company with offices in eleven cities worldwide, offers a wide range of solutions for its client base.

Custom-built games—offered as promotional tie-ins alongside client products—are project Director Dave Clark's particular specialty at the company's Lombard, Ill., office. Clark has been developing these games for his company's extensive client list for several years.

The games run on a small, card-like device with its own processor and liquid crystal display (LCD) and are usually bundled with another product as a promotional tie-in. The small LCD device features several game-play buttons, full-color printed backgrounds and 8-bit sounds. One-bit game-play icons are etched directly into the LCD glass and logic for the game play is embedded directly onto the chip.

"These chips offer a great way for our clients to provide comparatively low-cost games to their customer-base, without having to depend on whether or not those customers have the right kind of computer to play the games," Clark said.

Clark says it is also helpful to developers when they do not have to consider a wide range of computer specs.

"Even though we must adhere to a very strict set of specifications, the chips take a lot of guesswork out of the development process," he said. "There aren't a lot of performance variables to consider in comparison to developing for Windows or the Mac, because everything is self-contained on the LCD chip. It's a very specific development process that we can't really stray from because the options just aren't available."

Although the games are eventually coded directly onto the LCD chips, stringent prototyping is done in Flash prior to production, allowing Clark and his team to step through all possible game scenarios *before* the actual hardware coding begins. Prototyping in Flash is a critical development step that offers a lot of flexibility Clark and his team would not have with hard-coded chips. Using Flash, they can flesh out the viability of conceptual details for each game, and—at the outset of a prototype's completion—they can often find out whether the game play is engaging.

One of our consistent themes is chance versus challenge," Clark said. "For example, when creating a simple soccer game, our first pass set up the user as an offense player trying to score on a goalie. Our initial thought was that kids want to feel the thrill of scoring. In that prototype, the goalie was completely controlled by Flash, so if a player waited long enough in one spot, an opening would appear that would allow them to shoot at the goal. We very quickly discovered that there wasn't much challenge to waiting around for an opening in the goal and we really wanted to keep the player moving, so we decided to turn the game around and make the player the goalie, transforming their challenge to blocking all incoming shots and forcing them to constantly move the goalie and use their own skill. So, in this case, chance was waiting for the opening in the goal, versus the challenge,

THE MARKETING STORE'S GAMES RUN ON DEVICES WITH THEIR OWN HARDWARE.

(Continued)

(PROfile: Continued)

which was anticipating where the shot would come from next, keeping the player active and always moving."

Since the games run on their own custom-built hardware, there is no wiggle room for mishaps once they go into mass production. It is in everyone's best interest to get it right the first time, as developmental mistakes are costly and time consuming. That is really where Flash offers the biggest advantage.

"Creating the games in Flash saves time and money since we don't have to manufacture multiple rounds of demo boards overseas, which is time consuming and expensive," Clark said. "We still manufacture demo boards but only *after* the client and licensor have signed off on the Flash games. The Flash simulations ensure that game-play details are communicated clearly to the chip maker. If we didn't use Flash to create the game simulation, and the chip maker relied merely on a written outline, they may misinterpret a function of the game."

Flash prototypes also allow Clark to easily subscribe to the developer's mantra: "Test early and test often." Once completed, prototypes are typically small enough in file size to e-mail, making distribution to appropriate parties fast and easy.

"We begin the initial round of testing in the office," Clark said. "Typically, one game level is complete when office testing begins. Co-workers play the Flash games and try to break them. I take their comments regarding game speed, number of actions to perform, collections, avoidances, shots fired, number of lives allowed, and so on. Then I use the comments to refine the game. Occasionally the games are shared with the licensor to get their feedback. I also want to make sure that a game is bug free before it is presented to a client. It also needs to be bug free for the chip maker, so that there aren't any communication issues."

The time The Marketing Store saves in creation and distribution of prototypes often allows it to do child testing.

"Children are brought into our office, where we have a focus testing room, and they get to see and play the Flash versions of the games,"

SINCE THE GAMES RUN ON THEIR OWN HARDWARE THERE IS NO WIG-GLE ROOM FOR ERROR ONCE THEY GO INTO MASS PRODUCTION.

Clark said. "We get comments from the kids about what they did and didn't like, and what they might like to see added to the game."

Children in Clark's neighborhood often get in on the action.

"I bring my laptop over to their home and have them test drive the games and get feedback," he said. "We use the kid testing to get feedback on the plastic housing designs that surround the LCD chipsets, as well. Back in the office, we meet and discuss what options should be added or cut from the games based on the kids' feedback."

The Flash prototypes also speed up the process by getting a functioning game into the hands of a client or licensor faster, allowing a longer lead time for revisions or improvements.

"Code changes are much easier and faster to complete in Flash than having to wait and pay for a new demo board from the chip maker, and then hope that the changes are correct," Clark said.

From the time a game idea is born to the point at which final Flash files are provided to the chip maker, each game typically goes through a round of prototypes with an occasional second prototype if there are still issues.

Although The Marketing Store also does implement a round of hardware demo boards created by the chip maker, the ease of network-enabled distribution and the ability to make changes quickly and easily makes Flash the perfect tool for prototyping its games.

"If we didn't use Flash for prototyping," Clark said, "we could easily add several weeks of development time and exorbitant amounts of money to our development process every time. The advantages make it a no-brainer."

Dave Clarke is a project director at The Marketing Store.

CASE STUDY:
Prototyping and Scope Creep Redux

The Navigation Banner

The first element Mightybytes prototyped after the comps were approved was the site's header banner.

"We decided early on that the primary navigation banner would be created in Flash," Kristala Pouncy said. "The animation required for the baby head was a perfect candidate for Flash, but the Neo-Futurists weren't sure they could envision how the animation would be executed, so we thought it best to show them."

Sharon Greene said, "It was really important to us that users of the site could find what they were looking for easily. When we looked at the first comps we felt that the center of the page drew all the attention and that you couldn't even see the main navigation buttons. We imagined someone looking over the shoulder of a friend with a laptop at our homepage. We wanted that person to be able to point and say, 'Click that button. It has the info I need.' These were the categories we spent so much time selecting in those first architecture meetings with the Mightybytes team. They were the primary business reasons for the site to exist, so we

needed them to really pop. We loved the buttons Mightybytes designed for the secondary pages, and wanted something like that for the homepage."

"We had pretty specific ideas how we wanted button rollover states to look and what type of animated elements would work well in the header. Unfortunately, our verbal descriptions of those elements just weren't doing them justice. It was obvious that was our weakest communication link and needed to be addressed as quickly as possible," Greene said.

The biggest challenge in building the header banner in Flash was file size. Once the file was built it weighed in at nearly 200K. When published, this probably would not be a problem for users accessing the site with a broadband connection, but it definitely would be for anyone else.

"At first we kept the graphics in vector format," Pouncy said. "But it quickly became apparent that the number of edges needed to keep the somewhat dirty look and texture would prove to be a problem in keeping file size down."

The solution was to flatten many of the layers and shapes in the original Illustrator file into an optimized raster graphic. Once that change was implemented the file size was reduced considerably.

"If this was a corporation we probably wouldn't have considered Flash for the site's primary navigation," Pouncy said. "But given the client, using Flash allowed us to have a little more fun with animated elements on the banner."

Prototyping continued throughout production with regular client input. Frequent communication between Mightybytes and the Neo-Futurists on various prototype functionality ensured benchmarks and deadlines were met.

PROTOYPING THE NEO-FUTURISTS' HEADER BANNER PROVED TO BE THE BEST WAY TO SHOW OFF MIGHTYBYTES' ANIMATION INTENTIONS.

CHAPTER 11

Design Production

Objectives

IN THIS CHAPTER YOU WILL LEARN:

1. HOW TO APPROACH DESIGN PRODUCTION.
2. HOW TO GET THE MOST OUT OF A TEMPLATE DESIGN.
3. HOW TO APPLY NAMING CONVENTIONS TO YOUR DESIGNS.
4. THE LOGISTICS OF PRESENTING DESIGNS FOR REVIEW.

DEFINED, REFINED, REDESIGNED

The refined screen comps you initially created for the project should have prompted discussions and correspondence regarding how well the design and communication aspects of the project are working. Likewise, a functional prototype typically facilitates a dialogue, the result of which should give you an idea of how best to move forward. Now it is time to design the project's remaining screens.

Concurrent Design and Production

Many designers or developers will move forward concurrently with design production and interactive production, so the appropriate parties can get an equal taste of how a screen will look and how it will function. Others will create layouts for every screen and require approval on each before progressing into any production or development. Each approach has its pros and cons.

How you address design and interactive production on a project should be largely driven by a number of factors:

- ◎ The format of your final deliverable
- ◎ The complexity of your project
- ◎ Your relationship with those whose approval you require

Deliverable Format

Are you creating a Web site? A Flash project? Will your content end up on DVD or CD-ROM?

FIGURE 11-2
SPECIAL DELIVERY: YOUR FINAL DELIVERABLE'S FORMAT WILL LIKELY DICTATE HOW YOU PRODUCE DESIGN ELEMENTS FOR YOUR PROJECT MOVING FORWARD.

Depending on your authoring environment, each carries with it a unique set of production requirements in order to deliver a product that must run in a variety of browsers, play on a standard DVD player, or utilize the latest version of the Flash Player.

Designers may initially use tools like Photoshop or Illustrator to create layouts for Web pages, but typically they migrate to a Web-specific layout program, such as Dreamweaver.

"Sure, you can create button rollovers using programs like Fireworks, or Photoshop pretty easily," said freelance Web designer Christina Weisbard. "But those programs don't come close to offering the range of options you have for rapidly developing Web pages using something like Dreamweaver and a few well built custom scripts."

FIGURE 11-1
YOUR DELIVERABLES THUS FAR SHOULD HAVE PROMPTED MANY DISCUSSIONS ON HOW BEST TO PROCEED.

FIGURE 11-3
WEB DESIGNER CHRISTINA WEISBARD EMPLOYS A VARIETY OF TOOLS TO CREATE WEB SITES. SHE MIGHT START OUT IN ILLUSTRATOR OR PHOTOSHOP, BUT EVENTUALLY SHE MIGRATES TO DREAMWEAVER FOR IMPLEMENTATION.

Some say the jury is still out when it comes to design versus production on Flash projects. Old-school designers might be more comfortable using the tools built into Illustrator or Photoshop prior to authoring in Flash, while others prefer to stay in Flash from the start. Any of these programs will allow you to export screen layouts as images for approval. The benefit of using Flash is that, once your artwork is in the program, you can quickly create a functional prototype.

Additionally, many CD or DVD authoring programs, such as Director, Encore or DVD Studio Pro, might require that you flatten layers in the graphic files before importing them into the authoring environment, making a case for presenting screens as individual images for review prior to creating a prototype. Once those files have been flattened and brought into their respective authoring environments, making artwork changes becomes a harried, time-consuming, and

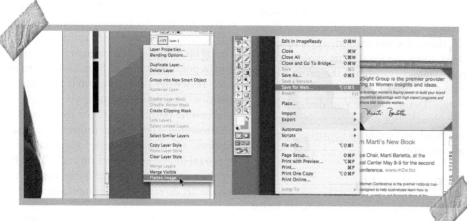

FIGURE 11-4
THE ABILITY TO EDIT ORIGINAL LAYERED SOURCE FILES AND SEE YOUR CHANGES REFLECTED IMMEDIATELY IN OPTIMIZED OR FLATTENED WEB GRAPHICS IS A HUGE TIME-SAVER.

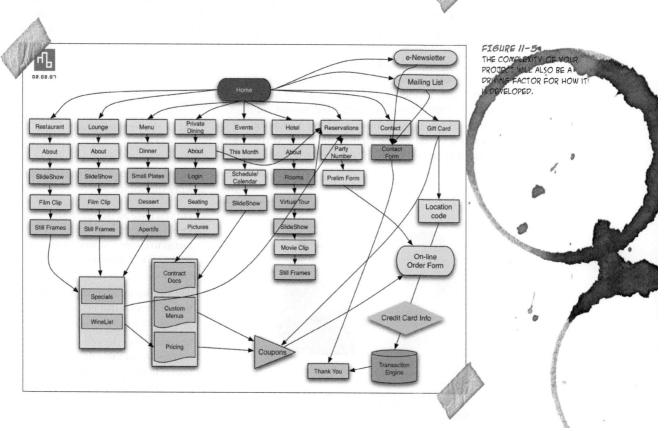

FIGURE 11-5
THE COMPLEXITY OF YOUR PROJECT WILL ALSO BE A DRIVING FACTOR FOR HOW IT IS DEVELOPED.

complicated process. If a program has "round trip editing" capabilities, like most of Adobe's Creative Suite, a simple key command will allow you to edit the original layered source documents and immediately see your changes reflected in all applications, making this less of an issue. Getting approvals on every screen layout before importing them into an authoring environment may work to your advantage in this case.

Project Complexity

A more complex project featuring many information screens will require more development time, documentation, revisions, and inevitably more reviews. This makes a case for prototyping first, even if the project is not completely defined or the designs are not very far along. "Define before you design" is the smart approach, but on larger, more complex projects those two methods sometimes are not mutually exclusive.

Client Relationship

You can also gauge the review process based on your relationship with other parties involved. If you know that a certain decision maker is prone to changing his mind on a whim or revising project scopes multiple times, you should build a round of screen layout approvals into the process before going into final production. If the said decision maker signs off on all design and layout elements prior to production, you have a legal leg to stand on should he change his mind as the project progresses. On the other hand, if yours

is a mutually collaborative and longstanding relationship, then move forward with design and production concurrently. If both sides can maintain a consistent level of flexibility, it will benefit all parties involved.

Screen by Screen

The primary purpose of creating information screen layouts is to give everyone involved an idea of how the screens will look and acquire approval of them. Rapid prototyping will show functionality from the outset, but design is typically not the focus of functional prototypes, rapid or otherwise. Typically, the focus here is on design and arrangement of information, a point that should be made clear to anyone reviewing the presented layouts. In addition to creating layouts, you should also concentrate on managing how the screens will be presented and, if the project has a large number of screens, how you will track approval of and comments on each. The effort you put into presenting the initial designs during the art direction phase should be reprised.

Once completed, the screens can be presented as flattened images, Web pages, PDF documents, or whatever format will work to ensure they can be reviewed, commented upon, and revised in a timely manner.

Where to Begin

The format of the finished product will decide how to proceed when creating screen designs. However, you should first review the initial revised comps you presented and ask yourself the following questions:

- ◎ Do you have all the necessary media elements (text, graphics, logos) to create a layout for each screen? If not, how quickly can you get them?

- ◎ Are all your elements organized and named in ways that make sense to you and other parties involved?

- ◎ Can you apply the initial designs or elements from those designs across your remaining screens?

- ◎ If so, what is the best method to do so?

FIGURE 11-6
THE RELATIONSHIP YOU HAVE WITH YOUR CLIENT WILL NO DOUBT AFFECT HOW YOU APPROACH DESIGN AND INTERACTIVE PRODUCTION AS WELL.

FIGURE 11-7
CHECK YOUR ASSET LIST TO MAKE SURE YOU HAVE ALL THE ELE-
MENTS NEEDED TO CREATE THE PROJECT'S DESIGN ELEMENTS.

FIGURE 11-8
LOREM IPSUM GYPSUM: A MISSING DESIGN ELEMENT SHOULD NOT IMPEDE YOUR PROGRESS.
JUST DROP IN A PLACEHOLDER UNTIL YOU GET THE REAL THING.

◎ If not, what alterations must you
   make to create a template or general framework that will work
   for most, if not all, of your
   remaining screens?

◎ How can you make subtle alterations to your template, so not
   every screen looks the same?

In Your Element(s)

Before you start designing, make sure you
have the elements to create what is required.
Missing an element or two should not hinder
your progress—you can always drop a placeholder or Greek text in until you have the
final asset needed—but you should possess
the majority of elements for every screen.
Cross-reference your script and asset list with
the files organized on your hard drive to
check what might be missing. If you have
been keeping both documents up-to-date,
they should reflect what media assets you
have—including the filenames—and those
you are missing. They will be helpful guides
to creating screen designs.

If after an asset review you are still missing
elements necessary to complete the design
process, you should assess whether it will
affect your ability to meet the next deadline.
If so, alert the appropriate parties, find out
how quickly you can acquire the missing
assets, and discuss extending the deadline.

Files and Folders: The Name Game

We have already covered the importance of a
solid naming convention strategy. Before you
dive into design production, revisit your files
and folders and make sure they are consistent.
If you have been lax in keeping your script
and asset list up-to-date, check your file directory. Appropriately named files should reside
in a directory structure that is intuitive and
makes sense, allowing quick and easy access
to the assets necessary for each screen. Make
sure everything is organized in places that are
intuitive both to you and others, and named
in such a way as to adhere to conventions outlined in the project. Also, make sure to keep
copies of original files in an obvious place in
case some are accidentally overwritten.

Sometimes it is necessary to create a directory
for each project screen, inside which lies a
copy of each custom media element associated with that screen—header, subhead and
body copy, photos, video clips, audio files,

FIGURE 11-9
REVISIT YOUR FILES AND FOLDERS TO MAKE SURE DIRECTORY STRUCTURES AND NAMING
CONVENTIONS ARE CONSISTENT.

FIGURE 11-10
ORGANIZING YOUR MEDIA
ASSETS BY SCREEN NUMBER
CAN SOMETIMES MAKE IT
EASIER TO FIND ELEMENTS
YOU WANT TO INCLUDE IN
A LAYOUT.

logos—as well as your final screen design, if applicable.

After you have reviewed the project directories and cross-referenced the necessary files, update the script and asset list, and then save a version with the current date. Remember, the script and asset list should serve as your most detailed checklists, and they should be kept current with proper naming conventions.

Work That Template

It will save you time to create layouts based on a general design template, because you will not have to design every project screen from scratch. Hopefully you kept this in mind when you created and revised the initial comps, as it will make template creation that much easier. If not, use elements from the approved designs to create a generic screen template that can be used across as much of the project as possible.

Creating Templates

Templates can be created any number of ways depending on the tools you use and the format of the project's final deliverable. Content management systems, such as Joomla, or Web publishing platforms, such as Movable Type, allow you to define areas within a Web page where content can be swapped based on any number of defining factors (i.e., current date or whenever the page is loaded into a browser). There are a number of approaches in Flash where content can be loaded dynamically into templates from a database or XML document. Hand coding or using tools like Dreamweaver will allow you to accomplish similar tasks, as will Director. Most DVD authoring programs have design templates built into the application and offer ways in which you can create your own custom templates, as well. But before you can use any of

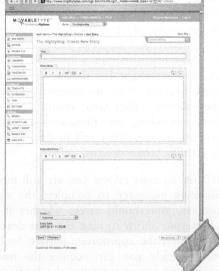

FIGURE 11-11
CONTENT MANAGEMENT
SYSTEMS LIKE JOOMLA OR
WEB PUBLISHING SYSTEMS LIKE
MOVABLE TYPE USE DESIGN
TEMPLATES TO ALLOW YOU TO
EASILY AND QUICKLY ADD NEW
CONTENT WITHOUT HAVING TO
CREATE A NEW PAGE DESIGN.

FIGURE 11-12
DESIGN TEMPLATES CAN SAVE YOU PRECIOUS TIME AND MONEY ON A PROJECT. THEY CAN ALSO MAKE YOU LAZY. WHEN USING THEM, TAKE SOME EXTRA TIME TO CUSTOMIZE YOUR SCREENS SO THEY DO NOT ALL LOOK EXACTLY ALIKE.

the technologies to create dynamic data applications, you need to make your initial layouts design template-friendly.

Specific applications aside, every design template features defined areas within a layout wherein one piece of content can be easily swapped for another. In the design stage, you should focus primarily on the position of elements and the overall "look and feel" of your screen layouts based on approvals you have received on the design comps. Although usability should always be in the back of your mind, mainly pay attention to appearance and consistency in color, font size, image usage, and layout of elements. Once you have hammered out a layout that will work for most of the screens, then you can focus on how best to make it work with the content.

Don't Be Lazy

Do not let the convenience of using design templates make you lazy. Consistency is essential to good design, but do not make your screen layouts so consistent you cannot discern one screen from the next. It can be tempting to create a design template and simply dump content into it, but remember, the goal is to engage the users, not bore them with screen after screen of information that looks the same or is repetitive. If budget allows, take the extra time to add unique elements to each screen or build scripts to randomly load content. Screen-specific elements or randomly loading images will ensure your content remains fresh.

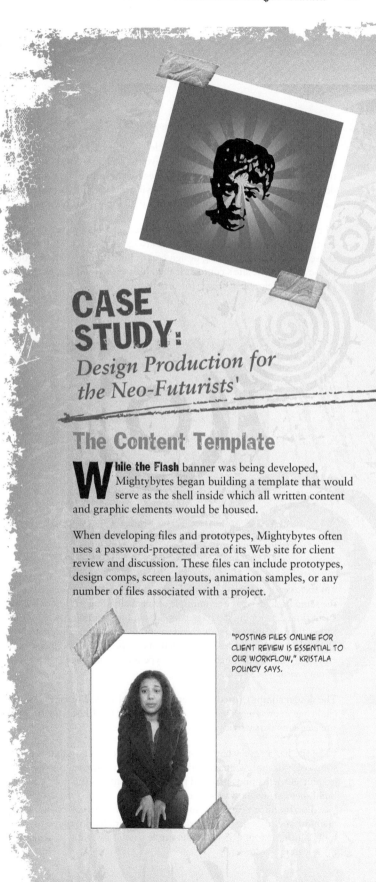

CASE STUDY:
Design Production for the Neo-Futurists'

The Content Template

While the Flash banner was being developed, Mightybytes began building a template that would serve as the shell inside which all written content and graphic elements would be housed.

When developing files and prototypes, Mightybytes often uses a password-protected area of its Web site for client review and discussion. These files can include prototypes, design comps, screen layouts, animation samples, or any number of files associated with a project.

"POSTING FILES ONLINE FOR CLIENT REVIEW IS ESSENTIAL TO OUR WORKFLOW," KRISTALA POUNCY SAYS.

"Sometimes if we are working on a video project or an interactive piece that requires a lot of different screen layouts, such as a kiosk or a Flash training module, we will post review files for the individual proposed design solutions for each screen. These will either be JPEGs posted to the client area of our Web site or multi-page PDF files," Kristala Pouncy said.

The Neo-Futurists' site was being developed on a new server with a new hosting provider. Rather than post files to its own server, Mightybytes chose to convert the existing design comps into a template that would house most of the site's content. It then posted the template to the Neo-Futurists' development server for review.

SHELL GAME: MIGHTYBYTES CREATED A TEMPLATE FROM ITS DESIGN COMPS TO USE AS A SHELL FOR GRAPHIC AND WRITTEN CONTENT. USING A DESIGN TEMPLATE ALLOWED MIGHTYBYTES TO RUN THE DESIGN PRODUCTION AND PROGRAMMING PHASES CONCURRENTLY.

"In the case of the Neo-Futurists' site, where many of the screens shared the same basic design with multiple elements loading in randomly, we spent time developing the page template and integrating it with Joomla rather than creating individual screen comps. Using a design template allowed us to run the design production and programming phases concurrently and use the shell as a prototype for regular client reviews," Pouncy said.

The design comps existed as layered Illustrator files. Mightybytes' first challenge in creating a template was to convert the Illustrator files into site elements that would work well on the Web.

"The site has a somewhat non-traditional background in that it isn't a solid color or a tiling image," Pouncy said. "It is instead four separate graphic elements that surround the page content. As such, we needed to build them in such a way so they would stretch, resize, or move about based on monitor resolution and browser window size. They also had to maintain the site's design integrity as it was initially presented as well. It took a little custom CSS [cascading style sheets] finessing in order to pull off a seamless solution."

The next challenge was to flesh out the content container. Header and footer images that contained the tape and rough, ripped page imagery were created and optimized for Web delivery, and CSS were used to resize the body content shell based on the amount of content it held. By using clashing table cell colors, Mightybytes was able to see how different cells were affected by the CSS and thus designate areas inside which content would reside, so it could create a unified template.

The animated Flash banner prototype was integrated into the content template, although navigation functionality was not yet implemented. Footer navigation would be consistent on every site page, as would a pair of dice, so those were built into the template. Buttons with rollover states were created from Illustrator layers and a randomize function was built into the dice imagery.

"We used a number of dice images and a randomized PHP function to facilitate a different roll of the dice every time a page loads," Pouncy said. "It is a small touch that will probably go unnoticed to the typical user, but one we think fits into the overall philosophy."

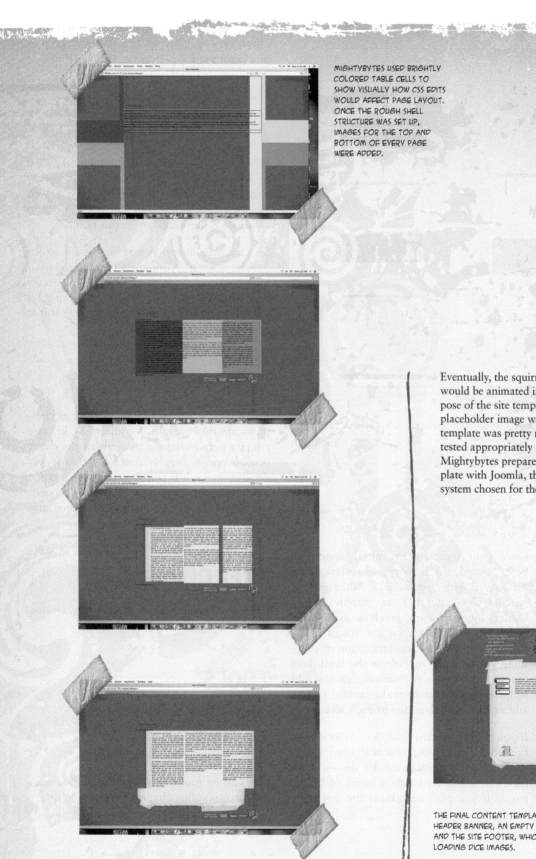

MIGHTYBYTES USED BRIGHTLY COLORED TABLE CELLS TO SHOW VISUALLY HOW CSS EDITS WOULD AFFECT PAGE LAYOUT. ONCE THE ROUGH SHELL STRUCTURE WAS SET UP, IMAGES FOR THE TOP AND BOTTOM OF EVERY PAGE WERE ADDED.

Eventually, the squirrel in the lower-left corner would be animated in Flash, but for the purpose of the site template a hand-sketched placeholder image was used. With that, the template was pretty much complete. Once it tested appropriately on the requisite browsers, Mightybytes prepared to integrate the template with Joomla, the content management system chosen for the site's back-end.

THE FINAL CONTENT TEMPLATE INCLUDED THE ANIMATED HEADER BANNER, AN EMPTY AREA FOR PAGE CONTENT, AND THE SITE FOOTER, WHICH INCLUDED RANDOMLY LOADING DICE IMAGES.

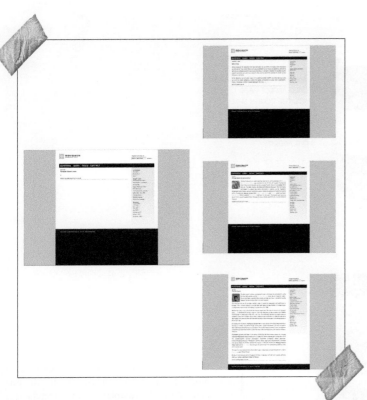

Screen Production

Once your template or initial design has been created, use it to create review comps for screens with custom data. Add any page-specific elements, such as graphics, place-holders for video clips, product shots, or bio portraits, to each screen for rough layout that include a visual representation of everything you want to include in the final deliverable. Be sure to regularly reference your script and asset list to make certain you are adding the right elements to each screen.

If you plan to present your designs as a basic, functional prototype, you will need to add click-through interactivity. To do so, insert the flattened screens into a series of HTML pages. If you plan to present the designs as

flattened images for review only (no functionality), save each layout as a flattened graphic in a common image format, such as JPEG, or add them to a PDF.

Presentation and Approval

When you are satisfied with the initial round of screen designs, present them for review either in person, by posting them to a Web site, or attaching them to an e-mail. A design rationale is not necessary at this point.

Set up a time to review and discuss the screen designs in detail. After you have received feed-back on the designs, revise them as necessary or mark them as approved. Be certain to get a written approval for each design, even if it is just an e-mail confirmation.

CONCLUSION

Design production is one of the crucial communication phases of a project. Make sure you are detail-oriented throughout the entire process and in regular contact with any key decision makers. If you are able to maintain a hiccup-free revision and approval process, readying files for production and programming should be a breeze.

EXERCISES:

Create a template design from initial comps. Prepare design layouts for a review.

TOOLS

Sample documents included on the CD-ROM that comes with this book:

◎ Sample screen layout templates

Files can be found in the folder labeled with the corresponding chapter number and title.

CHAPTER 12

Production and Programming

Objectives

IN THIS CHAPTER YOU WILL LEARN:

1. THE IMPORTANCE OF STANDARDIZING PRODUCTION ELEMENTS.

2. DIFFERENCES BETWEEN WEB, FLASH, AND DISC-BASED PROJECTS.

3. HOW TO ORGANIZE AN ASSET LIBRARY OR SERVER.

4. HOW TO USE A SCRIPT, ASSET LIST, OR FLOWCHART TO DRIVE A PROJECT.

5. IMPORTANT TEAM ENVIRONMENT CONSIDERATIONS.

6. TIME TRACKING AND PROGRESS REPORT TIPS.

COME TOGETHER

The production phase is when a project kicks into high gear. If you have been diligent since the project's inception, the materials generated thus far should support what you need to accomplish during this phase. Your flowcharts, scripts, asset lists, and other related items will be referenced throughout production and will be essential in helping you make key decisions about how the application or Web site will be put together. Assets should be well organized in easy-to-find locations and adhere to naming conventions outlined earlier in the project. Perhaps more important, however, is the fact that project production is where your organizational and communication skills will most come into play. How you build the project will play a factor in its success and how you communicate the production process to key decision makers will be essential to your success.

FIGURE 12-1
YOUR ORGANIZATIONAL AND COMMUNICATION SKILLS WILL COME MOST INTO PLAY DURING PRODUCTION AND PROGRAMMING.

If you are a project or production manager you will not need to write the ActionSript for a Flash game or create a site style sheet. A programmer will handle those tasks. However, you will need the following: the skills to manage the ActionScript and style sheet creation process, the knowledge to understand a project's production and programming requirements, the organizational wherewithal to set regular project benchmarks and deliverables (and of course meet them), and the communication skills necessary to keep everyone happy and on track.

Make it Modular

Whether you are building a Web site, a Flash application, or a CD-ROM or DVD, you should keep your files as modular as possible. You already separated the content into small, manageable pieces when you created the project's flowchart, script, and asset list. Take advantage of that legwork and build the project files in a similar manner. In other words, create individual screens of information as separate, externally loaded .swf files or build navigation systems that can be changed once and deployed site-wide. When possible, keep your graphics, code, video, and audio files, in external libraries or directories that are loaded on the fly. That way, when a client makes a request, such as "I need a new image on screen sixteen," it will take minutes rather than hours to make that change.

Building the project in a way that allows developers, designers, or people involved with production to work concurrently on it will facilitate a fast and efficient production process. Revisions will be easy to facilitate and you should be able to provide regular prototypes for review, which will ultimately make your boss or client happy. If you adopt this practice, you will save significant development time, and you will make content updates easy to maintain.

FIGURE 12-2
MANY HANDS: MODULAR PRODUCTION REQUIREMENTS THAT ALLOW MULTIPLE DEVELOPERS AND DESIGNERS TO WORK ON FILES AT THE SAME TIME MAKES FOR A FAST AND EFFICIENT WORKFLOW.

Thirty-One Flavors

Although all projects consist of a production phase, how that phase is defined varies depending on the intent, design and development applications used and what the end deliverable consists of. That said, the purpose of this chapter is to find commonality in a range of production tasks across a variety of projects from the perspective of a project or production manager.

The broad topic of interactive development includes such a wide array of production skills and tools that it would be impossible to cover them all in one chapter of this book. Be they a sketchpad, scanner, and text editor, Web 2.0 collaborative sites that offer desktop application functionality, or studio apps like Dreamweaver, Flash, and Photoshop, the tools and skill sets you use are up to you and your team. How you manage the creation process is what we will focus on.

Additionally, while server-side development has become an integral part of both Flash and Web applications, we are most worried about the relationships between client, developer, and user. Thus, when referring to online projects, we will focus on the content inside the browser, the "presentation layer" the user sees rather than how the application is built.

FIGURE 12-3
WHAT THE USER SEES WILL MOST AFFECT HOW THE DEVELOPER AND CLIENT GET ALONG DURING PRODUCTION.

Individual vs. Team Production

Production will vary significantly between individual and team environments. While an individual developer may get bogged down by handling too many specific production tasks—such as programming, animation, or video editing—at once, a team will no doubt be plagued by the hassles of version management on production files. Managing which files are current and which should be archived can be a monumental task. It is frustrating to work for several hours on a file only to find that it is three days old. See the sidebar "Version Apps" for a list of tools available to help with version management.

FIGURE 12-4
PRODUCTION WILL VARY SIGNIFICANTLY BETWEEN INDIVIDUAL AND TEAM ENVIRONMENTS.

File Management

Effective management of files and versions is crucial on larger projects where the sheer volume of files generated during production can easily become an organizational nightmare. Clocking development time on out-of-date files is both sloppy and time-consuming. The more time you waste, the more you run the risk of missing a deadline or going beyond budget.

If you are not using a specific application to assist with file management, a well-organized file server can help. Keep every file associated with a project in a central location that is easily accessed by anyone involved in production. Each project's directory structure should be intuitive and it should be clear to all involved where any file generated during production should be kept.

Version Apps

It can be a mind-numbing experience if a file you are working on turns out to be outdated. Fortunately, a number of applications are available to take some of the headaches out of keeping your files up-to-date and organized.

FIGURE 12-7
EXTENSIS PORTFOLIO HELPS YOU KEEP TRACK OF VERSIONS BY CONSTANTLY UPDATING ITS FILE DATABASE AND GIVING INDIVIDUAL USERS THEIR OWN PERSONALIZED WORKSPACE.

Portfolio software, by Extensis, promises database-backed driven catalogs that help to organize any job. Fast cataloging allows you to start working with added files immediately, with the added feature of file format support for most programs used to create files. Each user in the workgroup has her own space in which she can manipulate files for her specific task. Scratchpad galleries are another special feature that allows users to sort, edit, or merge files from one location or many locations. Digital photography and

movies are easy to work with as well since each edit is recorded and ordered. File sharing is made easier with the Screen Preview feature. The program also comes with video tutorials, HTML help, and sample catalogs. For more information and a 30-day trial, visit *http://www.extensis.com.*

Microsoft's Visual SourceSafe, part of the Visual Studio programs, offers an easy-to-use solution to managing changes to files when used in conjunction with the Team Foundation Server, a central part of Microsoft's Visual Studio Team System. This system forms a complete collaboration platform with which to work. Other features include Unicode and XML support, remote access over HTTP, backward compatibility, and 4GB capacity. For information about this program, visit *http://msdn.microsoft.com/vstudio/products/vssafe/default.aspx.*

Surround SCM, by Seapine Software, offers a central repository to help manage changes to files, portals to communicate with team members, and advanced security systems to aid in projects. The program works for both small teams working in one location and large corporations working in several locations. The program does not impose a branching process on the user, but offers advanced branching features so the user is given complete control. It offers a user-friendly interface and a number of robust features. The program can be reviewed at *http://www.seapine.com/surroundscm.html*

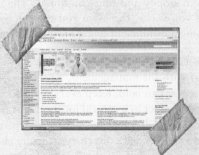

FIGURE 12-8
VISUAL SOURCESAFE HAS BEEN BUNDLED INTO MICROSOFT'S VISUAL STUDIO TEAM SYSTEM FOR A COMPLETE COLLABORATION PLATFORM IN WHICH TO WORK.

FIGURE 12-9
SEAPINE SOFTWARE'S SURROUND SCM PACKAGE ALLOWS TEAMS BOTH SMALL AND LARGE IN ONE PLACE OR SEVERAL DIFFERENT CITIES TO COLLABORATE ON PROJECTS.

FIGURE 12-5
KEEPING YOUR FILES ORGANIZED AND APPROPRIATELY NAMED IS
EXTREMELY HELPFUL IN A TEAM ENVIRONMENT.

Remember: Remind all parties involved with a project to upload each day's work to the server at day's end.

Stray Files

If you use a file server to house the files associated with a project make sure to maintain the file organization on a daily basis.

FIGURE 12-6
SLOPPY SERVING: AT THE END OF A LONG DAY IT CAN BE EASY TO
FORGET THE IMPORTANCE OF KEEPING DRIVES AND DIRECTORIES
CLEAN ON A PROJECT.

The Clock is Ticking

It is so easy to get slowed down by the minutia of debugging code, compressing video, or figuring out which button goes where on what screen. Before you know it, the deadline is only days away and you still have 50 percent of the project to complete.

If for any reason you think an aspect of a project is going to hinder you from making a deadline, let the appropriate parties know as soon as possible. A week's notice will be much more appreciated than a day's notice.

FIGURE 12-10
IT IS EASY TO GET BOGGED DOWN IN THE MINUTIA OF PRODUC-
TION. DO NOT FORGET THAT YOU HAVE A DEADLINE TO MEET.

Revisiting Your Tools

Possessing the right developmental tools and knowing their strengths and weaknesses is mandatory to the success of a project. You chose your development tools when you were defining the project and its teams. Now you need to make sure you made the right choices.

Ask yourself the following questions:

- Will I need to edit photos, draw objects, code, edit or compress video, animate elements?
- Will the tools I have chosen export to the correct media format necessary for the deliverable?
- Are there other tools available that would make the job easier or faster?

It is great to try new techniques. Some projects may require new technology and unique development tricks to set them apart from competitors. These things can make the difference between mediocrity and excellence. Interactive media is after all a constantly changing, always evolving field that requires a long-term

FIGURE 12-11
MAKE SURE THE TOOLS YOU DECIDED UPON EARLIER IN THE
PROCESS ARE THE RIGHT ONES FOR THE JOB. IT IS EASIER TO
SWITCH TOOLS BEFORE YOU BEGIN PRODUCTION THAN IT IS WHEN
YOU ARE IN THE MIDDLE OF IT.

dedication to learning. When you venture into uncharted waters, however, make sure to allot ample time for learning, so you can confidently ensure smooth implementation of these skills into the production process. You should have all the possible kinks worked out before going into production, so mistakes will not put you behind schedule.

Standardize Production Elements

You should have already decided upon most of your specs, such as supported video size and screen resolution. Just as you revisited your tool choices, however, you too should reconsider how each production element, such as text, graphics, videos, and audio, will fit into the workflow. Be certain to pay attention to the supported file formats of tools you intend to use and make sure they will work with the formats necessary for the deliverable. Be certain as well that all files associated with the project adhere to a standard set of naming conventions and are organized in a directory structure that makes sense to the parties involved.

Standardizing production elements, such as video clip size, animation specs, and audio levels, based on your technical specifications will lend cohesiveness to the production and give the finished product a professional sheen. Just as you checked the script for consistency in language, style, and voice in Chapter 6, you should apply the same standards to all remaining production elements. Remember, "garbage in = garbage out" is a good rule to keep in mind. In other words, if your original files are of questionable quality, then chances are those you export will be as well.

When attempting to standardize your production elements, consider the following:

Text

If you use a word processing program to write or edit copy for a project, make sure the text is in a universal format your authoring environment, design application, or code-wrangling tool will support. Some programs will attempt to keep formatting when importing or copying/pasting text from a word processing program. Depending on the application you use to put a project together, this could mess up your code and copy in the final deliverable. Choose a format for text headers and body copy for the project that will alleviate errant characters or awkward formatting and stick to it throughout production. Sometimes this can be as simple as opening your document in a text editor and converting it to plain text before copying and pasting into a studio application like Dreamweaver or a content management/publishing system like Joomla or Movable Type.

Graphics

Decide on a set of standards for your graphic files, including bit depth, color space, resolution, etc.

- ◎ **Bit depth:** Will 32-bit graphics suit your production needs? Will you be required to downsample them to 24, 16, 8 bit or less for final delivery?

- ◎ **Color Space:** Are your source graphics in CMYK color? When you switch them to RGB or indexed color are there noticeable or unacceptable shifts in color?

- ◎ **Resolution:** Are any provided source files at 300 dots per inch when they should be 72 (Mac) or 96 (PC) for screen resolution?

- ◎ **Bitmap vs. Vector:** Are the files you need to be resolution-independent in a vector-based format?

Audio

Make sure you have congruity in your audio levels and formats. Unfortunately, audio production is sometimes overlooked by designers and developers who are focusing more on a project's form and function than on the aural experience. Sweetening your files can be a time-consuming necessity, especially if they were provided from various sources or recorded at different times with different equipment. Inconsistent audio can be one of the most jarring detriments to an enjoyable user experience, so make certain you pay proper attention to its production.

- ◎ **Format:** If audio files are provided to you in different formats, such as WAV, AIFF, and MP3, you may want to convert them to the same format before you begin production. This will alleviate the risk of a particular format not being supported by your authoring environment and help you make all audio files sound alike, especially if you are authoring on multiple machines.

◎ **Levels:** Make sure your audio levels are consistent on all files. If not, use an audio editing program to adjust them and ensure they sound similar.

◎ **Bit depth:** Inconsistent bit depths across audio files can cause variations in audio levels. If your final deliverable will support 24-bit audio, try to keep the files at this resolution, as they will sound better. If you must downsample to 16- or 8-bit files make sure all are at the same bit depth.

◎ **Kilohertz:** As with bit depth, keep your files at the highest kHz supported by your final deliverable and make sure they are consistent to ensure best possible output.

◎ **Stereo/Mono:** Find out if your final deliverable will support stereo files (most will these days) and again, keep your files consistent.

Animation

If elements within the production will transition on and off the screen via animation, you should decide what kind of animation treatment will be applied to them and apply it across the board for consistency. Standardizing your approach to animated elements will give the project a visual consistency and a professional polish.

◎ Transition Style: Decide if it will serve the project to keep its transitional elements consistent with one another. Will you fade elements on and off the screen or use a reveal or wipe? Should each fade be exactly twenty frames or should you vary the length between elements? Does it make more sense to custom animate every element on or off screen using its own unique style? Put

some thought into this prospect, so whatever you decide is reflected in the final output.

◎ **File formats:** If you use a variety of programs to animate project elements, make sure you can output to a format that will work within the final deliverable's format and make sure the format will not adversely affect the project's overall file size, and performance. Also, be certain to create directory structures to house source files in case you need to edit or revise the original files.

Video

Figure out how the project will fare in the head-spinning battle between a dizzying array of video playback formats. The video the project uses will be driven primarily by the target user profile and tech spec. Make sure the format you choose will work on the user's machines.

◎ **File Format:** Obviously, you want as many users as possible to view the video content. What is installed on their machines will affect their ability to do so. Will you require them to have system-level playback architecture, such as QuickTime and Windows Media, or will a plug-in, such as the Flash Player, suffice? See the sidebar "Video Formats: Alphabet Soup" for specifics on various formats and how they will affect playback.

◎ **Frame rate:** Broadcast video typically plays back at 30 frames per second (fps). Actually, it is 29.97 fps, but for the purpose of computer playback for short clips you need not worry about that extra .03 frame. If your video will go back to tape that is another story, especially if it is long format. What you do need to worry about is whether your target machines can support that frame rate. Try encoding a video sample at 30 fps and 15 fps and running each on a test computer that represents typical target user machine spec. Does the higher frame rate give you acceptable

Video Formats: Alphabet Soup

AVI, MOV, FLV, SMIL: the acronyms are enough to drive you crazy, and it seems new ones are added every day. How is a self-respecting interactive producer supposed to keep up? It is not yet known who will win the battle to control video playback on computers. However, one thing is for certain: The format you choose for your project must be compatible with as many of your target users' systems as possible, so choose wisely.

Here are the facts on a variety of current video formats and the specs they generally support:

◎ **Flash Video:** Many interactive developers are turning to Flash for video playback due to its cross platform feature parity and the Flash Player's ubiquity on the Internet. Flash's ability to export self-contained executables for both Mac and PC makes it an attractive option for CD-ROM and drive-based applications as well. Each new version of the Flash Video Encoder (included with Flash Professional) improves the quality of Flash video as well, a consideration that caused many quality-conscious video producers to avoid Flash as a viable playback option in early versions.

◎ **Windows Media:** This format was made for Windows by Microsoft, so if your machine falls under that spec, you have nothing to worry about. Although there is a Windows Media Player for the Mac, implementation of features in new versions of the player lags significantly behind development for Windows. Telestream has a product series called Flip4Mac, which is a set of Windows Media Components for use with QuickTime. Flip4Mac allows users to view Windows Media files without having to open up a separate player. Encoders are available at *http://www.flip4mac.com*. Free Windows Media encoders are available from Microsoft's Web site, *http://www.microsoft.com*.

◎ **QuickTime:** Apple's answer to the video playback conundrum, QuickTime is available for Windows users as well via a download from *http://www.apple.com*. QuickTime comes in two flavors: standard and pro. QuickTime Pro, available for $29.99, has the added benefit of being able to play back and convert a wide variety of media formats.

◎ **RealMedia:** Once a promising forbearer of video's future on the Internet, Real Networks has lost much of its market share over the years. In 2005 the company reached agreements worth $761 million in an antitrust settlement with Microsoft, and the company has expanded its product and service offerings in efforts to stay competitive. RealPlayer is available for both Windows and Mac machines. Media encoders can be downloaded from *http://www.real.com*.

playback? If not, consider encoding the rest of the videos at a lower frame rate.

- ◎ **Dimensions:** Figure out what physical pixel size your video files will be—such as 640 × 480, 320 × 240, etc.—and stick to those dimensions for all files unless the project requires otherwise. Remember, older machines will have a difficult time playing back larger files, so plan accordingly.

- ◎ **File Size:** As with the physical pixel dimensions of a video, the larger its actual file size, the more difficulty older machines will have playing it back without chops and stutters. When encoding videos try to find a balance between video quality and file size that performs acceptably on the target machines.

- ◎ **Streaming vs. Progressive Download:** Will your video reside on a server? If so, will you need custom server configuration to facilitate its delivery? Will compressing your video files for progressive download and posting them to a standard Web server produce the playback performance you need or should the files be housed on a dedicated streaming server?

Code

If you decided on programming languages and development environments for the project in the tech spec phase, they may need to change now that you are in production. In some cases, as with a Flash project, the language choice might have been obvious. Any number of elements—your server structure and operating environment, authoring application, or content management system—can significantly change the way you develop a Web site and which tools or languages you will use to develop it. Make sure you know what these are prior to starting production and that those you have chosen are able to accomplish their assigned tasks.

Also, standardizing certain commonly used scripts within the project and making them readily available to you or other developers through external files will streamline workflow and save production time. Keeping your code modular and loaded from external files or style sheets will allow multiple developers to work on the project files at the same time and allow you the control over changing and revising individual elements without affecting the overall structure.

If you have existing scripts used in past projects that will be appropriate for the current project, put them some place they can be easily accessed. You will likely need to customize them for them to work within the framework of the current project. Developers on forums across the Internet regularly share code they have written for particular tasks, so take advantage of that. All a developer might ask is that you give him or her credit in the commented lines of your code in return, a small price to pay for the time you will save when building applications and projects.

If you do not have a library of commonly used scripts, you should start building one. Presumably, you plan to build upon and improve your skills as well as the tools you will use to continue this type of work, right? Reusing scripts when you can makes sense for a practical project workflow. Plus, it is a Web 2.0 world out there. Borrowing widgets, media elements, and snippets of code from other content providers is common practice. Just remember to credit the appropriate players.

The Asset Library

Most interactive media authoring applications, such as Flash, feature a library or project window in which you compile the elements necessary to put a project together and get it ready for export. If yours is a Web project, Dreamweaver has a site creation wizard meant to help you build the directory structure of your site as well. Even if you are using just a text editor and some CSS or JavaScript tricks to build a site, you should still have an organized set of assets for the project. The production files or the executables they export will be distributed with the final deliverable, so make sure they are built in a efficient manner.

Your library of source materials in a program like Flash, which features a library panel as part of its interface, should, if possible, mirror the organizational structure of files on your hard drive. Assets should be sorted by file type and/or by section of the project, so you can find any elements quickly and easily. Consider following the project's standard naming conventions closely here.

Sample questions to ask when putting a project asset library together include:

◎ Will you need to encode audio or video assets before importing them into the authoring environment or can you work with the original uncompressed files?

◎ If you will work with original, uncompressed files, how will this affect export time?

◎ Do you need to flatten or optimize any graphic files before you can use them in the authoring environment or development app? If so, consider how you will handle making changes to those files.

◎ Does your development app have "round-trip editing" features, so you can easily alter source files and see the changes reflected immediately?

◎ If there are no round-trip capabilities, how will this effect export time?

Structure Setup

Once the general directory structure is set up within your asset library, begin to populate it with the assets. Import graphic files for universal elements, navigation, and individual screens, and file them appropriately. Place audio, video, and other media elements where they belong in the library. Make sure everything is readily available and organized in an intuitive manner.

Adjust application settings so the project files are configured in a way that will facilitate rapid editing and, if applicable, collaboration by multiple parties. Create universal elements common to most screens, such as navigation, content management system templates, timeline markers, instance names, and chapter markers, before addressing the needs of individual information screens. Depending on the size of the project, this process could take several minutes or several weeks. Timing relies on factors such as how many people need to access files simultaneously, and how many information screens are included in the project. Remember, you are only adjusting file settings in the authoring application to reflect the needs of the project.

Once the project's production elements have been organized, you can begin authoring the production files. Begin creating the interactivity for the initial information screens or home page, applying the design template across as many screens as applicable. If you are using some type of back-end content management system, begin integrating its custom template tags with the design elements.

PROfile:
The Trendsight Group

Marcia Sutter,
The Trendsight Group
Working with Content Management Systems

The Trendsight Group is regarded as an industry leader on marketing to women. Started by speaker and author Marti Barletta, the company is the premier provider of Marketing to Women insights and ideas and helps its clients leverage women's buying power to build brands and gain competitive advantages.

Marcia Sutter, Trendsight's Client Services director, uses Joomla to manage and edit content for the company site at *http://www.trendsight.com.*

"Joomla allowed us to play an active role in our site's development process without having to become developers ourselves," Sutter said. "Although we don't use some of its more complicated features, the ability to have control over all written content is a huge asset for us."

"Once the initial site template was in place," she said, "I was able to add, subtract, or edit copy content without having to bother the developers, who were busy working on other elements like video, graphics, and programming."

Now that the site is live, Sutter uses the site's administrative application to manage all content, including speaking and conference announcements, published articles, press, and Barletta's blog, *GenderTrends.*

"It is so helpful to have control over what is live on the site and what waits in the wings. I can set dates to make certain content live and can un-publish any content within seconds from anywhere there is a Web browser and a live Internet connection. It is very helpful for keeping our content timely and gives users a reason to come back to the site for multiple visits," Sutter said.

In addition to the dynamic content inherent to the Joomla content management system, the site was also built so a variety of images and client testimonials appear randomly in specific areas every time the page is loaded. This makes the site content appear more dynamic and always changing.

"All in all, I find the CMS easy to use and administer," Sutter said. "I would definitely recommend that other companies develop their sites in this manner."

Marcia Sutter is Client Services Director at The Trendsight Group.

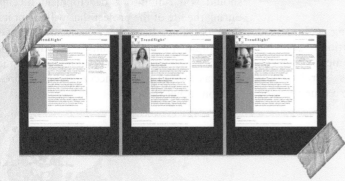

AREAS ON EACH PAGE OF TRENDSIGHT.COM ARE POPULATED WITH UNIQUE CONTENT EVERY TIME A PAGE LOADS. IMAGES ON THE LEFT SIDE OF EACH PAGE LOAD RANDOMLY AS DO TESTIMONIAL QUOTES ON THE RIGHT SIDE OF EACH PAGE, WHILE THE CENTER HIGHLIGHTS THAT SECTION'S UNIQUE CONTENT.

Your Faithful Documents

As your project begins to take shape, the documents you have created should prove as invaluable tools to answer most production questions that might arise. If you were detailed enough in creating a script, asset list, tech spec, etc., building the site or application should be a clear, intuitive process.

Of course the documents you reference will be a bit different between Web and Flash projects. On a Flash project you might find that the script and asset lists will offer the most help when putting together the project. A Web site, on the other hand, might rely more on a thorough and detailed navigational flowchart.

Go through each screen of the flowchart, script, and asset list, adding functionality as you move along. Place graphics, code buttons, create forms, etc. As you finish small sections of content, post or distribute them for review. Should any questions arise that cannot be answered by your documentation, approach the appropriate party immediately for an answer.

Tracking Time

Tracking your time with any efficiency is a great safeguard against problematic production, because it will help you provide a breakdown that accounts for your work in case something goes wrong. Of course you hope nothing goes wrong, but you should plan for it to be on the safe side. Additionally, regularly tracked time will allow you to gauge your profitability on a specific job and cross reference it with what you estimated, other jobs of a similar nature, etc.

There are many time-tracking widgets and free or shareware applications available online and most project or company management software, such as Project or Quickbooks, typically include a time-tracking feature. Or, if you prefer, keep a simple Word, Excel, or text editor-based timesheet in which you jot your hours whenever possible.

Progress Reports

Although it is easy to get caught up in an ever-growing list of production tasks, always keep the appropriate parties abreast of developments and overall project status on a regular basis. Frequent status updates will reinforce their decision that you were the right choice for the job and will help facilitate the goal of establishing a long-term relationship. No matter how successful or well deployed your final deliverable is, if you disappear from a client's radar at any point during the development process it is a pretty safe bet she will never forget that. Frequent updates will also help the client do her job, since, most likely, she also has to report to someone on the status of the project.

You should also make sure the client is able to actually view or regularly interact with the files you are working on. Remember rapid prototyping, which has been mentioned several times throughout the book? It is built on the premise that applications and Web sites are built from the ground up with constant client input and deployed quickly and with regular frequency to ensure the integrity of the final deliverable.

In some cases it may be difficult to do this, but frequent communication is a key ingredient to success on projects.

Regular updates will also lessen the blow should you run into a development hiccup during the life of the project that will affect its final deadline. If a client knows you have come up against a particularly difficult issue to debug, she will tend to be more forgiving if she was alerted to the hiccup earlier in production rather than later.

CASE STUDY:
Production on the Neo-Futurists' site

Production and programming for the Neo-Futurists' site took place concurrently with multiple other project phases. A significant amount of programming was required to convert the design template from an Illustrator file into something that could work well on the Web and integrate seamlessly with Joomla. The content management system was installed and configured while graphics for the randomly loading areas within the site were produced and revised. Simultaneously, the banner that provided the site's primary navigation was developed and animated in Flash. These tasks occurred under a tight timeline, so production was not allotted the luxury of fully completing one task and then starting the next.

A big part of the early production process consisted of building a library of CSS and PHP functions from which to pull when building pages. This was helpful for several reasons.

"Creating a style sheet and library of functions allowed us the freedom to easily recycle elements housed in one central location rather than embedding them into each page," Kristala Pouncy said. "It also gave us flexibility to swap out site elements on the fly, if necessary, which saved us production time in prototyping and development."

Installing and configuring Joomla, then integrating the template figured prominently in early production as well.

"Joomla has a number of configuration settings that need to be made during the installation process and must work seamlessly together before you can even consider integrating the application with your design template. You have to spec out your server and create a database using phpMyAdmin and MySQL. You need to define an installation directory, configure the recently created database, set user names and passwords and set up global configurations, such as language, time zone,

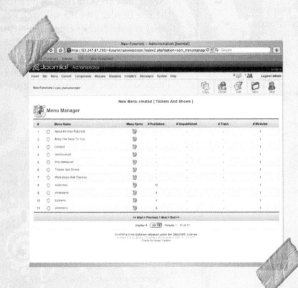

MIGHTYBYTES USED THE NEO-FUTURISTS' SITE MAP TO DEFINE CATEGORIES THAT WOULD MAKE UP THE SITE'S PRIMARY NAVIGATION AND SECOND LEVEL CONTENT ITEMS FOR EACH SECTION.

DEVELOPER POUNCY NOTES THAT SETTING UP AND CONFIGURING JOOMLA IS A MULTI-STEP PROCESS THAT MUST BE COMPLETED BEFORE CUSTOM DESIGN TEMPLATES CAN BE APPLIED.

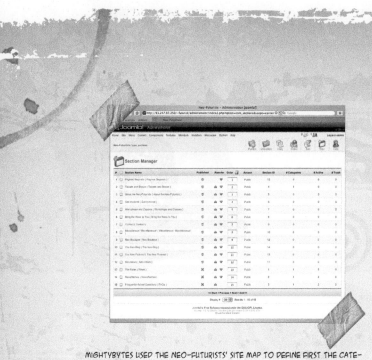

MIGHTYBYTES USED THE NEO-FUTURISTS' SITE MAP TO DEFINE FIRST THE CATE-
GORIES THAT WOULD MAKE UP THE SITE'S PRIMARY NAVIGATION AND SECOND
LEVEL CONTENT ITEMS FOR EACH SECTION.

and so on. Once that has been completed without any errors, Joomla is installed and you can begin the process of configuring it to work with your site structure and integrating it with your template," Pouncy said.

After Joomla was installed, Mightybytes began setting up site categories, content items, menu items and unique modules based on the project site map. Upon completion of the site structure within Joomla, the company then began integrating Joomla with its design template.

"When creating a Joomla-driven Web site and integrating it with your template, you have to make two key decisions right up front," Pouncy

said. "You have to decide what content you will give your client control over from within Joomla and what content will be part of the universal design and thus cannot be altered."

In the case of the Neo-Futurists' site, Mightybytes wanted the client to have control over the majority of the content, so the majority was created with Joomla integration in mind.

"With the exception of Flash elements like the site header and the squirrel, nearly every other regularly changing page element, including random press quotes, 'Meet the Neos' imagery, and second-level buttons were all integrated with Joomla, so the Neo-Futurists could have maximum control."

To integrate Joomla with the Neo-Futurists' design template, Joomla-specific tags were added to the template page's header. Mightybytes worked out the conditional logic that deciphers which page the user is on and feeds content accordingly. There is a Dreamweaver extension called Mambo Toolbar that can assist in this process. Once the tags were in place, the template document was imported into Joomla and a portable network graphics (PNG) preview file was created. Additionally, Mightybytes created an XML document to categorize filenames associated with the template and integrated that with Joomla as well.

"After you have applied the imported template you should test everything created thus far to make sure the site is not spitting out any PHP or other code errors," Pouncy said. "When you are able to test the template/Joomla integration error-free, you can then begin importing content. We tested the integration numerous times until we got it right."

When a functioning template within Joomla was completed, Mightybytes called upon the Neo-Futurists to begin bringing the company's written content into Joomla.

"Mightybytes had us over for a really brief rundown of our new site's content management system, and they showed us how and where to put in copy," Sharon Greene said. "The training wasn't very intense at this point because we knew our role was merely to get the content put into the system, not to make it look pretty or function properly. Mightybytes

AFTER CONVERTING YOUR DESIGN TEMPLATE TO A WEB-FRIENDLY FORMAT AND ADDING JOOMLA-SPECIFIC TAGS TO ITS HEADER, YOU MUST PHYSICALLY IMPORT THE TEMPLATE DOCUMENT INTO JOOMLA, CREATE AN XML DOCUMENT FOR FILE NAME CATEGORIES, AND APPLY THE TEMPLATE DOCUMENT TO JOOMLA.

While the Neo-Futurists brought written content into the site, Mightybytes focused on implementing the remaining elements.

"We set up external links to the Neo-Futurists' blog, podcasts, contact management and payment systems, programmed the random dice function, and animated the squirrel outside of Joomla since none of those elements were going to change," Pouncy said. "Most of the remaining tasks on our end then involved integrating random loading graphic elements into various modules within Joomla. And of course testing. Always testing. Multiple browsers. Multiple machines. Multiple platforms."

made it clear that they would take care of that and give us more advanced training down the line."

Pouncy said, "We gave the Neo-Futurists Super Administrator-level access right off the bat because they are a pretty tech-savvy client. In the past we have set up less proficient clients as merely editors or publishers in Joomla, which restricts the amount of access they have to the application's administrative functionality, but we gave them complete access while simultaneously making it clear that we would give them complete training at a later date."

After the Neo-Futurists completed a round of content input, Mightybytes began formatting the content to make it consistent with the rest of the site.

"Essentially we just went in page by page and applied previously defined styles for our library to any content elements that required it," Pouncy said. "We changed hypertext link colors, made headers bold, changed font sizes, and so on across the board. At that point most of the remaining tasks fell under testing and minor revisions."

With what could be construed as a solid alpha of the site complete, Mightybytes and the Neo-Futurists began testing each link and every function on the site and making revisions accordingly.

CONCLUSION

If you regularly post files for review as the project progresses, even if those files are nowhere near completed, your client will rest easier knowing work is moving along. When you do post files for review, be certain to include a specific list of what they do and do not include in your progress report. If it is a prototype of just one small content section, mark it as such. If only two-thirds of the buttons are working, make sure to tell everyone. Remember, successful deployment of production on a project depends on constant communication between the parties involved and intermittent progress reports.

EXERCISES:

Schedule regular review sessions on project progress. Use time-tracking tools to track profitability on project. Post prototypes for review. Create progress reports.

TOOLS

Sample documents included on the CD-ROM that comes with this book:

◎ Production Checklist

CHAPTER 13

Testing, Revision Tracking and Quality Assurance

Objectives

IN THIS CHAPTER YOU WILL LEARN:

1. WHY YOU SHOULD THOROUGHLY TEST YOUR PROJECTS.
2. STANDARD TESTING PROCEDURES.
3. HOW TO DEVELOP AND USE A TESTING MATRIX.
4. HOW TO TRACK REVISIONS.
5. THE PROS/CONS OF INTERNAL VS. EXTERNAL TESTING.

READY, SET, TEST

Sadly, testing is a development step often overlooked by the inexperienced. Many developers spend so much time developing that they do not allot enough time to thoroughly test their work prior to a deadline, an oversight that can significantly affect the quality of their deliverables. Be sure to test all features and functionality throughout project development, so by the time you have a solid build ready for review there should be a process in place for managing revisions and cross-referencing required functionality with your project scope and technical spec. After all, if your project does not perform acceptably on the target machines, what is the point of developing it?

Not every project will require the extensive testing outlined in this chapter. However, every interactive media project *will* require you test

FIGURE 13-1
SLOPPY TESTING CAN MAKE FOR A FRUSTRATING USER EXPERIENCE.
MAKE SURE YOU ALLOW ENOUGH TIME TO DO IT THOROUGHLY.

and debug it thoroughly using the functionality outlined in your scope document and technical spec as general guidelines. Whether you do this yourself or outsource it is up to you. You may consider contracting the entire process to a dedicated testing and quality assurance (QA) facility. This will help you achieve an objective take on where the project's strengths and weaknesses lie and where it may need improvement. Or you could share it with a few friends on a number of computers and engage in the debugging. The scope of the project should dictate how extensive your testing regimen is.

Testing Defined

Functionality, compatibility, component, regression, usability, and master: the list of interactive media testing types sounds more at home in a psychology textbook than it does here. These testing scenarios, however, can help you gauge both the project's bugs and defects and its effectiveness in different scenarios with the target user. Read the following sections to see which process is right for your project.

Functionality Testing

This is as self-explanatory as it gets: Testers ensure the project's required features function properly based on its flowchart. Project performance is tracked, as are load times and navigational elements. Functionality testing is extensive and focuses on a variety of the project's performance aspects.

FIGURE 13-2
TESTING THOROUGHLY CAN ALLEVIATE PROBLEMS SUCH AS THE ABOVE FORMATTING ISSUES BETWEEN BROWSERS.

Compatibility Testing

Functionality testing typically also includes compatibility testing, wherein the project is checked for feature parity and consistency across platforms, browsers, operating systems, and multiple computers to ensure it runs efficiently on required systems and interface elements look and perform consistently.

Component Testing

Component testing, also part of functionality testing, focuses on individual segments of the content and how they work in the overall structure of the project. Cohesive performance and an intuitive relationship between individual sections of the project will increase the chances of an enthusiastic reception upon its release.

Regression Testing

Regression testing also falls under the functionality testing umbrella. Regression testing is typically undertaken on a second or third round of tests and focuses on project bugs only. Kind of like a spot check for the project, it is often accomplished on the same machine where a bug was originally found.

Usability Testing

Based on your information architecture, usability testing helps make the project more effective for users. The goal with usability testing is to find out how intuitive the project is to the people you are designing it for. In other words, you literally sit in a room with several target users and watch them click through the content, paying attention to how well they understand and follow the flow of information. Usability testing is typically more effective earlier in the production process, because the deeper you get into development the more expensive and complicated it becomes to change the user interface and overall structure of the project.

Focus groups can be very helpful when usability testing as well. They allow you to quickly obtain high-level usability testing results from a very specific group of people with demographics that reflect those of your target user. A thorough focus group will help you understand where weaknesses in the

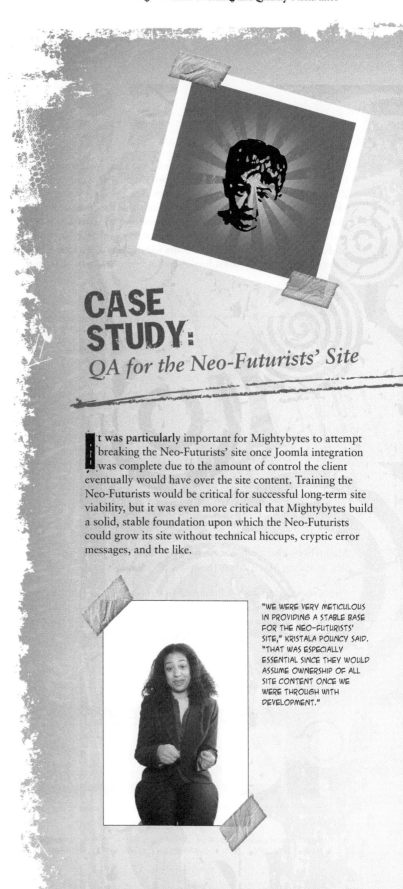

CASE STUDY:
QA for the Neo-Futurists' Site

It was particularly important for Mightybytes to attempt breaking the Neo-Futurists' site once Joomla integration was complete due to the amount of control the client eventually would have over the site content. Training the Neo-Futurists would be critical for successful long-term site viability, but it was even more critical that Mightybytes build a solid, stable foundation upon which the Neo-Futurists could grow its site without technical hiccups, cryptic error messages, and the like.

"WE WERE VERY METICULOUS IN PROVIDING A STABLE BASE FOR THE NEO-FUTURISTS' SITE," KRISTALA POUNCY SAID. "THAT WAS ESPECIALLY ESSENTIAL SINCE THEY WOULD ASSUME OWNERSHIP OF ALL SITE CONTENT ONCE WE WERE THROUGH WITH DEVELOPMENT."

"After completing what we felt was a solid site beta, we distributed testing forms in-house, which in this case were just Microsoft Word documents," Kristala Pouncy said. "Several people clicked through each page on multiple machines to check content integrity. Each time they ran across an inconsistency in style, functionality, or formatting, they marked it down and reviewed the completed forms with appropriate parties to get the problems rectified. Once all those issues were resolved, we let the Neo-Futurists review the site for a final round of minor cosmetic changes."

LINKS TO MULTIPLE VERSIONS OF THE NEO-FUTURISTS' SITE WERE SENT TO USER MAX CROWE FOR HIS OPINIONS DURING DEVELOPMENT.

Mightybytes also made certain to periodically send links to external parties, including Max Crowe, the Web site's target user.

"Max provided us with helpful feedback throughout the development and testing process," Pouncy said. "As we finished rounds of key revisions to the site, we sent a link over. His feedback was essential to getting the Neo-Futurists the kind of Web presence they wanted."

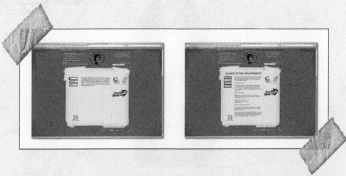

MOST REVISIONS THAT CAME ABOUT FROM TESTING WERE MINOR COSMETIC ENHANCEMENTS TO THE SITE'S AESTHETIC APPEAL, SUCH AS CHANGING BUTTON AND HYPERTEXT STYLES.

Given the number of previous Joomla sites on Mightybytes' track record and the amount of direct client collaboration, the revisions that came from the testing process were expectedly light. Nearly all revisions were cosmetic in nature and typically required minor CSS tweaks, resizing of images for pixel accuracy, etc.

"Successful implementation of a complete template in Joomla was really the biggest testing hurdle for us," Pouncy said. "Once the Neo-Futurists got their content into Joomla the rest of our tasks were, for the most part, simple formatting tweaks and other minor revisions. That's not the case on every project, however. Some Web projects, particularly those with complex database or e-commerce requirements, can take weeks or even months of testing before they are ready for prime time."

After the final round of testing passed muster with the Neo-Futurists, Mightybytes readied the site for launch.

"TRACKING BUGS CAN BE EXTREMELY FRUSTRATING BUT OUR TENACITY PAID OFF IN THE END," POUNCY SAID.

project lie and provide valuable insight into user behaviors, perceptions, attitudes, and where they may see the project fitting into the greater scheme of things (i.e., the market and your competition).

If focus groups are not an option, quick usability testing can be done one-on-one in a small setting.

Master Testing

Another self-explanatory testing routine, this is essentially functionality and compatibility testing of everything on the final release candidate. Usability testing should be long over and testers should focus on the project's viability as a completed entity, paying careful attention to the possibility of (usually minor) performance deficiencies.

The Testing Environment

You should have established the technology profile of a baseline user earlier in the project. Be certain to test the project on multiple machines that represent as many conceivable configurations included in that profile as possible. Analyze the project's performance on a number of computers with multiple iterations of Windows, or Mac OS, varying amounts of installed RAM, and with different speed processors. If the content is meant to run on mobile devices or DVD players, the same process applies. Most importantly, make sure it runs on the machine that represents your technology's low-level cut-off point. This is of particular importance if you plan to publish system requirements somewhere on the packaging of your CD-ROM, DVD, or on a page of the Web site.

Remember, the single most important computer or device the project *must* perform acceptably on is the one whose spec will be published on the product. That is the computer spec your client signed off on at the project's beginning. In other words, if you have established that the project must perform acceptably on a Windows 2000 machine with 128 MB of RAM and at least a 400 MHz processor and have published that fact somewhere on your product, then you better make certain it achieves the standard it is supposed

to under those circumstances. Otherwise, you will set yourself up for a maelstrom of disappointments, not to mention legal ramifications or the hell of any unhappy client or boss.

Testing your project's functionality on the machine you developed it with will do little to ensure its performance on the computers it is intended for, since a designer's or developer's machines usually feature more bells and whistles than those of the average user. Hence you will need to either procure (or at least gain access to) a variety of machines that represent a wide array of configuration possibilities. Once you have established, the machines you will test on, it is time to do the testing.

The Testing Matrix

To thoroughly test a version of the project, it will be helpful to use a testing matrix to track what needs to be fixed or revised. A testing matrix is a document, spreadsheet, PDF, or Web form that gives you the following information:

- ◎ Date/round of testing (first round, second round)
- ◎ Name and contact information for tester
- ◎ Build or version number of project
- ◎ Spec of testing machine
- ◎ Required functionality checklist
- ◎ List of custom questions specific to any areas of weakness that have been noted in previous builds
- ◎ Detailed description of discovered bugs and circumstances under which they were found

Typically, testers sit with the product and the testing matrix in front of them and fill it out as they progresses through the content. As with most interactive media documents, testing matrixes should be comprehensive and informative, covering in detail all aspects of project performance and providing testers with the information necessary to implement functionality revisions and improve the final deliverable. A good testing matrix should feature a required functionality checklist and a list of questions customized to address specific

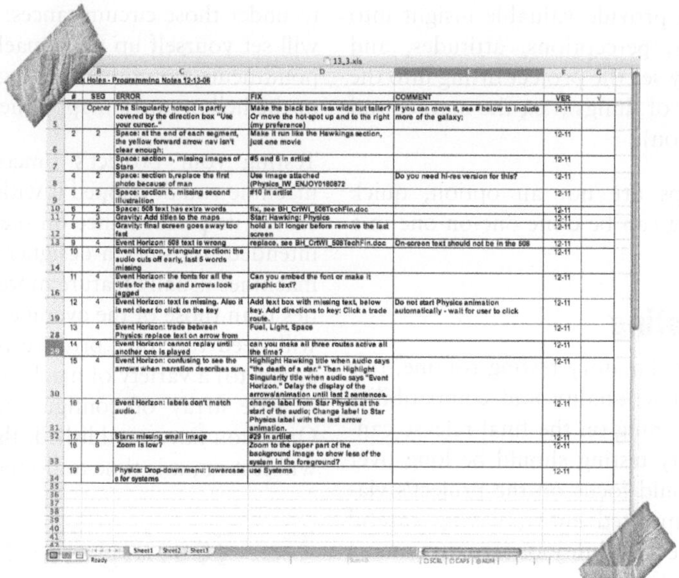

FIGURE 13-3
TESTING MATRIXES ARE ESSENTIAL TOOLS FOR PROPER TESTING OF ANY INTERACTIVE MEDIA
PROJECT. THEY CAN TAKE MANY FORMS BUT ALL SHOULD ARM YOU WITH THE INFORMATION
NECESSARY TO THOROUGHLY DEBUG AND REVISE YOUR PROJECTS.

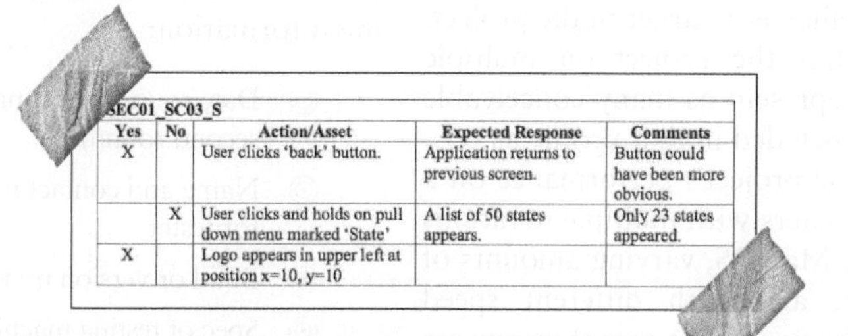

SEC01_SC03_S				
Yes	No	Action/Asset	Expected Response	Comments
X		User clicks 'back' button.	Application returns to previous screen.	Button could have been more obvious.
	X	User clicks and holds on pull down menu marked 'State'	A list of 50 states appears.	Only 23 states appeared.
X		Logo appears in upper left at position x=10, y=10		

ACTION/ASSET, EXPECTED RESPONSE, AND COMMENTS COLUMNS IN A
TESTING MATRIX:

concerns you may have about the project's performance, design consistency, or usability. The checklist lets you cross-reference any required functionality for all screens of the project, such as whether the "back" button functioned consistently each time it was selected or if the company logo was placed in exactly the same spot throughout. The custom questions will help you target specific problematic areas you have noticed during production.

Building a Checklist

The checklist in your testing matrix should include detailed information, preferably broken down by individual screens, about the project requirements in a format that will allow you to organize feedback quickly and efficiently. Every navigational direction in the flowchart and all the details outlined in the script and asset documents should be addressed in a way so testers can make sure all function and aesthetic elements are in place. A typical way of organizing this data for functionality may be to include "Action," "Expected Response," and "Comments" columns with "Yes" and "No" check boxes beside each. Audio and visual assets can be listed by naming conventions used in the script or by brief descriptions beside each check box.

Custom Questions

If a design element or piece of required functionality has been giving you problems throughout development, you should include any custom questions you may have about its performance at the end of the checklist. These should be specific queries targeted at problematic areas in the project that have arisen during development or usability questions specific to the current interface. Make them specific and easy-to-understand but do not give away to much information about the project. Remember, the content needs to stand on its own. Once the project is complete, users will not have the benefit of you holding their hands every time they access the site or launch the application. If you are testing with paper and pen, remember to leave plenty of space for comments and suggestions.

Bug Standards and Priorities

It is a good idea to standardize the types of deficiencies testers may run across when working with the project and provide a dedicated area within the testing matrix to describe the nature of these bugs.

Consider the following criteria when standardizing deficiencies:

- ◎ **Feature Failure:** Does the bug cause a certain required feature to fail?
- ◎ **Crash:** Does the bug cause the application or browser to crash?
- ◎ **System Crash:** Does the bug cause the entire computer or device to crash?
- ◎ **Data Loss:** Does the bug cause any loss of data?
- ◎ **Interface:** Does the bug require an interface redraw or design change?

Priority:

It also helps to standardize priority of bugs found in the project. Although the goal is to fix all problems found in the content, if the deadline is fast approaching it might be best to get the big problems out of the way first.

Consider these categories when prioritizing bugs:

- ◎ **Showstopper:** Is this a global bug that will make release of the project impossible?
- ◎ **Serious:** Is the bug one that will keep a particular screen or section of the content from functioning properly?

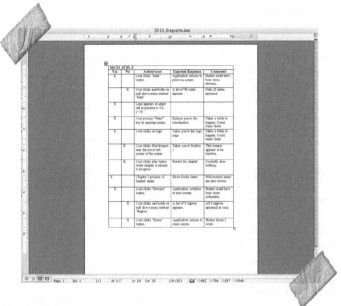

FIGURE 13-4
THE CHECKLIST IN YOUR TESTING MATRIX SHOULD INCLUDE AS MUCH INFORMATION AS NECESSARY FOR APPROPRIATE TESTING OF ALL SCREENS.

◎ **Inconvenience:** Is the bug an annoyance that, while not essential to project performance, compromises its professional viability?

◎ **Cosmetic:** Does the bug affect the visual integrity of the project?

Finishing Touches

Whether you include the most recent copy of the script, asset list, or navigational flowchart as reference elements for testers will depend on the nature of the testing. Usability testing will dictate that the content speak for itself. Testers doing a thorough functionality test, however, may benefit from the advantages of extra documents that explain how the content is *supposed* to behave versus the reality. In this case, you may want to add a column to the testing matrix that references appropriate file naming conventions.

Test Away

After you have completed the matrixes and set up a time/place to perform project testing, get to it. Try as hard as you can to break the project, crash the browser, or freeze the application. With the mouse and keyboard as your weapons, generally beat it to a pulp on as many machines as possible using as many resources as possible, all the while tracking how it reacts to your assault. Make certain you document the exact navigation path taken to find specific bugs, including which buttons were pushed, the menus accessed, and the forms that were filled out. By the time you are done you should have a list of issues to address before entering the next round of testing.

Tallying Your Results

The results of your testing should be tallied and compiled in such a way that when presented to the programmer or development team it is intuitive and clear what the next step will be to implement revisions and fixes. Typically, you want to create a single, unified report with high priority items at the top of the list.

FIGURE 13-5
TALLY THE RESULTS OF YOUR TESTING IN A DETAILED REPORT TO REVIEW WITH YOUR CLIENT.

Exterminate

Use the tallied results of your testing as a checklist to begin implementing bug fixes and functionality revisions. The amount of time this will take will vary based on the complexity of the project and the number of bugs found. Decide where the most problematic areas of the project lie and figure out a plan to rectify each. Begin with global issues that affect the overall feasibility of the project and work your way in toward individual concerns on each screen. Once you have addressed each issue, start over.

Lather, Rinse, Repeat

To continue to the next testing phase, rebuild the application, post new files to a server, or burn a new disc and alert the appropriate parties to the presence of new files. If you have been using an external testing facility, let them know new files are on the way and discuss a timeline for results from the next round of testing. Repeat this process until no bugs are found and the project is ready to progress to the next development phase. Seasoned testers will tell you that if you have not found any bugs you are not looking hard enough, so be mindful of the fact you might have to repeat the testing process several times.

Other Testing Options

Now that you know what is included in the typical testing process, you might decide to consider additional options. Perhaps you do not want to deal with this level of meticulous detail as you weather the production process. Maybe you have realized it might be best to bring in a third party for an objective viewpoint. Or perhaps you want to streamline the process to rid yourself of some paperwork. Following are a number of additional options to the age-old paper and pencil approach to testing.

Web and Software-based Testing Tools

Since the previously outlined processes of using standard word processing and spreadsheet tools can be laborious and paper-intensive, many interactive production companies have migrated their testing processes to the Web using custom online applications and commercially available software packages. Testing results are automatically tabulated in a database, so the online applications can generate custom reports in many different forms. This can be a time-saving asset as it gives all parties instant access to both individual and compiled results and streamlines the testing process. See the sidebar "Tracking Tools: Web-based Testing" for information on some of the commercially available products.

Internal vs. External Testing

If you as the designer, developer or project manager have decided to undertake testing above and beyond what is required in the standard development process, remember that even for a relatively simple project it can be a drawn-out, laborious process. You will need to test every button, link, rollover state, animation, text box, and audio/video element for all the screens, and you could quite possible miss key requirements. You want to make sure you facilitate a thorough and comprehensive environment for testing to ensure the final product fulfills or exceeds the project

Tracking Tools: Web-based Testing

There are several software tools that can help you locate and exterminate those pesky bugs in the project and track project revisions.

TestTrack Pro, by Seapine Software, has many amenities to help you get a handle on the laborious task of bug tracking. Its client/server architecture and database engine will help manage many testing issues, tasks, and team members at anytime and anyplace. It is set up to perform across a number of platforms, allowing users the flexibility they need in which to

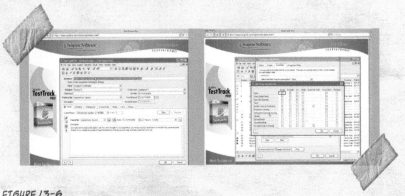

FIGURE 13-6
SEAPINE SOFTWARE'S TESTTRACK PRO'S CLIENT/SERVER ARCHITECTURE CAN HELP AN ENTIRE TEAM TRACK AND MANAGE BUGS OR OTHER INCONSISTENCIES ON AN INTERACTIVE PROJECT.

work. The software offers a team-based approach, allowing managers to assign and follow up on tasks while providing capabilities for the team members to communicate with one another. The manager is also able to decide workflow and can set up the process by which tasks are assigned. Fields can be customized and renamed to fit your program's needs. Open interfaces allow the program manager to easily integrate it into the development process. Options are also available to allow customers access to information and processes within their project. For more information on TestTrack Pro, visit *http://www.seapine.com*.

Borland's StarTeam application family offers many of the same basics as TestTrack Pro, such as ease in communication among team members, flexibility in accessing and using the program, and options in how the tasks are assigned. It also allows you to choose a solution to fit the size, geographical distribution, and work style of the project. Four different packages are available to help fit the need of the project. Each package progresses in its offerings from basic tracking and communication systems via a browser-based Web client, to systems that aid in tracking the specific details and the ability to customize an application to fit your specific needs. All four systems can be viewed at *http://www.borland.com*.

The eRoom products offered by the EMC Corporation at *http://www.emc.com* offer

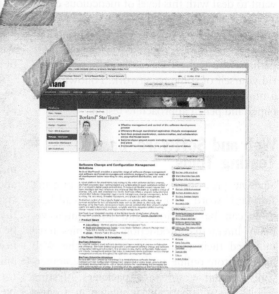

FIGURE 13-7
BORLAND'S STARTEAM HAS CUSTOM SOLUTIONS TO FIT YOUR PROJECT OR ORGANIZATION'S SIZE.

a wealth of applications to fit the needs of any project. Such features as user-defined dashboards, integrated instant messaging, and desktop, office, and e-mail integration help to streamline the many processes in a project. Gantt charts and planning features will help you see each task and record milestones while version control and portal integration make the eRoom products highly adaptable to many different situations.

Trials and tutorial or "at-a-glance" videos of each program are available on each company's site as well as a bevy of information to help guide you in the decision-making process.

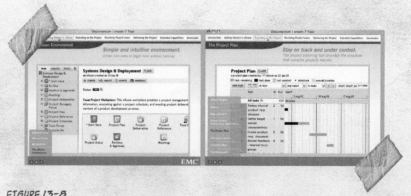

FIGURE 13-8
IN ADDITION TO TESTING FEATURES, EMC'S EROOM PRODUCT LINE HAS A LARGE NUMBER OF CHARTING AND PLANNING TOOLS AS WELL.

requirements you have defined. If it means bringing in external forces you may want to consider it.

External testing facilities are typically more methodical in their testing and will give you contextual information of bugs they find as well as step-by-step directions of how to re-create the bug. Since this is what they do, they tend to be more focused, more objective, and more detailed than an individual tester, and they can be useful allies when testing the project. They provide both an objective viewpoint and a complete arsenal of tools and experienced testers to test the project's usability and functional elements down to the minutest detail.

Testing Facilities

The following is a list of several agencies that offer testing services for the differing needs and types of interactive projects:

Altone Services Inc., Antioch, Calif.:
http://www.altone.com/

Critical Path Software, Portland, Ore.:
http://www.criticalpath.com/origin.html

Professional Multimedia Test Centre, Belgium: *http://www.pmtctest.com/*

Recommended Test Labs Inc., San Francisco, Calif.:
http://www.testlabs.com/

SWAT Lab, Minneapolis, Minn.:
http://www.swatlab.com/

T-est Pte. Ltd., Singapore:
http://www.t-est.com/

Test Partners, United Kingdom and San Francisco, Calif.:
http://www.testpartners.co.uk/

VeriCode Inc., Ashland, Mass.:
http://www.vericode.com/

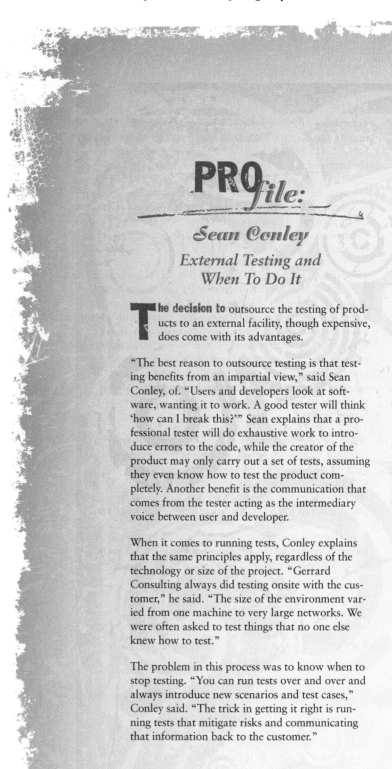

PROfile:

Sean Conley

External Testing and When To Do It

The decision to outsource the testing of products to an external facility, though expensive, does come with its advantages.

"The best reason to outsource testing is that testing benefits from an impartial view," said Sean Conley, of. "Users and developers look at software, wanting it to work. A good tester will think 'how can I break this?'" Sean explains that a professional tester will do exhaustive work to introduce errors to the code, while the creator of the product may only carry out a set of tests, assuming they even know how to test the product completely. Another benefit is the communication that comes from the tester acting as the intermediary voice between user and developer.

When it comes to running tests, Conley explains that the same principles apply, regardless of the technology or size of the project. "Gerrard Consulting always did testing onsite with the customer," he said. "The size of the environment varied from one machine to very large networks. We were often asked to test things that no one else knew how to test."

The problem in this process was to know when to stop testing. "You can run tests over and over and always introduce new scenarios and test cases," Conley said. "The trick in getting it right is running tests that mitigate risks and communicating that information back to the customer."

(Continued)

(PROfile: Continued)

The quality of customer service is an important consideration for the external software tester, especially those looking for repeat business. The formality level depends on the environment and the project. "You need to listen to the customer and not overwhelm them with the process if that is not what they really need," Conley advises. At times his job becomes challenging when having to ask developers who hire him to tidy up their project before submitting it. "Sometimes people need to help themselves before asking for outside help," he said.

The decision to outsource testing is one that is best made early in the development stage. Conley says that testing should start long before any code is written. When testing begins later in the development process, after a problem is found, it often takes a long series of questions to find out keys to the specific problem. "Usually we were asked way too late, after the customer thought that testing is something they might need to do," he said. "In an ideal world we would have been asked in very early and reviewed requirements and technical specifications with all concerned parties."

While the communication process varies from customer to customer, Conley says that most often a testing company will agree upon deliverables with customers on a weekly or sometimes daily basis. These deliverables includes data that will help the producer to make an informed decision on whether or not to go live, and what future risks they have.

Sean Conley is a freelance software testing consultant and a former Software Testing Manager for Evolutif.co.uk (now Gerrard Consulting).

Even Creepier

Be prepared: The results of your testing could very well bring up additional requests for project enhancements and features that might be considered out-of-scope. Unless you have meticulously explained it to him or her, (which should have been an integral part of your proposal) a client (or boss) may not know the difference between bug fixes, content revisions, and scope creep. Make sure he or she does and has a response in place regarding how you will address these issues as they come up and how they fit into the overall proposal, budget, and timeline.

Remember, additional features you might not have included in the proposal can vastly improve the final project and may be worth pursuing. They can also send the project careening out of control. It is up to you to find the fine line that separates these two situations.

If possible, you need to fix every bug that crops up during testing, but at some point you will need to decide on a cut-off point for any more revisions or additional features. Make it very clear when and where that point is.

Revisit Status and Progress Check

While revising the project based on test results, revisit where you stand in the overall development process. Cross-reference the current status with where you said you would be at this stage in the proposal. If you implement the first round of revisions from user testing do you expect to be done with the project? If so, start preparing the files for final review. If not, what is left to do? How many more rounds of testing will you go through? Are you still on track with the deadlines? How about the budget? After you have answered these questions, prepare and distribute a status report or progress e-mail, so everyone involved is aware of where you stand in the overall scheme of project development.

Software Options for Screen Recording

In the case of the Newark InOne project, a tool like Adobe Captivate would have made all the difference in creating movie captures of recorded screen activity and saving them as small Flash files. Unfortunately, Captivate was not available at that time, so Mightybytes used SnagIt, a still frame capture application, and animated elements on the timeline. Screen recording applications can be useful assets when creating training modules, especially if the training topic is computer-based. Following are several options for making effective screen captures.

Adobe Captivate

Adobe Captivate allows users to create effective simulation-based learning content with little to no programming knowledge or multimedia skills. The program contains rich features for creating screen recordings, but it does not stop there. A library of interaction components that support an easy-to-use dialog box-driven creation process allows for fast and easy production of interactive simulations in a number of formats. A library panel allows users to organize clips and easily drag and drop content from one section of a project to another, saving production time and lending ease to project management.

Scenario-based learning simulations are easy to create with features that allow users to record their actions, including keyboard and mouse activity. Audio and screen captures can be recorded simultaneously. AutoText captions allow you to add captions to your simulation describing important actions.

Editing features include a visual timeline that offers control over the timing of objects, captions, and audio. A visual branching view allows you to map out multiple learning paths based on different instructional scenarios. Items can be transferred from the library to your timeline with drag and drop ease.

Developers can design their own customizable workspaces and storyboards with built-in tools as well.

The program even supports SCORM-compliance (Sharable Content Object Reference Model) for integrating data with Learning Management Systems (LMS) and has features for quizzes, scoring, and instructional feedback.

Captivate is a great tool for creation of simulation-based learning modules and goes well beyond simple screen recording and capture features. A free 30-day trial is available at *http://www.adobe.com/products/captivate/*.

Camtasia Studio

Camtasia Studio, by TechSmith, offers the ability to record, edit, and share high-quality screen-based video across multiple delivery platforms. The program boasts capabilities for creating high-quality content by recording screen grabs, audio, voice narration, picture-in-picture, and Webcam video. Editing features let you add callouts, titles, credits, zooming, panning, and additional audio tracks with export capabilities to QuickTime, Flash, and a number of other video formats. The Production Wizard allows you to choose the best format and settings for your specific audience.

Camtasia Studio contains features that make it easy to blend different types of content into your videos without using multiple tools. Ease-of-use in both the recording and editing tools allow users to publish and share recordings in multiple formats with a single production process. Built-in Screencast.com integration offers a number of simple content hosting solutions as well. For more information, visit *http://www.techsmith.com/camtasia.asp* and *http://www.screencast.com/*.

SnagIt

The creators of Camtasia Studio also make SnagIt, a screen grab application. SnagIt allows you to select anything on your screen and capture it to a variety of image formats. Once captured, images can be edited using a variety of options that include a full-featured paint tools panel, edge effects, resizing, scaling, cropping, etc. Screen capture can be shared through e-mail, posting to a personal Web page, or included in an instant message.

For more information about SnagIt, visit *http://www.techsmith.com/snagit.asp.*

NEWARK INONE CREATIVE
DIRECTOR MATT ULBERT

CASE STUDY:
Newark InOne Search Engine Tour

The Need

After integrating a new search engine into its company Web site, electronics distributor Newark InOne contracted Mightybytes to build a guided interactive tour that would showcase the new technology's features and train users on how to take advantage of its key features.

"We offer literally hundreds of thousands of products on our Web site," said Matt Ulbert, creative director. "Over time we found that the site's existing online search technology wasn't getting users to the products they needed quickly or in an intuitive manner. We implemented a much more robust and feature-rich search engine to address this need but very quickly discovered that our user base required a tour of all the new features they might not know they could take advantage of when searching for products."

Newark InOne's Web site averages 30,000 visits per day from three major customer segments: electronic design engineers, maintenance/repair/operating (MRO) technicians, and purchasing professionals. These three segments use the site differently, but each demands an efficient use of its time.

"An ongoing challenge for us is to create a great user experience for these customers," Ulbert said.

NEWARK INONE'S SITE AVERAGES 30,000 VISITS PER DAY FROM ELECTRONIC DESIGN ENGINEERS, MRO TECHNICIANS, AND PURCHASING PROFESSIONALS.

"THE EXTENSIVE AMOUNT OF ANIMATION AND AUDIO REQUIRED FOR THIS PROJECT NECESSITATED THAT IT BE DEVELOPED USING FLASH," POUNCY SAID.

The need for this tool extended to Newark's U.K.-based parent company, Farnell InOne, and another subsidiary, MCM InOne, since they also had implemented the new search technology.

"Since this was a tool that would require re-branding for multiple companies, we wanted to build the interface in a way where we could easily swap out graphics, colors, audio files, and so on in as easy a manner as possible," said Kristala Pouncy from Mightybytes.

The Specs

Mightybytes had several meetings and conference calls with various company decision makers to define how the project would be deployed and what kind of requirements would drive its production.

"We wanted this to be an engaging tool for our users rather than merely graphics and words on a screen," Ulbert said. "Animation and voiceover were requirements on our end from the get-go. It was critical that this piece be received by our customers as a value-added service and *not* marketing hype."

THE NEED FOR THIS PROJECT ALSO EXTENDED TO NEWARK INONE'S UK-BASED PARENT COMPANY FARNELL INONE AND MCM INONE AS WELL.

Technical requirements and client requests led to the decision that the project be developed in Flash.

"Since the project had to load quickly and featured a significant number of animations and audio voiceover files, we decided early on in production that Flash was the best delivery format," Pouncy said. "We could have developed the content using a screen recording application to save development time but at the time we created this tool, most commercially available applications on the market could export only to either video or proprietary formats that required custom browser plug-ins. Neither was an optimal solution. Newark InOne wanted their content to load quickly and unfortunately at the time we developed this tool, applications like Adobe's Captivate, which can export small SWF files, weren't viable solutions yet."

Ulbert said, "Even though we envisioned the piece as very linear, we wanted to produce it in a way that would allow us to easily repurpose portions of it for future use."

Market penetration of Flash Player version 6 was significant enough at the time of development that Mightybytes and Newark InOne agreed it was the best version for exporting content to reach target users.

Newark InOne also requested that the content be viewable on monitors with 800-by-600 resolution, so it was decided that the Flash files would be created at 700-by-560 pixel dimensions.

"Our Web analytics package lets us watch client system data, such as OS, browser versions, and screen resolution," Ulbert said. "At the time we developed this tool, 800-by-600 was the resolution that most of our customers used to visit our site, so we planned accordingly."

The Content

"Writing effective scripts for this project was key to its success," Ulbert said. "There were fifteen screens of information total and each screen had to clearly convey a specific topic related to our search engine functionality. Since this content was going to be posted to the Web, the information needed to be conveyed in as terse a manner as well."

To make navigation options easier for users the content was broken into four primary sections. Each section had several screens of information related to specific elements of the master heading's broader topic. It was planned that users could get to any individual information screen in two clicks.

"In addition to addressing the challenge of breaking content down into manageable and intuitive chunks, we also needed to phrase each topic in somewhat conversational tones as the script would be delivered as voiceover as well as text on the screen," Ulbert said.

Newark InOne employed a two-column script format typical of most video projects. Information was broken down by screen and naming conventions were applied for all necessary file references. Voiceover text was housed in one column with screen names and assets in the other. References for procuring individual required visual elements were provided to Mightybytes in the script as well.

"Newark InOne provided us with a very specific script we could use to acquire screen grabs," Pouncy said. "It broke down not only which page on the site would yield the appropriate elements for us to take screen grabs, but also outlined in detail which buttons, form elements, and so on would produce the required results. This was extremely helpful once we moved into production. With so many files to juggle and essentially three similar but different tools to create for the company's various subsidiaries, naming conventions were critical to keep everything organized."

The Design

When creating design comps for the search engine tour, Mightybytes opted for a simple tab-based navigation system that would allow access to all content with just a click or two and would be easy to update from one company to the next.

"Since most of the screen real estate would be taken up by animated screen grabs, we kept the tool's navigation simple and unassuming with just enough room for appropriate navigation and text content needs," Pouncy said.

A recent enterprise-wide re-branding campaign involved new logos, unification of company names, company-specific color panels, etc.

Newark InOne provided guidelines around which Mightybytes could build the design comps with these brand-specific requirements in mind.

"Newark InOne provided us with a very clear and concise brand standards manual that outlined the specifics of what our design could and could not do visually," Pouncy said. "An easy to follow PDF file provided at one of our early meetings helped ensure that color, image and font choices we made reflected those used on each site and adhered to the company's exacting brand standards."

After several reviews and minor design revisions Ulbert and his team at Newark InOne gave Mightybytes permission to move into production.

"WRITING EFFECTIVE SCRIPTS FOR THIS PROJECT WAS KEY TO ITS SUCCESS," NEWARK INONE'S ULBERT SAID.

The Production

Gathering assets and organizing files were among the first tasks Mightybytes undertook once it began the production phase. Server file and directory structures were set up to house content as it was developed. Each company's live Web site provided resources for visual elements while the completed script offered a springboard for recording audio elements. Design comps served as the basis for creating an organized library of global navigation and design elements and developing the overall Flash file structure.

"We built the application's file structure in a modular manner for several reasons," Pouncy said. "Creating individual Flash files for each information screen not only hastened the production workflow by allowing multiple developers to work on the project at a time, but also facilitated faster content loading from screen-to-screen on the presentation end as well."

In addition to a master "shell" file that housed global navigation and interface elements, separate Flash files were built to house content elements, such as audio, text, screen grabs, etc., that were specific to individual information screens.

Screen grabs from each company's Web site played a prominent role in the final deliverable. Newark InOne provided the first set of

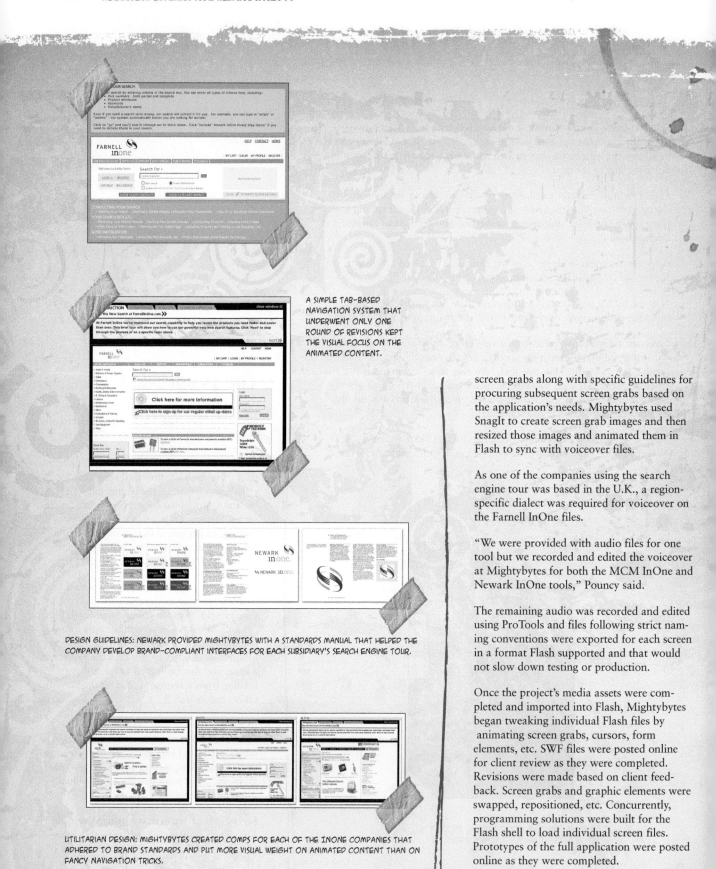

A SIMPLE TAB-BASED NAVIGATION SYSTEM THAT UNDERWENT ONLY ONE ROUND OF REVISIONS KEPT THE VISUAL FOCUS ON THE ANIMATED CONTENT.

DESIGN GUIDELINES: NEWARK PROVIDED MIGHTYBYTES WITH A STANDARDS MANUAL THAT HELPED THE COMPANY DEVELOP BRAND-COMPLIANT INTERFACES FOR EACH SUBSIDIARY'S SEARCH ENGINE TOUR.

UTILITARIAN DESIGN: MIGHTYBYTES CREATED COMPS FOR EACH OF THE INONE COMPANIES THAT ADHERED TO BRAND STANDARDS AND PUT MORE VISUAL WEIGHT ON ANIMATED CONTENT THAN ON FANCY NAVIGATION TRICKS.

screen grabs along with specific guidelines for procuring subsequent screen grabs based on the application's needs. Mightybytes used SnagIt to create screen grab images and then resized those images and animated them in Flash to sync with voiceover files.

As one of the companies using the search engine tour was based in the U.K., a region-specific dialect was required for voiceover on the Farnell InOne files.

"We were provided with audio files for one tool but we recorded and edited the voiceover at Mightybytes for both the MCM InOne and Newark InOne tools," Pouncy said.

The remaining audio was recorded and edited using ProTools and files following strict naming conventions were exported for each screen in a format Flash supported and that would not slow down testing or production.

Once the project's media assets were completed and imported into Flash, Mightybytes began tweaking individual Flash files by animating screen grabs, cursors, form elements, etc. SWF files were posted online for client review as they were completed. Revisions were made based on client feedback. Screen grabs and graphic elements were swapped, repositioned, etc. Concurrently, programming solutions were built for the Flash shell to load individual screen files. Prototypes of the full application were posted online as they were completed.

The Testing

Once the first search engine tour was prototyped, the issue of content load time arose.

"The navigation and animation were pretty straightforward thanks to detailed documentation on the client's part," Pouncy said. "The first issue we noticed once a prototype was built was that each screen still took a

NEWARK INONE PROVIDED DETAILED DOCUMENTS OUTLINING WHICH WEB SITE PAGES TO PULL SCREEN CAPTURES FROM AND HOW TO RUN EFFECTIVE PRODUCT AND ATTRIBUTE SEARCHES TO PRODUCE THE APPROPRIATE RESULTS.

WITH OVER FORTY-FIVE SCREENS OF INFORMATION TO KEEP TRACK OF FOR THREE DIFFERENT COMPANIES, KEEPING PRODUCTION FILES ORGANIZED WAS A NECESSITY.

A SAMPLE SCREEN CAPTURE PROVIDED BY NEWARK INONE USING TECHSMITH'S SNAGIT.

significant time to load. We spent a lot of time finessing the balance between acceptable image and audio compression and load times."

Although building a modular file structure that utilized multiple individual per-screen Flash files assisted somewhat in the content loading process by easing the up-front load time, there were still noticeable lags as each screen loaded.

"The number of audio files and bitmap images in the search engine tour proved to hamper even the fastest connections," Ulbert said. "The wait time for each screen to load was unacceptable on the initial prototypes. We wanted to decrease load time overall while still maintaining high-quality standards for the media. Image and audio quality were paramount to the project's success."

The solution came in the form of a custom loader that sequentially brought content into the application in the background while the first few information screens played in the foreground.

"Rather than waiting for each screen to load individually as a user clicked through the application or loading all the content at once up front, which would create an even longer initial load time, we opted for a solution that loaded content in sequential order one screen after another," Pouncy said. "With this solution the user would only have to wait for the first screen to load. Subsequent screens would load in the background as the first screen played. This improved file performance considerably since by the time screen one was done playing the next one in the sequence was already loaded and ready to play."

This solution proved effective but not perfect. Problem: If a user went immediately to screen nine upon accessing the application, then the custom loader was rendered useless because it started with screen one and moved forward.

"Our final resolution was to code the loader in such a way that if a user clicked on a navigation option other than the 'Next' button, the loader would automatically reconfigure itself to begin loading content from whatever screen option they selected forward," Pouncy said. "Since most people would view the content in some kind of sequential order, we

"OVERALL, THE SEARCH ENGINE TOUR WAS VERY WELL RECEIVED," ULBERT SAID.

MINIMIZING LOAD TIMES WAS A CHALLENGE THAT REQUIRED SIGNIFICANT TESTING.

found that building a loader that could essentially jump around from screen to screen and load sequential content accordingly provided the best solution to afford most users a seamless content experience."

The Deliverable

The Farnell InOne search engine tour was created and tested first, Newark InOne followed, and MCM InOne's tool was developed third. Once the files functioned properly on the testing server Mightybytes delivered final Flash and HTML files to each client via File Transfer Protocol.

"We posted a banner on our site's home page and announced the tool's availability through e-mail marketing campaigns to our customer base," Ulbert said. "Overall, the search engine tool was very well received."

CONCLUSION

Once you have completed your final round of testing, create one last list of minor revisions and/or bug fixes that will move you toward a release candidate of the project. Remember, if you have not found any bugs, you are not looking hard enough. By now, depending on how many rounds of testing you have weathered, any bugs on the list should be minor alterations: typos, pixel adjustments of onscreen elements, recompressing a video or audio file, and the like. If any bugs under the "showstopper" category on your list still exist, you should repeat the full testing process once you have addressed those issues. If your content is sound upon another round of testing, create a release candidate.

EXERCISES:

1. Write a Test Plan for the sample project.
2. Create a custom testing matrix.
3. Test a broken site.
4. Do quickie usability testing for the test project or any Web site and compile your results into a report (watch someone else navigate through a Web site).

TOOLS

Sample documents included on the CD-ROM that comes with this book:

◎ Sample testing matrix
◎ Sample Test plan

Files can be found in the folder labeled with the corresponding chapter number and title.

CHAPTER 14

Final Revisions, Launch, Promotion and Maintenance

Objectives

IN THIS CHAPTER YOU WILL LEARN:

1. HOW TO DEVISE AND STICK TO A REVISION CUT-OFF POINT.
2. WHAT TO INCLUDE IN A RELEASE/LAUNCH CANDIDATE.
3. WHAT CONSTITUTES A FINAL DELIVERABLE.
4. WHEN TO DELIVER A COMPLETED APPLICATION/SITE VS. SOURCE CODE.
5. LAUNCHING YOUR SITE, DISTRIBUTING YOUR PRODUCT.
6. STRATEGIES TO EXTEND YOUR SERVICES BEYOND AN INITIAL CONTRACT.

THE HOME STRETCH

Only a few steps remain before your project reaches completion. But it is not time to break out the confetti yet.

FIGURE 14-1
READY, SET: YOU SHOULD BE IN THE FINAL
STRETCH OF YOUR PROJECT'S LIFE CYCLE NOW.

Your extensive rounds of testing should have generated a final "To Do" list. Once you have addressed issues on that list, you can compile what hopefully will be the final project files for one last review. If your testing has been thorough, this release candidate could become the final version 1.0 of the project.

The Cut-off Point

At some point during production and the testing, you will need to decide on a cut-off point for revisions and bug fixes. Obviously, you need to fix all the bugs before you can realistically say you are done, but if you have planned and built the project correctly, this will happen concurrently with the approach of your final deadline. As you start winding down, there are a few things to consider.

The Final Files

After you have addressed the issues that arose from testing and are certain the project meets previously outlined requirements, compile what could be the final version of your project. Review said version in detail with the key decision makers and agree upon whether it meets everyone's standards as a final master build. If not, address any dangling issues and regroup. Once you have completed a final build the appropriate parties can agree on, you need a written sign-off from said parties, as this build becomes your master.

What's in a Master?

With the final written sign-off in your hand, the project is ready for release. Package your deliverables in the format upon which you have agreed and get ready to upload them or hand them off to the appropriate parties.

FIGURE 14-2
ONCE YOU HAVE RECEIVED A SIGNOFF, PREPARE TO MAKE THE
FINAL FILE TRANSFER.

Web Site Launch

By the time your site is ready to launch, hopefully all you have to do to make it live is transfer files to a new directory or point the domain to your new IP address. If you have a client who is taking care of the launch details, provide her with a zipped or stuffed archive of all files properly linked with defined directory structures, so she can easily extract and go.

Publish Settings

If you are using an interactive authoring program, such as Flash, make sure to double check the publish settings of your application to ensure they reflect the needs of your final

FIGURE 14-3
PUBLISH THIS: MAKE SURE YOUR PUBLISH SETTINGS REFLECT THE
PROJECT'S NEED BEFORE DOING A FINAL EXPORT.

deliverable before engaging in a final export. Sometimes it is common practice to alter publish settings during development for quicker movie testing or exporting to a different format than what your final will be, so verify that your settings are in order.

Burn Disc

If you are working on a CD-ROM or DVD project, make certain your files are in the right place before you select the "Burn Disc" command. Even if you have tested previous discs, you should still test every disc burn to ensure data integrity was not compromised during the burn. You do not have to click every button or play every video. However, you should make sure the disc auto-runs if it is meant to and that you did not have a bad burn.

You should include a separate set of graphic files for labels and packaging if the project will leave your hands bound for a duplication facility. Make sure to size the label and packaging graphics accordingly.

Deliverable: Application vs. Source Code

In the proposal phase you should have decided whether you will provide the source code and graphics along with the final deliverable. However, once you near project completion you also need to consider what files you will turn over and how you will provide them.

Providing source files versus a compiled application or Web site is a typical scenario to address if you are a vendor working with a client. This scenario is not so much an issue if you are an onsite freelancer or company employee, as such a situation usually requires a "work-for-hire" contract in which you must hand over all files created during the term of your employment immediately upon their completion. A work-for-hire setup is doubly detrimental for the person who created the media, as it usually strips her of the right to use samples as portfolio pieces.

Holding onto the source files provides you with the opportunity for future contracts, since a client needs to return items for alterations, future revisions, or maintenance. Retaining rights to your files allows you the freedom to use certain elements from the project in future projects, a definite time-saver, and as promotional or portfolio items. Obviously previously copyrighted images, stock photos, licensed music or sound effects, and logos are exempt from this, but it certainly applies to code, original graphics, music or photography, and any other elements you have created from scratch and retain ownership of.

The reality of this situation in the corporate communications world is that many clients either do not understand licensing logistics or they only want a "work-for-hire" scenario. Although it is in your best interest to retain ownership of your work, you have to weigh the pros and cons of relinquishing it with those of maintaining the relationship. Is the relationship worth it? If so, polish up your negotiating skills to make sure you may include the files in your portfolio even if you cannot retain ownership of them.

If you have agreed to provide source files, you need to compile them. Make sure to include all source files separately from the compiled application, presentation, or Web site. You should also include a "Read Me" file that outlines what is included in each directory on your disc or downloadable archive. This will ease your transition out of the project and hopefully save you from panicked phone calls months later.

Looking Ahead

As the project nears completion revisit how you intend to promote and maintain your work. Review your initial proposal or the project scope document. Did you include language outlining how you will promote the project? What about regular maintenance? Have you outlined a plan to keep the content fresh and bug-free? If not, you need to consider these things. Pitch your ideas before the project is completed, so that once it is done you can immediately begin getting the word out and establishing a regular maintenance routine.

IF YOU BUILD IT, WILL THEY COME?

After wrapping up the production phase, you are one step closer to the finish line, but it still requires a little more tender loving care before you send it out the door. How will you ensure people can find the Web site? How can you direct potential customers to a place where they can buy the DVD or CD-ROM? What if the content becomes dated in a few months? What if you discover a factual error that was overlooked during production? Or worse yet, what if a new browser or operating system is released that does not support your content? Such situations should be considered before the project is finished.

In addition to all the production challenges inherent to building a robust interactive media application, any fully realized project also includes a solid promotion and maintenance plan. A comprehensive strategy for helping people find the fruits of your labor and a process to keep content fresh and approachable are essential to ensure the project has an extended shelf life and always maintains a fresh perspective. If you adopt a plan to overcome these hurdles, you can guarantee the project has a competitive edge. If you have created your content for a client or other outside party, presenting her with options beyond project completion emphasizes your strategic problem-solving abilities and will ingratiate you to her more than your whiz-bang production skills already have.

Pixel Polygamy

You will reap the most benefit from building and nurturing successful relationships with your clients, so they come back for repeat business. This works best if the relationship is mutually beneficial, something you will know upon completion of your first joint venture (if not sooner). Digital media creators who can handle all the negotiations, production hassles, and potential developmental pitfalls and walk away with their relationships intact or even flourishing are the ones who will succeed over time. Repeat business is what will keep your career flourishing (or keep you from getting fired) and making that work takes foresight and strategic thinking. Not only should you want to do your best to create solutions that exceed expectations, but you should also make yourself an invaluable resource and a necessary asset for your client or boss' success. Anticipating their needs before they do will help make that happen.

Promotion

To devise and implement a successful promotional plan for the project, turn to your user profile. You already defined who your typical user is. Now figure out how best to get your content in front of her. Although this is not a book about how to start your own ad agency or public relations firm, a few universal tried-and-true tricks can be the ticket to getting your content in the right hands.

FIGURE 14-4
A FEW TRIED AND TRUE PROMOTIONAL TRICKS CAN INCREASE YOUR USER BASE SIGNIFICANTLY.

Web Projects

If your project is Web-based, there are a number of things you can do to increase traffic to the site. Consider the following tactics:

- ◎ **Register with Search Engines:** Using an online tool for search engine submission is an easy and cost-effective way to submit your site's content to multiple search engines at once.

- ◎ **Online Ad Campaigns:** Although significantly more expensive an endeavor than registering your site with search engines, a strategically placed online ad campaign can get your content viewed by targeted potential users and can increase appropriate traffic to your site. A quick Web search will give you a wide variety of companies that will help with your online banner ad campaign. The digital advertising packages found at *http://www.doubleclick.com/us*, for instance, offer a variety of ways to build and distribute online ad media that targets the people you want to reach.

- ◎ **Search Marketing:** Search engine marketing tools, such as Yahoo! (formerly Overture), allow you to sponsor search engine results so you can connect with potential users who are searching on terms relevant to the content of your Web site. Charges are typically based on actual click-throughs.

- ◎ **E-Newsletters:** Create an e-mail newsletter campaign wherein e-mail teasers lead recipients to your site to get the full content. Just remember, unsolicited e-mails are often considered spam by their recipients and rarely receive an enthusiastic reception. For more information, see the sidebar titled "Spam Free."

- ◎ **Viral Marketing:** It is a challenging prospect to create e-mail content that is inspiring enough to warrant users to forward it to their friends. If it works, your content can circulate to thousands or even millions of users around the Web

Spam Free

Although it may be tempting to purchase a bulk e-mail list to promote your content via an e-newsletter, people rarely appreciate unsolicited, impersonal e-mails. Be mindful of who will receive your product announcements and if possible, create an opt-in solution so they have the choice whether to subscribe to your announcements.

Constant Contact *(http://www.constant contact.com)* is one of many reputable resources for creating and managing newsletters or product announcements. You can upload your contacts to its online database and manage your account from any Web-enabled browser.

Whatever e-mail management option you choose, make sure it is reputable and will suit your needs in terms of cost, ease-of-use, and features.

in a very short period of time. However, Web-savvy users are a very wary lot and do not take kindly to blatant marketing messages being directed at them. It is the quickest way to stop your viral marketing plan in its tracks.

- ◎ **Social Media:** Community-based sites like mySpace, YouTube, LinkedIn, and Second Life all offer plenty of opportunities to get the word out about your project. Post to forums and blogs, register with sites like Technorati and SoFlow, or use online tools like *http://www.salesforce.com* to help promote your content. Most of these sites are free and the only resource they require is your time.

- ◎ **Direct Mail:** Create postcards, a brochure, or other promotional mailers and send them to target users. Direct mail can be a successful strategy if your mailing reaches the right hands.

Disc or Drive–based Projects

If the project is not on the Web, your first step might be to make it available to the Internet community. This is not to say you should repurpose the content for Web delivery (unless you want to), but rather consider providing information about the project online. Creating a Web site that showcases the project, features content samples, or allows people to purchase the entire application online will widen the audience significantly. Previously mentioned tactics, such as direct mail campaigns or e-newsletters, can be helpful strategies as well.

Maintenance

The maintenance process will be different for each project and will change based on a project's long-term needs. Due to the immediacy of their content, Web sites tend to require more regular maintenance than disc or drive-based projects like CD-ROMs or DVDs. Some projects, such as speaker support presentations or trade show kiosks, may have a short-lived shelf life or one-time-only usage and thus require no maintenance beyond the initial setup and configuration.

For projects that do require long-term upkeep, you can maintain a relationship with the client (if the client is your boss you may not have a choice), building upon and maintaining the project over time. Or, if there are no in-house capabilities to promote and manage the project long term, you can refer the client to outside partners who will take care of these services.

The Plan

Approach the promotion and maintenance of the project as you would any other production step. First, review the language you wrote in the initial proposal on this topic. Does it need to be revised to accommodate changes in the project spec? Use what you have to facilitate a dialogue between you and key decision makers that covers any revised needs now that the project has been completed. Include those needs with your original proposed long-term services to create a comprehensive strategy for addressing upcoming creative and technical concerns as well as any promotional considerations. Outline this in written detail and begin to negotiate the terms by which you will perform the necessary duties.

Even though you included provisions for these services in the initial proposal you should address ongoing project tasks as a separate contract with your client.

Payment Plans

How you define the workload and set up a fee structure is your preference and depends on how you negotiate those terms with involved parties. Sometimes it is appropriate to set up a weekly or monthly retainer fee or allotted number of hours over a set period of time for maintenance duties with the understanding that exceeding those hours will result in additional billing or further negotiation. Other times it is suitable to track your time on an hourly basis and report it to your boss or client. Either way, you should set up a contract or job description separate from the initial proposal that covers your activity over a set period of time based on your negotiations.

FIGURE 14-5
ALTHOUGH GETTING PAID FOR A JOB WELL DONE IS A GREAT FEELING, SETTING UP A FEE STRUCTURE FOR ONGOING PROMOTION AND MAINTENANCE WORK CAN KEEP THE MONEY ROLLING IN OVER TIME AND WILL HELP YOU BUILD SUCCESSFUL LONG TERM RELATIONSHIPS WITH YOUR CLIENTS.

Training

Sometimes the best way to make a smooth transfer of ownership (of the project) from your hands to your client's is to train her to maintain the content and integrity of the project. This does not mean your relationship with her is over once the training ends. If you played your cards right, she will be gracious you have supplied information requisite to her job performance and happy to take over a small portion of the ongoing tasks. In addition, she might also be eager to pass off responsibilities not in her job description.

CASE STUDY:

"Launching www.neofuturists.org"

The tested and fully functional Neo-Futurists site beta received thumbs up all around. With its completion, Mightybytes and the Neo-Futurists got ready for the final push toward launch.

FACE-TO-FACE TRAINING PLAYED A SIGNIFICANT ROLE IN GETTING THE NEO-FUTURISTS READY TO ASSUME SITE OWNERSHIP," POLINCY SAID.

Neo-Prep

Prior to switching domains over to the new server and launching the site, Mightybytes made sure the Neo-Futurists Theater Company were prepared to take over the site's upkeep and maintenance.

THE COMPLETED SITE AT WWW.NEOFUTURISTS.ORG.

"I'VE REALLY NEVER LEARNED ANYTHING LIKE THIS AND . . . ALL I CAN SAY IS THAT, IF I CAN LEARN TO UPDATE THIS SITE, THEN ANYONE CAN," GREENE SAID OF THE EASE WITH WHICH SHE PICKED UP JOOMLA PRODUCTION TECHNIQUES.

"We had one last Neo party at our office prior to the site launch where we demystified as many of Joomla's menu and functionality features as possible," Kristala Pouncy said. "We shared tips and tricks we had discovered in being heavy users over the past couple years and tried to foresee any hurdles they might come up against in daily administration of the site. The training was pain-free thanks to some Neo-Futurist members possessing basic Web development skills and having an understanding of how the site was built due to past meetings and training sessions."

"Mightybytes shared their Joomla and development expertise with us until we felt comfortable walking out of that training session and taking ownership of the site's content," Sharon Greene said. "They also made sure we felt comfortable giving them a quick call should we get stuck on something that was over our heads, which we appreciated. Our Webmaster and managing director are very Web-savvy folks, they learn quickly, write HTML and are used to doing all sorts of content management. I knew they could learn Joomla easily. But I've really never learned anything like this and was worried that I would fail. However, it's become really important to me that I don't need to rely on other members of the organization to communicate with our audience. So I knew I had to try. All I can say is that, if I can learn to update this site, then anyone can. I really like that there are fewer barriers between me and the people who want to see our theater."

File Finessing

To this end, Mightybytes facilitated a discussion about site meta tags, search engine optimization, and how best to promote the launched site.

"We had a couple last-minute tasks to accomplish before going live," Pouncy said. "But they were quick and painless. Meta tags and keywords can, of course, be added to site pages at any time during development. Sometimes we ask our clients right up front to give us ten words that they think best describe their company, and those end up in the keyword list that goes live. Other times we wait until the project's end to have this discussion because it provides us with the perfect opportunity to come full circle and bring up the promotional and marketing opportunities we included as part of our initial proposal. We also want to give the client an opportunity to express their thoughts on how to define their business in twenty words or less."

Earlier in the production process the Neo-Futurists supplied Mightybytes with a list of keywords for search engine optimization. Those were added as meta tags and a Joomla module for search engine-friendly URLs was installed. On the agreed-upon launch date, Mightybytes transferred the domain name pointers to the new location and the site went live.

"After the launch, we pointed the Neo-Futurists to a couple good sites for batch registering their site with various search engines and had several discussions with them about promotional opportunities," Pouncy said.

Promotional Opportunities

Upon launch, the Neo-Futurists planned to promote the new site to its audience through a number of channels.

"We'll put ads into our own programs and send a series of e-blasts to our mailing list," Greene said. "We'll blog about it and maybe even post something in our space itself about the process. The members of our community who hang out on our blog will probably be the first to notice and explore the re-design and tell their friends. When we are running two shows a night about 550 people hold our programs per weekend. We are also part of the Chicago theater community, and that community has its own press and Web sites. We'll probably send out a limited press release about it and see if any of the journalists who cover the theater scene want to do an article about our process as a way of educating other mid-sized theaters."

LOVE FEST: "WE'VE REALLY ENJOYED WORKING WITH THEM AND LOOK FORWARD TO BRINGING THEIR NEW SITE TO THE NEXT LEVEL SOMETIME IN THE FUTURE," POUNCY SAID.

"WE'LL PUT ADS INTO OUR OWN PROGRAMS AND SEND A SERIES OF E-BLASTS TO OUR MAILING LIST," GREENE SAID OF THE NEO-FUTURISTS' PROMOTIONAL EFFORTS. "WE'LL BLOG ABOUT IT AND MAYBE EVEN POST SOMETHING IN OUR SPACE ITSELF ABOUT THE PROCESS."

Pouncy echoed Greene's thoughts on promotion.

"Mightybytes immediately put a link to it and a 'Featured News' item on our own home page and sent a few targeted e-mails to key people in our address book who we want to see the work," she said.

As version 1.0 of the site was launched, the Neo-Futurists were heavy into writing grant proposals to help fund further enhancements to the Web site as well as many other company endeavors.

"We've really enjoyed working with them and look forward to bringing their new site to the next level sometime in the future," Pouncy said.

CONCLUSION

Although the successful promotion and maintenance of a project may not be an integral part of its actual production, it can be a very beneficial facet of its overall life. Keeping the content fresh as time progresses and safeguarding it against technological obsolescence will help ensure its viability for the long haul and your relationship with the client.

Now that you have successfully managed an interactive media project from start to finish, take a moment to review each step outlined in this book and think about how they may apply to future projects. Are there things you could do more efficiently next time? Do you see opportunities to combine steps and save time? The tasks outlined in this book should provide a framework around which to keep interactive media projects in line. But they are only a framework. Each project you undertake will bring about its own unique set of challenges and present different ways to integrate effective communication into your workflow. As time passes, you should be able to take on bigger and better projects with ease by applying the steps you learned herein. Good luck!

EXERCISES:

1. Burn release candidate disc or launch Web site.
2. Create sample banner ads.
3. Register with search engines.
4. Write a list of steps in managing an interactive media project.

TOOLS

Sample documents included on the CD-ROM that comes with this book:

◎ Sampe e-newsletter banner ads

Files can be found in the folder labeled with the corresponding chapter number and title.

INDEX

A

B

C